PETE BUTTIGIEG

SHORTEST WAY HOME

JOHN MURRAY

First published in the United States of America in 2019 by Liveright Publishing
Corporation, a division of W. W. Norton & Company, Inc.

First published in Great Britain in 2019 by John Murray (Publishers)
An Hachette UK company

1

Frontispiece: The South Bend River Lights over the St. Joseph River.
Designer: Ellen Cipriano

A CIP catalogue record for this title is available from the British Library

Hardback ISBN 9781529398045
eBook ISBN 9781529398076
Trade Paperback ISBN 9781529398052

Printed and bound in Great Britain by Clays Ltd, Elcograf S.p.A.

John Murray policy is to use papers that are natural, renewable and recyclable
products and made from wood grown in sustainable forests. The logging and
manufacturing processes are expected to conform to the environmental
regulations of the country of origin.

John Murray (Publishers)
Carmelite House
50 Victoria Embankment
London EC4Y 0DZ

www.johnmurray.co.uk

Everyone's own homeland is Kashmir to him.

—AFGHAN PROVERB

CONTENTS

SHORTEST
WAY HOME

I

REMEMBERING

Factories were our cathedrals,
pushed up out of the great plains.

MICHAEL COLLINS

1

The South Bend
I Grew Up In

Dawn comes late here along the western limit of the Eastern Time Zone, so far from the coast that our first sunrise of the year arrives after eight in the morning. Most January days are cloudy, making sunup a hidden and gradual process, less a moment of daybreak than a cold shift away from the illuminated night, in which the cloud ceiling and the snow cover reflect the sodium streetlights between them into an orange glow so bright you can read the paper outside at four in the morning.

So the first hint of morning actually makes things seem darker, as the amber night light yields and the sky deepens into a kind of electric indigo. The species of light evolve around you, from luminous ambience to discrete points of light along the horizon, the general giving way to the specific.

Looking at this scene from the fourteenth-floor windows of the mayor's corner office, it's easy to imagine that you are in the wheelhouse of a ship at sea. Adding to the effect, if it's windy out, the air pushes and pulls the picture windowpanes, making a noise far out of proportion to the wind's actual strength, as though the entire building is buffeted by a great gale. A few snowflakes whirl out of the air and fly up across the reflection of your fluorescent-lit face, and you feel like touching a piece of furniture to make sure you are steady.

It was that kind of deep winter morning on New Year's Day 2012, my first day as mayor of South Bend, a city of one hundred thousand people in northern Indiana. My hometown. Peering out across my empty desk into the lingering blue of a slow-motion midwinter dawn, the sky no longer orange but not yet gray, I pondered what to do with my first few minutes of unscheduled time.

Day One had commenced early with a visit to the Street Department garage to encourage the plow crews, and a stop at Memorial Hospital to greet Caleb, the first newborn of the new year. Now I was upstairs in my new office, and there was plenty on the schedule for the rest of the day, building up to the formal swearing-in ceremony set for that evening. But in this unstructured moment, what exactly should I do? Go over the speech one more time? Open my new city government email? Check the weather again, I quickly decided, and find out how the plows are doing.

Snow, of course, can be a beautiful thing. It is the great benefactor of children, promising canceled school and hot chocolate and down-hill sledding. But it is the mortal enemy of any mayor it touches. One day's worth of bungled plowing is all that stands between a mayor and political disaster. At a minimum, as Mike Bloomberg experienced, a rough or mishandled snowstorm can bring days of criticism; at worst, as Chicago's Michael Bilandic and New York's John V. Lindsay learned the hard way, it spells career oblivion. Even after it melts, mayors curse the past winter's snowfall, because it invariably refreezes to become the progenitor of a mayor's other great enemy and prey: the pothole.

AS I LEARNED GROWING UP, snow can be a great unifier in a place like South Bend. When a storm is past and the glinting winter sun emerges, so do we with our shovels, and as water drips from icicles along garage gutters we appear in our alleys to dig out our cars. It becomes a social activity based on cheerful neighborly commiseration. Snow furnishes the grounds for conversation—and even though we pride ourselves on being able to handle it, a good enough snowstorm can supply conversational fodder for weeks or even years to come. Like rain for the English, snow to a South Bender is worthy of intensive discussion even though, or perhaps because, it is so familiar.

Ask anyone who is old enough to remember, and they will tell you all about the Blizzard of '78. According to my parents, it was still the universal conversation starter even two and a half years later, when they arrived on College Street with their U-Haul from Texas, not long before I was born.

"Have you heard about the Blizzard of '78?" someone would ask as you were pumping gas, waiting in the checkout line at Martin's Super Market, or slicing into your roasted chicken at a dinner party. And once the question is asked, it makes no difference how you answer. Prepare to hear about the Blizzard of '78.

BY LATE JANUARY THAT COLD YEAR, there were already a couple feet of snow on the ground. Forecasters knew a storm was coming on that Thursday, January 26, perhaps a serious one, but no one realized it would be historic. The mayor was traveling, so Pete Mullen, the city controller, was in charge by default.

By the time he arrived at work, as the snowfall gathered speed, it had already been a terrifying day for Pete. He had started his usual morning routine—shower, shave, putting on a suit—and was getting some coffee when he paused to check on his two-week-old infant and realized that the child had stopped breathing. The baby was scarlet-red; no air was coming out of his mouth. Pete turned him over and patted him on the back. Still nothing. Sprinting upstairs with the infant in

hand, he woke his alarmed wife and handed the child to her while grab-
bing the phone to call 911.

Soon there were police cars, a fire truck, and an ambulance at the
house—as Pete recalled, "When they hear it's a baby, they pull out all
the stops to get there." It wasn't snowing yet, at least not much. A para-
medic stuck something in the baby's throat and opened his passageway,
and soon he was healthily inhaling and exhaling. Pete rode in the ambulance to the emergency room at St. Joseph Hospital, where the family's
pediatrician was waiting, while Mary Lou waited anxiously at the house
with their other kids. Once it was confirmed that the boy was all right,
the doctor offered to give Pete and the baby a ride home, then take Pete
to the office.

So by the time he arrived on the fourteenth floor at noon, Pete Mullen
was already drained. But it was clear now that this storm was going to
be a big deal. I can picture Pete looking out at the same view I see now,
noting the shrinking visibility—first you can't see the West Side anymore, then all you can see are the buildings across the street, then just
the courthouse down below, and finally nothing at all but a dull white
glow where your view of the city ought to be.

By midafternoon, Pete was telling everyone to get home but be
ready to come in the next day. Not willing to risk leaving the office and
being himself unable to get back, he found a couch and spent the night
there, waking up five hours later with his suit still on. As the winds blew
snow into drifts ever higher, stranding cars and burying neighborhoods,
Pete would stay in the office for two more nights, manning the city's
response. On Thursday, temperatures fell to zero and winds peaked at
fifty-five miles per hour as the bulk of what would be a three-foot snowfall struck the city head-on. But it was the drifts that set records, piling
up ten feet or even more.

The Chevy dealership downtown loaned the police department
some of its four-wheel-drive vehicles for emergency personnel to get
around. If you were lucky (or unlucky) enough to be working downtown

on the emergency response, you might rate a lift home. Once or twice a day they would get Pete home to check on his family and get a change of clothes, a process that involved dropping him off at the corner of his block and calling his wife to tell her to expect him as he trudged up the unplowed street in nearly chest-deep snow. Almost an hour later, he would make it to the door of his house, panting, five doors down from where he had been dropped.

City resources were not enough, so Pete arranged to contract with every individual he could find who owned a pickup truck with a plow. By Saturday, the snow had abated, but the stress level was mounting as people began to run out of food and supplies at home. Main roads were beginning to clear, but much of the city remained buried. From a National Guard helicopter, Pete saw how many houses were covered up to the windows. On the campus of Notre Dame, students were jumping out of third-story windows with glee, and daring each other to try it from higher.

People who really needed to be somewhere got creative. An Israeli dignitary who had been stuck in town for far too long was transported by snowmobile to the LaPorte County line, there to be conveyed, somehow, to Chicago and on to Tel Aviv. When Pete finally made it to Martin's Super Market, which had a skeleton crew selling whatever perishables they had left, he passed half a dozen horses tied up in the parking lot.

Pete wasn't the only one sleeping at work. Charlie Spiher, the director of the Mar-Main Pharmacy downtown, knew that people would need him, snow or not, and found a way to keep the pharmacy operating as everything around him shut down. He couldn't let people go without heart medication or dialysis supplies. A few days into the emergency, he realized he had run out of what had suddenly become his most popular item: birth-control pills. I can't find statistics to prove it, but locals speak of the hospital resorting to placing maternity beds in the hallway to accommodate an autumn baby boom, nine months after the storm.

As normalcy reasserted itself in the weeks to follow, a new problem arose: *where to actually put all the snow*. Around here, it may stay below freezing for weeks, so the snow doesn't just melt. That winter's snowfall came to 136 inches, millions of cubic yards of snow that had to find someplace to go. It was forbidden for environmental reasons to push it into the river (which moves so quickly that it never fully freezes over, even on subzero days). Downtown, a stalled development project (now a bustling hotel and office building) had led to a semi-permanent giant hole taking up a city block, known to locals as the Hole. This turned out to be the simplest place for the whole downtown's-worth of snow to be dumped. A radio station hosted a contest to see who could guess when the last of the snow would be gone; the winner guessed a date in May.

FOR MY NEWLY ARRIVED PARENTS-TO-BE, these blizzard stories must have really been something. They had come from El Paso, Texas, where they had lived and commuted to work at New Mexico State University in nearby Las Cruces. This was high desert at the foot of the Organ Mountains, and snowflakes were rare and short-lived. The daughter of an Army officer who retired at Fort Bliss in El Paso, my mother had attended high school in a sun-washed building less than two miles from the border with Juárez in Chihuahua State, Mexico. No river valley could be more different from South Bend's than that of the Rio Grande as it shunts through El Paso in the concrete casing that keeps its banks from shifting—a river forbidden to meander like normal rivers, because it is not just a waterway but also an international border. Mom had lived in Indiana before, as a girl in Scott County, but that was on the other end, near Kentucky, so far south of here it might as well have been a different state.

For my father, who had emigrated from the island nation of Malta, the snow would have been even more exotic. They say the Alaskan Inuit natives have over fifty different words for snow, because they experience it so often and in so many different forms. The Maltese have none.

When he calls his sisters back on the island on a winter Sunday to trade family updates, he'll use the word "*silġ*," which means ice. So if this newly naturalized Mediterranean immigrant had anything in common with his wife from Scott County, Indiana, by way of El Paso, it was that neither of them was a child of snow country.

Yet, like the South Benders they were to become, they quickly learned to shovel snow. They taught themselves how to shift and brake differently when driving on snow, and adopted the cultural norm of talking with enthusiasm about memorable snows, even ones before their time, in an ever-escalating cascade of superlatives. Thus, when we celebrate my birthday each passing year, their story of that night in January of 1982 seems to grow in meteorological ferocity, the temperature further and further below zero and the snow cover ever higher above eye level, to the point that if you take them literally when they tell the story of the night I was born, it is an utter miracle that I made it out of the hospital—or indeed that anyone survived at all.

But somehow, with help from Maria Concetta Portelli Buttigieg, my weather-shocked Maltese grandmother, who made her first and only trip to America for the occasion along with my astonished young aunt Myriam, Mom and Dad successfully delivered me to their small two-story house on College Street on the northwest side of South Bend.

TO BE BORN IN 1982 is to be just old enough to remember the Soviet Union, and to have its fall be the first seismic geopolitical event of your lifetime. I remember the kid who dominated second-grade show-and-tell with a little chunk of the Berlin Wall, gray and rough on one side but smooth and painted on the other, a trophy from his father's business trip to Europe. And there was Ms. Martin repeatedly explaining to us why our maps and globes, with "Union of Soviet Socialist Republics" spread in impossibly stretched letters across the Siberian tundra, were now obsolete.

Coming into the world in the early 1980s puts you in that senior segment of the millennial generation that still remembers life before the smartphone. Today I couldn't tell you the number of the phone on my own desk, but I still know my friend Joe's number from sixth grade because I would punch it daily after school on a phone we had not yet learned to call a "landline." If I dial that number even today, one of his parents will still pick up.

I'm young enough that I don't always use a TV set to watch television, but old enough that you might catch me using the phrase "flat-screen TV," as if they sell any other kind. Only now can I make sense of the way my grandparents' generation used to talk of "color TV" long past the time when you could find a black-and-white TV for sale anywhere in America.

From my freshman dorm room in late 2000, the most high-tech thing I did every morning was log on to South Bend's WNDU.com and look at the two-inch-square, low-resolution still image from the webcam on their transmission tower aimed at the Golden Dome, updated every few minutes—a grainy but comforting link to home. Websites didn't have much to them back then, I can see myself telling my grandchildren one day. But things moved quickly. By senior year, as I was banging out my thesis on an early-model iBook, a few sophomores in another dorm were creating a website patterned after the "face books" that Harvard passed out at the beginning of the year so that we could figure out who was who in the dining hall.

Being in your thirties today means you have lived more or less half-and-half with Democratic and Republican presidencies, known twenty years of peace, and fifteen of war. It means you were grazing the boundaries of adulthood when we all experienced the sudden reversal of what some fashionable scholars had taken to calling the "End of History" after the close of the Cold War. That shock came my sophomore year, a crisp September day in Boston, as it was in Manhattan, when history thundered back into being. It wasn't hard to tell by sundown that everything would be different, that irony and apathy wouldn't dominate our years after all, that our generation would go to war just as our parents' and their parents' did.

History was back, and in hindsight it's obvious that we had actually never been living outside its rhythm. But in the horror of that sunny Tuesday, all we could make out was the onset of a major shift. I remember thinking that suddenly our generation's project had been abruptly reassigned—that yesterday we had been absorbed in Clinton-era concerns around globalization, the distribution of wealth, and the consequences of technology, but now we were being plunged into a different realm, dominated by things like warfare and terrorism.

Today, it has come full circle; we see how often war and terrorism are driven by the dynamics of globalization, the distribution of wealth, and the consequences of technology. Like laws of physics, these forces were animating our affairs all along—which should have been no surprise to people from a place like South Bend, a city wrestling such forces long before economists and newspapers gave us terms like "globalization" and "Rust Belt."

By THE TIME MY PARENTS' U-Haul appeared on College Street in May of 1980, little remained of South Bend's industrial heyday but a widespread plague of empty factory buildings. I grew up among them, unable to fathom the tragedy encoded in their condition. From the back seat of the car on the way to Martin's, I scarcely even asked about the enormous brick structure with the even taller white smokestack that we would pass after the turn onto Elwood Avenue. Ghostly, it presided over the junction where our residential area met the strip mall containing our go-to grocery store, along with Osco Drug, a Little Caesar's, and a Laundromat. Only years later would I go around the back of that giant brick brewery to explore the parking lot, bounded by an ex-railroad with waist-high weeds poking up between the ties, and look up at the several stories of ruin, with one outer wall gone completely, exposing floors in naked cross-section like you'd see in footage of war zones, topped by inexplicable trees growing from somewhere on the fifth floor.

Why do I not recall talking to classmates about the acres of collapsing Studebaker factories we would pass on the way to school along Michigan Street? If I had grown up somewhere else and arrived to see this, I would have noticed little else. I don't think it was taboo to speak of it. It was just unremarkable, since we'd grown up in its midst. We were used to it, it was part of the furniture.

Yet somehow none of this made it feel like a bad place for a child to grow up. The collapsing structures had their place in the larger texture of our neighborhoods, which also included well-kept parks and decent houses with lawns and hedges and flowers. We didn't think of the empty factories as the scenery of a post-industrial bust town in the 1980s. We didn't think of them at all. They were just there, a visual set, accompanied by the soundtrack of life in South Bend: crickets in the summer, crows in the fall, and all year long the echoing horns of trains rumbling through in the night on their way to Chicagoland.

AND IF THERE WAS RUIN in some corners of the city, there was majesty in others. There was the gleaming Golden Dome of the University of Notre Dame, the library with the mosaic mural of "Touchdown Jesus" overlooking the stadium, and the stadium itself, the "House that [Knute] Rockne Built," which I vaguely understood to be a historic and hallowed place even before I understood what football was and what it meant around here. Its orange bricks, colored a little differently than most of the rest of campus, signaled something important. Fidgeting with my seat belt on days when Mom or Dad brought me along to campus, I could turn and gaze up at the mysterious structure, try to fathom the bizarre geometry of the underside of the concrete risers ("Dad, why is there an upside-down stairway?"), and sense that this place, neither civic nor religious, was somehow both.

Growing up in any place with a lost golden age, you absorb its legacy in fragments, hearing once-great names—Oliver, Morris, Bendix, Studebaker—without being able to match them to anything living. You take them in at first without comprehension, like the names of saints. Only as you grow older, with more education and context, do you begin to picture how such giants of industry must have thrown their weight around their city, and what it might have been like as our factory precincts heaved with tens of thousands of workers at a time.

A century ago, city boosters burst with pride as they celebrated and marketed South Bend. A 1901 book published by the *South Bend Tribune* begins:

> South Bend! No inland city on the American continent has attained greater renown or displayed more fully those sterling virtues of modern manhood and human progress, than this beautiful city located on the banks of the magnificent and picturesque St. Joseph River.

A bit more factually, a 1919 *Pictorial Souvenir of South Bend* made a series of impressive assertions:

> It is, of course, generally known that Studebaker's plant is the largest vehicle factory in the world and that the Oliver Plow Company is the largest plow factory in the world, but it is not generally realized how many more of the city's establishments are among the largest of their kind.

It goes on to document the fact that the Folding Paper Box Company had "the largest paper box factory in Indiana and one of the largest in the world," and that the Birdsell Manufacturing Company housed the "largest makers of clover hullers in the world." South Bend companies made brooms, cigars, spark arresters (whatever that is), gears, gloves, white ice, ice cream, mattresses, plows, stoves, rubber, shirts, tents, dowels, bicycles, and fishing tackle, among countless other products.

And, famously, there were the pocket watches. The South Bend Watch Company made products so precise that at trade shows they would freeze a watch in a big block of ice where you could see it still ticking faithfully inside. An old advertisement has an image of the watch in the ice, but for me the most remarkable thing in the ad is something else that strikes you as you read its big letters:

SOUTH BEND WATCH
FROZEN IN ICE, KEEPS PERFECT TIME
SOUTH BEND WATCH CO.
SOUTH BEND, IND.

How powerful the very name of our city must have been. All you had to do to sell watches—besides put one in a block of ice—was name them after our city. That was enough, by way of branding: the name "South Bend" was a byword for workmanship and precision.

I'm proud to own a couple, one of them a 1909 model, which still keeps pretty good time if you wind it up. The company made over a million watches, but failed to realize how much was at stake when rivals began marketing the "trench watch," a World War I innovation that put watches on leather straps on men's wrists. The company lumbered along as though nothing had changed, producing some of the best-known pocket watches of the early wristwatch age. Their failure to innovate was fatal; the firm did not survive the Crash of 1929.

The easy lesson to draw from this is that you must innovate to survive. But you could find a more nuanced moral of the story: that keeping up doesn't always mean making something completely new. To survive, South Bend Watch wouldn't have needed to start making radios or computers. They just needed to adapt a good thing they already had, and refine their business. If they, and Studebaker, and some other companies, had managed to do this, I might have grown up in a different South Bend.

DOWN MICHIGAN STREET, just south of the Studebaker factory district, sits the United Auto Workers Local 5 hall, home to what was once America's largest auto union local. Like many auto workers' halls, it has a stage for speaking, with an American flag, a portrait of Walter Reuther on the wall, and a big UAW logo painted as a backdrop matching the smaller one affixed to the podium. But unlike any other local union hall I've seen, its concrete-block walls on either side are covered with murals depicting the union's story, including Studebaker's fall as seen from the perspective of the workers. One section shows workers making an uncertain departure from the factory grounds on the day that their jobs, and thousands of others, came to a sudden end.

Old-timers on the West Side can tell you what it was like on that gray December day in 1963, just weeks after the Kennedy assassination, when news got out that the company was about to shut down. Jack Colwell, who covers me to this day in his *South Bend Tribune* columns, was the bearer of doom in a story he broke as a cub reporter, under the headline: "AUTO OUTPUT TO END HERE."

Jack, who also teaches at Notre Dame and writes a weekly column on politics, is gentle and disarming, never breaking his smile as he toggles his gaze, now looking down at his notepad full of orderly script, now back up at you through his glasses as he listens intently. Like Mark Peterson, another experienced local reporter, he has a way of looking at you as if you are about to say something very interesting and important, which of course makes you want to oblige, rather than stick to your talking points.

Maybe that's how Jack got the scoop, a day before Studebaker planned to make the announcement from a safe remove in New York City. It was probably the biggest local story ever, but South Bend was not ready to hear it. Jack wrote later that some workers "were hostile toward carriers delivering that paper, that news, at shift end to Gate 1 on Sample Street," with one repeatedly yelling, "It's not official yet!"

Social science research hadn't yet confirmed that sudden job loss can be the psychological equivalent of losing a loved one, but everyone must have sensed the depth of harm this news would bring as thousands of jobs were wiped out in a matter of days. Some were defiant about the city's future, like Paul Gilbert, the clothing store owner, who told a gathering of civic leaders: "This is not Studebaker, Indiana. This is South Bend, Indiana." But there was no escaping the fact that we had become a company town without its company.

The decline was not instantaneous, but 1963 was like a fulcrum. There was Before, and there was After.

It is difficult for someone born twenty years later to truly picture Before, but you can see it in the bustle of our downtown on the old postcards. You can sense it in the grandeur of the big stone houses—castles, almost—that the local titans of industry built to live in. In old photos, you can sense that the *South Bend Tribune* was justified in describing the Oliver Hotel as "the best and most magnificent in Indiana" when it opened in 1899, complete with frescoes in the lobby and steam baths downstairs.

Nor were South Bend's charms just for the wealthy. Bob Urbanski was the son of a butcher in a big Polish family, like so many others on the West Side. He was clearly bright, yet he had been struggling to follow lessons in class, and his seventh-grade teacher realized it had something to do with his eyesight. "He moved me to the front of the class and asked some questions and met my father one day after school and talked to him," Bob remembered. It turned out Bob needed glasses. So his father took him to the eye doctor downtown, where he was examined and got his first prescription. He remembers emerging and seeing the splendor of the downtown for the first time: "And I walked outside and I looked to the north down Michigan Street and I was just awed. The lights weren't just a blur. It was like someone took a camera lens and . . . they were crisp, you could see the sign for Osco's and Spiro's and Milady Shop and Robertson's and Wyman's Department Store, all this stuff that was down there."

What young Bob saw was a dense cluster of clothing, furniture, and department stores that transacted the arrival of the modern American middle class. The avenue was packed, and on Mondays and Thursdays the shops would stay open into evening. As in the department store scene of *A Christmas Story*, it was a special occasion for kids to accompany their parents downtown to shop, "typically before Easter, or a new suit for a Communion, that sort of thing." Then they would return home to a West Side bustling with families moving among neighborhood groceries, churches, and taverns, as the aroma of half a dozen Eastern European countries' cuisines wafted into the city air.

At Christmas, fish head soup would be served, and, of course, there would be pierogies. Bob's grandma would make a hundred of them at a time, rolling the dough on a table, putting the cheese on them, folding them by hand. The kids would eat them right out of the boiling pot. "But my grandpa would take it, slit the thing, put butter in each one, then pour cream over it."

That was reserved for special occasions. But when bread could be truly fresh it could be a treat any day, so much that some days Bob's father literally couldn't wait to get the bread home from the Hungarian bakery. He would bring a quarter stick of butter from home with him when he went to pick up the boys from school downtown. If they saw the butter in the front seat, they knew they were going to the bakery, just in time for the hot bread to come out of the oven at three o'clock. "We'd go over there and get a loaf of it, and it wasn't sliced, we'd get to the car and tear it, and he had his pocketknife and he'd chop up butter and put it on if you wanted it." The day he died, Bob's father was making a pot of czernina, a Polish duck blood soup, stirring in the potato dumplings.

Children were raised not just by parents, but by neighborhoods. Gladys Muhammad, about the same age as Bob, remembers the LaSalle Park neighborhood: "You could go anywhere, next door anywhere, and eat, they'd just invite you in and eat, and if you did anything wrong, the neighbors would tell on you. . . . So everybody was real disciplined." Gladys went to Washington High School, which was racially integrated—but the neighborhoods were not. Red-lining hemmed in African-Americans like her to the LaSalle Park area colloquially known as "the Lake," after the pond at the bottom of the sledding hill there. Walking to school, Gladys would have to cross the railroad tracks, sometimes clambering through an open boxcar to get there. African-American residents couldn't live south of the tracks, though they were more than welcome to work, as her father did, alongside the Polish and Hungarian and Irish men on the line at Studebaker.

CERTAIN DAYS OF THE WEEK, you can still get pierogies, cabbage- or cheese-filled, at Joe's Tavern on the Near West Side, one of those neighborhood watering holes nestled between houses to one side and an industrial site across the street. But on your way there, you will pass by the hulking mass of the biggest factories we haven't torn down yet. Deeper into the neighborhood you will see the vacant lots where cozy homes used to host the family gatherings that Bob and Gladys remember from their childhoods. You will sense the slow decline that followed that pivotal December day.

It's our version of a story that played out, in some fashion, across the American Midwest. We've lost over thirty thousand people since the 1960s, the population falling to about a hundred thousand while our per capita personal income sank by 2010 to $18,805, half the national average. In parallel with a general out-migration from the region, to

Chicago or beyond, a local realignment gradually emptied the urban core. By the time I was born, shops and residents had started to flow from the heart of the city. You no longer went to get your first Communion suit from Gilbert's or Robertson's downtown anymore, you went instead to J. C. Penney at the mall in nearby Mishawaka. You no longer headed for the Hungarian bakery, you went to a new location that Martin's had strategically positioned on the road that leads out of down town toward the mall and the new subdivisions. Swiftly and inexorably, the cornfields and wetlands that ringed the outer limits of our metro area were marked for development and transformed into suburban plazas of chain stores and office parks, great angular islands in a sea of parking lots.

Even my elementary school, square and carpeted wall-to-wall, was located in an office park. By the time I sat in its airy second-grade classroom in 1990, the big family name in town had nothing to do with manufacturing. Now it was real estate, and the Cressy family had become prominent after Don Cressy put a big shopping mall northeast of town, on the other side of Notre Dame and outside the South Bend city limits. University Park Mall was not that close to the university, nor was there a park nearby, but by the time I was growing up here it had become the epicenter of our social and commercial life. Its popularity led to more retail and residential subdivisions around it, a big-box frontier of development pressing northward one cornfield at a time, almost all the way to Michigan.

I liked our house in the city, but envied the high ceilings, generous rec rooms, and huge sloping lawns of the well-off people I knew from school who populated these newer subdivisions. We were doing fine, but to a professor's kid, the doctors and lawyers seemed extravagantly wealthy. Most of them lived in Granger, a sprawling and unincorporated zone of spacious houses on winding streets with names like Clarendon Hills Drive and Hunting Ridge Trail that signaled affluence and a certain upper-middle-class taste. The most abundant animal species there is surely the Canadian goose, but you wouldn't know it from the street names. Within a square mile or two you can find Fox Pointe Lane, Fox-cross Drive, Foxdale Lane, Fox Chase Court, Red Fox Drive, Fox Trail, and so on, right on up to the state line.

South Bend proper was a different domain, filled with older East European West-Siders who kept pristine lawns in front of their small ranch houses, black families (unless they could afford the leap to Granger) mostly clustered in the Near Northwest and Far West Side, and the public servant class of cops and schoolteachers who would tend to avoid a neighborhood that didn't have sidewalks. And there was the occasional professor who eschewed suburban life for the charm of a historic house, or couldn't afford otherwise on a junior faculty salary, or just hadn't come under the sway of the Realtors then nudging people out to the suburbs as they scoped out options while moving in from around Dartmouth or Palo Alto. That's how my parents found the house on College Street that my mother spotted and swiftly purchased on a quick scouting trip from El Paso. As a child I had no idea that "West Side" would come to be considered "dangerous" by the denizens of Granger, and some in the city, too.

Later we moved to a brick house on Marquette Avenue, down the hill from St. Joseph High and therefore a convenient place for me to have friends over after school. It came back to me later that some parents hesitated to let their children come to our house, because it was "in the city." (If there was a racial layer to that phrase, I was too young to catch it.) In fact it was a perfectly safe neighborhood, full of kids and dogs, with families who went back for decades keeping an eye out for each other.

The houses were close together, about thirty to a block, under a leafy layer of treetops that shaded us in the summer, painted the neighborhood in fall, and left creaking branches for the wind to howl through in wintertime. When it was too cold to do much outside, I passed after-school afternoons in a finished room in the basement with my friends, growing pudgy on store-brand cola and popcorn as we took in *Star Trek* reruns or Bulls games, or bled off excess energy wrestling until a parent would come down to see what the ruckus was.

Our neighborhood was called, a bit grandly, the "North Shore Triangle," because it is bordered by the fast-flowing run of the St. Joseph River as it runs northwest at an angle, with the curving Angela Boulevard on the north and the busier, four-lane Michigan Street to the east. As the land inches down toward the river, the property values slope upward, forming a tidy triangular slice of the middle class about six blocks across. In the middle of that triangle is Nokomis Park, better known as Triangle Park, the general headquarters of my boyhood. The park didn't have or need any playground equipment or water features, just trees, a metal trash barrel, and an irregularly placed streetlight in the middle. Its simplicity made it perfect for me and my friends Joe and Ben—an adaptable field suitable for baseball, football, and battle. If it felt like time for an adventure, we could cross Angela and venture along the old coal line toward Saint Mary's College, veering off into the woods that led to a bluff over the river. You could get close to the water if you carefully maneuvered down the slope, but if you weren't careful a patch of clay would take your leg all the way up to the knee. You could get your leg back, with help from friends pulling mightily, but your shoe would be gone forever.

IT'S STILL A GOOD NEIGHBORHOOD, but it's rare for a house to be worth what it cost to build. Today the most expensive houses in the neighborhood, big ones on the river, can run as much as $300,000. The cheapest, one-story houses with vinyl siding and attached garages can be had for around $60,000. Chasten and I now live on the same block as Mom and Dad, and the mortgage payment on our large old house facing the river comes to about four hundred and fifty bucks.

About two miles up the hill gleams the gold leaf of the Golden

Dome. Those who have never visited may know little else about us than that we host the university, along with Saint Mary's and Holy Cross College across the street. Yet Notre Dame rose to real prominence only after our industrial fame had collapsed, and campus and community lived mostly separate lives for most of our history.

Still, if South Bend was never exactly a college town, we have long been a football town. I can still remember the first time, not yet five, when I witnessed tailgate country. Most of the accoutrements of tailgating are useless to a small child, which is probably why I have no memory of beer cans or chicken wings. But I do clearly recall a cake in the shape of a football, a cacophony of radios and gadgets playing the Notre Dame fight song, and everyone dressed in blue, gold, and green. Tailgating made no sense to me then, but I understood what a party was, and this looked like the biggest birthday party I had ever seen. Bundled up in my winter coat and accompanying my parents on a game-day walk around campus, I asked them what the big party was for. Matter-of-factly and in unison, they answered: "The game."

WHEN I TURNED SIX, I was deemed old enough to start going with Dad, who until then had brought our next-door neighbor Leon Helak, a police officer, to sit with him in his seats in the southwest corner, Section 21, Row 42, which his faculty status gave him the privilege of buying each year. I don't know when this literary scholar picked up his taste for American football, but it must go back in some way to his boyhood devotion to the great English soccer club Manchester United. After all, that loyalty meant he was totally at home as part of a roaring mass in the stands of a great stadium cheering for a team known by its deep and legendary tradition.

When the Man United team plane crashed on takeoff in 1958 in Munich, the disaster at once claimed the lives of my father's soccer heroes and cemented his lifelong loyalty to the team—much as a 1931 crash in Kansas both took Notre Dame Coach Knute Rockne's life and sealed his legendary status. Perhaps that's why my father's fondness for Notre Dame football showed no sign of the gap in affinity that you might expect to see between the Fighting Irish and a nonreligious Mediterranean intellectual. One afternoon thirty years after the Munich tragedy, he cheerfully guided his bewildered son up to his place on the weathered wooden bench to take in his first game, against Purdue.

It wasn't even close. Lou Holtz was coaching; you could make out his red hair even from our corner seats two-thirds of the way up. The quarterback, Tony Rice, ran thirty-eight yards for a touchdown and later threw a fifty-four-yard touchdown pass to the soon-to-be-legendary Raghib "Rocket" Ismail. The crowd roared when Ricky Watters returned a punt sixty-six yards to the end zone, imprinting on my young brain the idea that every kickoff must be a scoring opportunity. Clutching the program my father had bought me, a four-dollar extravagance so that we could check the players by number, I stood on my seat to see the field when the fans leapt up for a big play. I was watching what would become the national championship team of 1988.

Over the years the mysteries of the stadium began to decode themselves. I finally grasped that those strange concrete forms that had looked like upside-down stairways leading nowhere were in fact the underside of the stands. I began to understand the difference between the regulars, who kept the same seats for decades as my father would, and the ones who came in one game at a time after buying tickets from one of the scalpers standing out by the Toll Road exit. I learned about penalties, rushes, passes, touchbacks, and safeties. And amid the magnificent swearing of people sitting around us I started to gather how profanity may be abusive but also poetic.

I learned about hierarchy, too. There were "alumni," a word I came to associate with combed-over gray hair, blue blazers, blue-and-gold-striped ties, beige raincoats, and the smell of cigars. The nearer to the fifty-yard line and the closer to the field I looked, the more gray hair and beige coats. Our seats were more the domain of the "fans," sporting Notre Dame jackets and scarves and hats and socks. And of course there were "students," a mysterious kind of proto-adult whose ranks dominated the northwest corner of the stadium and who stood for the whole game.

Then there were the ushers—the same men each year—who conveyed in their yellow jackets and white caps such authority that it is peculiar to think that they were volunteers with day jobs, rather than full-time members of a football-oriented military order. Indeed, there actually *was* a football-oriented militaristic order, the elite and selective Irish Guard, consisting of tall, kilt-clad students in narrow bearskin hats, who marched out magnificently behind the band's drum majors and performed the flag honors at the beginning of each game.

Some things I did not understand, and wouldn't for years. At six, I could detect but not fathom the controversy when the students arrived at the vaunted 1988 Miami game wearing T-shirts that read CATHOLICS VERSUS CONVICTS. Nor could I then figure out what motivated my father's wrath when he turned to some fans in the next row, aggravated by their catcalling Tony Rice (our second-ever black quarterback) over his grade-point average, and said to one of them, "I'd like to see *your* grade-point average."

I could not then have comprehended the tension involved in the fact that my father was a man of the left, no easy thing on a campus like Notre Dame's in the 1980s. I would learn later that many of his closest friendships among the faculty were sealed amid the protests of his early years, such as the time he spoke out against the Reagan administration's covert support for human rights abusers in Latin America during the popular president's visit to campus. (All I knew at the time was that he took me to the airport to see Air Force One through a chain-link fence at the end of the runway.)

As reliably as most students were conservative, the humanities faculty members were overwhelmingly liberal. From dinner tables at the homes of my parents' professor friends I would hear words and names that would mean nothing to me then but in retrospect make it very clear what was on their minds: Reaganite. Intellectual. Iran-Contra. Lynne Cheney. Half the table talk was just faculty gossip, and that was pretty understandable to me by the age of ten or so because it wasn't that different from the talk at school. But the other part, the reference-laden intellectual and political discussion, was opaque. I would hear but not understand arguments over the uselessness of post-structuralism or the relevance of Hobsbawm's historiography, wondering what any of it meant and how anyone could be as passionate about it as the people seated at the dinner table who just a couple hours earlier were indulgingly asking me about my loose tooth or my baseball card collection. At first I tuned it out, awaiting the first opportunity to excuse myself from the table with the other kids and go watch TV (especially if the house we were visiting had cable) or play tag. Like the coffee they would pour to go with dessert, their style of conversation was an acquired taste. But the more I heard these aging professors talk, the more I wanted to learn how to decrypt their sentences, and to grasp the political backstory of the grave concerns that commanded their attention and aroused such fist-pounding dinner debate.

WHEN I WAS FOURTEEN, Mom and Dad sent me to St. Joseph High School, the Catholic school up the hill from our place, housed in a 1950s-era tan brick building sometimes confused for a light industrial structure due to the surprisingly high smokestack of its old incinerator. This offered its own sort of political education. At Saint Joe, we were brought up not only to learn Church doctrine on matters like sexuality and abortion, but also to understand the history of the Church as a voice for the oppressed and downtrodden. At all-school mass in the bleachers of the airy, aging gym, we would pray for the various places and peoples around the world experiencing oppression.

My adjustment to high school life first unfolded under the command of Father Bly, who presided from an elevated desk with a dog-eared Bible on it, as he had since the 1960s, teaching the Old Testament. He had reluctantly consented to the mixing of girls and boys a few years earlier, but had succeeded in refusing to allow his room to be renovated, so we sat in those fifties-style seats with the desk built into them, bolted on to the floor. With a sort of terrified reverence, we held still as Father Bly expounded on the wisdom of the ages, beginning with Genesis. As he lectured, he rarely budged from the stool behind his raised desk; rumor had it that with an imperceptible movement he could send that Bible flying into the forehead of any student caught sleeping.

Occasionally he would lighten things up by passing out copies from what must have been a mountainous library of *National Geographic* back issues, so we could look at pictures of the Holy Land or something else he considered interesting. Once, he distributed an issue that contained satellite photos of subdivisions and golf courses being built in the deserts of Arizona, made possible by irrigation schemes that diverted water from the Colorado River. You could see the giant green squares in the satellite imagery, surrounded by barren sand and mountains. There are whole towns in Mexico, he explained, where the riverbed now runs dry because the water is drained upstream in the American Southwest. Next came the moral of the story:

"This weekend, you will probably go to the University Park Mall, and you may run into some atheists," he pronounced, lingering on the consonants at the end of the word, hissing a little, atheisssttsss, without losing his aloof posture and hundred-yard stare.

"These atheists will tell you, 'There is no God, there is no heaven, and there is no hell.' And how will you answer them? You will tell them, of course there is a God, and a heaven and a hell. There must be a hell. Because *where else would you put the man who built this golf course!*"

• • •

IN GOVERNMENT CLASS, WE WERE shown the 1989 film *Romero*, in which Raul Julia plays the Salvadoran bishop assassinated in 1980 by right-wing paramilitary after challenging the ruling elites in El Salvador. Shocked that this could have happened within living memory with what looked like American complicity, I began paying more attention to human rights. The school had a small chapter of Amnesty International, which raised a few hundred dollars a year and conducted letter-writing campaigns. I joined and eventually became president of the six-or-so-strong group. Here came an early lesson in the realities of organizing—it was nearly impossible to get people to volunteer to help write letters to political prisoners at the little card table I put up outside the lunch hall, but we got hundreds to come to the Battle of the Bands organized to raise money for the club.

On balance, the school faculty was far from a liberal bunch. A monument to aborted fetuses on school grounds reminded us all that pro-life politics was an article of faith, and many teachers were skeptical of the perceived bleeding-heart tendencies of their more social-justice-oriented colleagues. Mr. Dubois, who taught gym and drafting, comes to mind. He spoke with a thick southern Indiana drawl, combed what remained of his white hair back, and usually called gym class to order by barking, "LAAAAAHN UP, YOU IDIOTS." Or occasionally, for variety, "LAAAAHN UP, YOU MORONS." Over time, I would come to understand that this was a way of showing affection. But you can see how, at least early on, this could be a little intimidating—especially since gym class was not my scene. It would be a good ten years or so before I experienced any real level of physical fitness, so the primary objective was to survive without embarrassment. I could handle myself in touch football just by throwing my weight around, because half my classmates had not yet caught up to my then-imposing five feet eight. But basketball was more nuanced and less forgiving.

Once, after I somehow made a basket, Mr. Dubois pulled me aside at dismissal and offered something that might be described as encouragement. "Butt-man," he began, "I see a lot of poh-tential in you. Keep working at it."

But some weeks later, he stopped to talk to me with something else on his mind: he'd heard I was getting mixed up in Amnesty International. Mr. Dubois was not fond of "Ay-rabs," so I could see where this was going. I stiffened, and told him that I was, that I was running our chapter now, and that I felt that was consistent with the values we were being taught in theology class. There must have been a little more force in my voice than either of us had expected, because he responded with a respectful nod followed by a cheerful snort: "Well, to each his own, I guess." He smiled and returned his gaze to his clipboard as he proceeded toward a new victim on the gym floor, a sophomore whom he had decided for some reason to nickname "Re-cruit."

By high school I had traded my oversized, thick glasses for contact lenses, but my eyesight was getting worse every year, smothering my childhood aspiration of becoming an astronaut or at least a pilot. But in the meantime I had begun to wonder what it would be like to be involved in public service directly, instead of reading or watching movies about it. Could political action be a calling, not just the stuff of dinner table talk?

I got onto every mailing list I could, and from every political persuasion, from the local Republican Party to the Democratic Socialists of America. I wanted to find out how people went about being involved in ways more impactful than lonely letter-writing campaigns. And I decided to try my hand at leadership in student government, first losing an election for student body treasurer but then winning one for senior class president. In an assembly in the dining hall, the five or so candidates for class president gave our short speeches, using a closed-top trash can as a kind of makeshift podium, and once the scraps of paper got counted up, I had won my first election.

I kept up top grades, and by senior year a flow of mailed college recruiting brochures accumulated into an avalanche on our dining room table. Sifting through them, I tried to picture a future as a college student. There was something distant and even intimidating about the imagery—confident, smiling, diverse students in sweatshirts chatting and laughing in small groups on tidy quadrangles, or walking cheerily with their backpacks through autumn foliage on slightly different variations of the universal college campus. It was hard to picture myself at ease like these students; I wasn't even at ease in the halls of my own high school, even as a class president. But the letters and brochures made it seem like the colleges were happy to have me. I applied to about ten of them, hoping above all for a shot at Harvard. The odds seemed long—I'd heard of even valedictorians from Saint Joe being turned away—but I had to make the attempt.

When I got home one day and saw a letter from Harvard on the mail table, I didn't get my hopes up too much. It was not a thick envelope. I feigned nonchalance, setting my backpack down before heading back to pick up the letter that might hold a key to my future, while my parents kept a discreet but unconvincing distance in the living room. I usually open letters with my finger, but this one deserved a letter opener. Pulling out the page of watermarked paper, I read the opening line over and over again: "I am delighted to inform you . . ."

Slowly, I allowed myself to believe the letter from this dean of admissions, and by the time I studied the bottom, with a little "Hope you will join us" written in ballpoint pen near the signature, it felt like the establishment had thrown its doors open and beckoned me inside.

All I had to do was leave South Bend.

I HAD NEVER BEEN TO BOSTON, but I wound up going twice during that last semester of high school. The first was a planned college visit after I got admitted, sleeping on the floor of a freshman dorm and learning what to expect from the campus, at least physically. The second was an all-expense-paid trip that came as even more of a surprise than the admission to Harvard.

At the urging of my teachers, I had submitted an entry to an essay contest sponsored by the John F. Kennedy Presidential Library as part of their annual Profile in Courage Award. Around South Bend, President Kennedy was on par with Lincoln. As the first Catholic president, he had won the undying loyalty of the white ethnic working class, and as the man who had invited America to shoot for the moon, he was the first example of presidential leadership that I had understood as a child. Participating in the contest seemed almost like a duty.

I worked for days on an essay about Carolyn McCarthy, who had run for Congress on gun policy issues after her husband was shot and killed on the Long Island Rail Road. I had nearly finished the essay when I went online to research a couple last details—and found out that the previous year's winner had written about the same person. I would have to start from scratch.

Rushing to come up with an alternate plan, I decided to write about someone I had found even more interesting, if a little more edgy politically. An obscure Vermont congressman, Bernie Sanders, had been reelected for years as a socialist—in a (then) generally Republican state. At a time when vagueness and opportunism in politics seemed to be the order of the day, here was an elected official who succeeded by being totally transparent and relentless about his values. "Socialist" was the dirtiest word in politics, yet he won because people saw that he came by his values honestly. Regardless of whether you agreed politically, it certainly seemed like a profile in courage to me.

Years later, when I was running for mayor, I would check my mailbox one morning and find a mass mailing from the local Republican Party (I guess I was still on the list) warning that Pete Buttigieg was dangerously leftist, citing the high school essay as proof. I wasn't too worried about it—by then even many local Republicans were support-ing me—but it prompted me to go back and find the essay.

It definitely reads like something written by a high schooler, start-ing with the opening sentence: "In this new century, there are a daunt-ing number of important issues which are to be confronted if we are to progress as a nation." Other comments fit the times then but no longer ring true—such as when I lamented that a strong conservative like Pat Buchanan "has been driven off the ideological edge" of an increasingly centrist Republican Party. But the basic premise still holds: that candi-dates for office can easily develop "an ability to outgrow their convictions in order to win power," and that Sanders was an inspiring exception.

Also impressive to me then was the fact that Sanders often worked across the aisle, collaborating with Republicans when possible and using his position as the only independent in Congress to drive dialogue on issues like trade. The lesson here, which Sanders himself would dem-onstrate some twenty years later when he ran for president, was that bipartisanship and appeal to independents was not the same thing as ideological centrism. I wrote that Sanders's "real impact has been as a reaction to the cynical climate which threatens the effectiveness of the democratic system."

I had forgotten about the contest until one day in March, when one of my teachers appeared, beaming, in the hall and pulled me aside after class. I had won first prize, she said, and would be flown to the library in Boston to meet the award committee and accept the scholarship money that went along with it.

A few weeks later, wearing a newly purchased suit (my first), I stepped into the soaring atrium of the JFK Library in Boston Harbor. Beneath its giant American flag, flanked by my parents, our principal Mr. Cassidy, and two teachers from Saint Joe, I was ushered to an eleva-tor and up to a reception room commanding views of the Boston sky-line, with planes descending toward the airport and ships crossing the harbor. It was unlike anything in Indiana.

My eyes widened as people I had only read about in the news milled about, holding soft drinks. The lanky and cheerful Senator Al Simpson, Republican from Wyoming, widely known as one of the wittiest members of Congress, began talking to me as if we'd known each other for years. (I was too new around politics to realize that for him this was a professional skill as well as a personal quality.) "You have to keep a sense of humor, otherwise they'll chew your ass and it'll get you down," he advised. A distinguished-looking journalist named John Seigenthaler casually mentioned that he had launched *USA Today*, while another elderly patrician gentleman dropped that he had once chaired the Democratic National Committee.

Dignified and quiet, Caroline Kennedy was standing a little apart from the other guests with her three children at her side, looking as much like an attentive mother as like the American political royalty she was. Then, I had my first experience of the feeling in a room when a very famous person walks in. The energy of the room shifted perceptibly, and I turned to see the arrival of Senator Ted Kennedy, "the Lion of the Senate." Moving slowly but with a kind of fire in his crisp blue eyes that made him all at the same time seem fierce and warm, he was heralded by the kids yelling, "Uncle Teddy!" as they rushed from Caroline's side into his enormous embrace.

Feeling at once elevated and humbled, I was suddenly aware of looking like an Indiana hayseed, a schoolboy shaking hands with an icon. I have no recollection of what either of us said, until the end of the conversation, when he offered me an internship the following summer in his Washington office. His voice, full of Boston *ah*'s, sounded just like that of President Kennedy challenging America to go to the moon and do other great things, "naht because they are easy, but because they ah hahd." In my mind, listening to the senator speak, I heard the strains of historic presidential leadership.

It felt like I had been handed a ticket to the major leagues.

II

LEARNING

To learn one must be humble.
But life is the great teacher.

JAMES JOYCE

2

City on a Hill

On the underground platform at the stop for Harvard Square, the approaching Red Line train made itself felt as well as heard. A breeze of air would push out of the darkness of the curving tunnel, a beat ahead of the rumble and the light from the lead car. Each time I sensed that little gust during my freshman fall, it brought with it the thrill of knowing I now lived in a city.

I know now that, by the standards of major global cities, Boston is mid-sized. Cambridge itself might be considered quaint. But to an eighteen-year-old freshman out of northern Indiana, navigating a subway unsupervised seemed nothing less than an initiation into the ways of the metropolis. I made an effort to blend in, entering the station weekly to catch the train for an internship at the JFK Library. As I trotted down the crowded steps, I would try to mimic the worldly and jaded affect of the commuters around me. But as I returned later in the evening, hustling past the florist and the Dunkin' Donuts and on up the stairs into the Square, my face would still have stood out amid the grumpy Bostonians, betraying the fact that I was as exhilarated by the idea of being in a "big" city as I was by the new marvels of college life.

I would emerge into the Square, eyes darting around the lively scene. There were the teenage punks, their expressions just a little too bored to be menacing, who loitered with skateboards off the entrance to the station. Always, someone would be passing out flyers, usually for something edgy like a Lyndon LaRouche for President rally or a Chomsky talk down at MIT. Nearby, at Au Bon Pain, lingered a mix of postdocs, autodidact geniuses, and drifters. Some of the outdoor tables had chessboards built into them, one permanently occupied by a man with a little sign inviting you to PLAY THE CHESS MISTER. Looking up overhead, I could note the time on a lighted display over the Cambridge Savings Bank building. I felt that telling the time by reading it off a building, instead of a watch, affirmed that I was now in a bustling place of consequence, as downtown South Bend had perhaps once been.

Past Out of Town News, where you could get exotic newspapers like *La Repubblica* or *Le Monde*, I would cross the street, where, unlike home, cars would actually yield to pedestrians. Across Massachusetts Avenue and through a gate, the loose energy of the Square suddenly gave way to the serene precincts of Harvard Yard. The darkening quadrangle bespoke a kind of meaningful silence (Henry Adams would say, "If Harvard College gave nothing else, it gave calm") as I trekked across it to my red-brick dorm, Holworthy Hall.

My room on the fourth floor was itself a wonder. It had hardwood floors and a wall of exposed brick, a style I'd only seen in fashionable restaurants and occasionally on television. There was even a fireplace (bricked up, but still), and a fire escape that, with some imagination and well-meaning disregard for rules, could serve as a balcony. A letter on your pillow had a list of everyone who had ever lived in your room, which in my case included Ulysses Grant Jr., Cornel West, and Horatio Alger.

No less impressive were the present occupants living up and down that staircase. They all seemed easygoing and normal enough at first, but soon it began to feel like the academy of *X-Men*: everyone had some concealed special power. Cate, on the second floor, could read books at four or five times the normal pace. Andrew, on the ground floor, could do a Rubik's Cube from any starting point in about a minute. Steve, my roommate, was like a science fiction telepath; he could dissect social interactions and predict with remarkable accuracy how the relationships among other freshmen we knew would play out with time. Pretty much everyone expertly played musical instruments, sports, or both. I had gone from the top of my high school class to wondering how I would measure up.

From out the big green door of our Holworthy Hall entryway, I could look into the faint fog of history that blankets Harvard Yard, knowing which dorms had housed which U.S. presidents, from Adams (Massachusetts Hall) to Kennedy (Weld). Subtle cues everywhere linked history with expectation. A stone lintel over one of the gates read ENTER TO GROW IN WISDOM, and on the other side DEPART TO SERVE BETTER THY COUNTRY AND THY KIND. Though the seventeenth century Puritans who founded the place wouldn't exactly recognize it these days, the basic message had not changed: you are among a select few admitted to this place, for the rare privilege of a fine education. And you had better put it to good use.

There were daily reminders that you were expected to be part of history, if not magnificently, then tragically. In Memorial Hall, after filling your belly with scrambled eggs, you emerged into a churchlike transept lit through stained glass and lined with marble panels bearing the memories of Harvard's Civil War dead by name, date, and place, each punctuated by a grave period.

The names all seemed characteristically Harvard. The place names seemed apt, too, almost as if those places had originally been named in the foreknowledge that a great many men would one day die there. I sometimes paused to recite a few of them, under my breath, between eating breakfast and going to class:

Peter Augustus Porter. 3 June, 1864. Cold Harbor.

Richard Chapman Goodwin. 9 August, 1862. Cedar Mountain.

George Whittemore. 17 September, 1862. Antietam.

William Oliver Stevens. 4 May, 1863. Chancellorsville.

I tried to envision being part of the Civil War generation of Harvard students—or for that matter the World War I and II soldiers remembered at nearby Memorial Church. What would it be like to wrestle with college education at the same time a nation was at war? In that fall of 2000, it was hard to picture; war seemed unimaginably remote and theoretical, something that happened only to populations of a different time and place. Still less could I imagine that, after graduating, I would ever have occasion to carry a weapon on foreign soil.

AS SOON AS I ARRIVED on campus, I started hanging around the Institute of Politics, better known as the IOP, a center for undergraduates that brought speakers and fellows from government, policy, and journalism for the purpose of inspiring young people to pursue public service. At various events, you would munch on cheese or pepperoni pizza with impressive fellows; that fall's slate included Rick Davis, fresh off managing John McCain's first presidential campaign, and Jamil Mahuad, the ex-president of Ecuador who had just been deposed in a coup. More formal events in the forum would host a Cabinet member or foreign prime minister, there to give a speech containing some significant policy pivot that would make headlines the next day.

At first the proximity of these figures was one more shot in the arm for an already healthy Ivy League student ego. But the more attention you paid to the leaders who came through, especially the most accomplished ones, the more you sensed that their effectiveness did not come from the playing-up of prestige. The IOP's director, the retired Senator David Pryor of Arkansas, embodied this: he specialized in putting you at ease. Slow-talking and plain-spoken, he cultivated the demeanor of a kindly bumpkin. Not very tall and just a little hunched, he would look at you with wide and gentle eyes and greet you in the Southern drawl you might expect of a former senator from Arkansas. Listening as you spoke, he would first furrow his eyebrows in concentration, then they would rise and his face would slowly open, as he took in whatever you had to say with interest and pleasure. Interacting with him, you would feel special—and disarmed, forgetting that you were face-to-face with the man who had outmaneuvered the segregationist former Governor Orval Faubus, mentored a young Bill Clinton, and dominated the politics of his home state for a generation.

This was the political education we really needed—the realization that success in politics was not necessarily about impressing people with your pedigree or intellect. Pryor's successor at the IOP, former Agriculture Secretary and Kansas Congressman Dan Glickman, had a similar humble streak, only with a Midwestern flavor. At a function or meeting with students, he would never fail to open by joking that he never could have gotten into Harvard, and I suppose we took that at face value rather than as flattery. In fact, Glickman had a law degree from George Washington University, had chaired the House Intelligence Committee, and was an authority on the modern role of Congress. As a freshman, you might have been lulled into thinking that you really were deserving of such compliments from this Cabinet secretary. By junior year, hearing the same sort of thing, you would have matured enough to realize you were the recipient of a kindness, the treatment that is instinctual to a politician who knows that you will be best to work with if you have first been made to feel good about yourself.

Politics was in the air freshman year, though in retrospect it seemed like an almost quaint kind of politics, preoccupied with arguments that hadn't changed much since the 1980s. I volunteered for Al Gore's campaign that fall, chauffeuring guests around Boston during the run-up to the presidential debate there, but the sense among many students was that Bush and Gore were barely distinguishable on domestic policy: center-left versus center-right. The biggest campaign-related excitement was the arrival of riot police on the outskirts of the debate site to contend with Green Party protesters who were marching and chanting, "Let Ralph [Nader] debate." When Bush ultimately prevailed in the Supreme Court and claimed the presidency, it still felt like little would change from the Clinton era.

National politics seemed sleepy compared to the scene on campus itself. In April 2001, a student group called the Progressive Student Labor Movement took over the offices of the university's president, demanding a living wage for Harvard janitors and food workers. That spring, a daily diversion on the way to class was to see which national figure—Cornel West or Ted Kennedy one day, John Kerry or Robert Reich another—had turned up in the Yard to encourage the protesters.

Striding past the protesters and the politicians addressing them, on my way to a "Pizza and Politics" session with a journalist like Matt Bai or a governor like Howard Dean, I did not guess that the students poised to have the greatest near-term impact were not the social justice warriors at the protests, nor the more buttoned-up types I would find at the Institute of Politics, but a few mostly apolitical geeks who were quietly at work in Kirkland House, the dorm across the street, cooking up a virtual version of the paper face books that Harvard would distribute on move-in day.

We knew, of course, that the new century would herald great technological change. So much ink has been spilled on the flood of tech's arrival that it is hard to say much about it that isn't repetitive. But even now, looking back, the swiftness of it is stupefying. In that fall of 2000, my freshman dorm room had a "cordless" phone linked to a wired base, from which I could dial a 1-800 number to use a long-distance calling card and then reach home in South Bend. One year later, I returned to campus with a Sprint flip phone whose monochrome display let you see the number that was calling you, and which remarkably charged the same no matter what area code you were calling. One more year passed, and I had in my pocket a tiny (as was the fashion then) T68i phone by Ericsson with a 101-by-80 pixel display boasting 256 colors. What most excited me about it, as a tech fan, was that it could connect to a computer, with a new technology called Bluetooth, and download your address book without you having to key in every name with the numeric keypad. A year after that, I began to see the occasional professional around town with her face glued to a BlackBerry, which could be used to read email. What could possibly be so compelling, I thought, on that little screen?

The front end of Harvard's own website, as of September 2000, was about one page long, and was all text except the Harvard logo and a rotating campus news photo the size of a postage stamp. To check email, you would open up a Telnet window and use a program called PINE to bring up an interface that resembled an Atari game. By 2002, the *Harvard Crimson* had occasion to run a story on the remarkable fact that newly arrived freshmen were checking their email almost exclusively by webmail.

As part of a side job for the IOP, I was entrusted in the fall of 2002 with an expensive digital camera, which I used to take photographs of visiting speakers like Serbian Prime Minister Zoran Djindjic and Senator Kennedy. By the following year, as Serbia reeled from Djindjic's assassination, most students had a digital camera of their own. Junior year I got a camcorder for Christmas, and brought it to campus to take video footage of dorm life—by senior year, to the great amusement of friends, I could edit it on my own laptop and burn it to a DVD. (YouTube would not exist for another year.)

"Social media" wasn't a term of art yet, though we did notice it beginning to emerge around us even before Mark Zuckerberg changed the way all of us relate to the Internet and to each other. There was MySpace, and something called Friendster, and a few others that I never got around to signing up for. For a brief period, online social networking seemed like it might be a fad. It was intriguing, but could meet the same fate as the short-lived Kozmo.com, a within-the-hour retail delivery service that was popular on campus during my freshman year but arrived fifteen years too soon. But something did feel different about that February of 2004 when the creation of thefacebook.com ricocheted around campus, and we came to view it as part of Harvard, like the *Crimson* or the Square. It became indispensable for checking on your friends and exchanging gossip, and began to overtake AOL Instant Messenger and even compete with email. (Texting was still sporadic, since you generally had to pay by the text.) Suddenly you could look up who was friends with whom—and who was seeing whom.

In the privacy of my room, out of what I told myself was curiosity, I could even search which users were men whose profiles said they were interested in men. Still years away from facing the reality of my own sexual orientation, I had no practical use for the information, but I was impressed that some of my classmates had no reservations about putting it online in this way. Only today can I imagine the comedy of traveling back in time to tap my twenty-one-year-old self on the shoulder and explain to him that one day he would use a Facebook-connected app *on a phone* to be introduced to his future husband.

ACADEMICALLY, IT DIDN'T TAKE LONG to decide that I should major in Harvard's program in History and Literature. Plenty of subjects had been interesting in school, but it was literature that had captured not just my mind but also my emotions. I had wanted to explore it deeply ever since reading Robert Frost's "The Road Not Taken" in Mr. Wylie's sixth-grade English class at Stanley Clark School. At twelve years old, it felt like sudden enlightenment when we learned that this poem wasn't just about two roads in a forest but about the choices we make in life. Once I'd figured out what a metaphor was, I saw them on every page of text. I wanted to read every great author, maybe even become a novelist. And doing History and Literature together meant that I could also study pretty much anything that had a past—ideas, politics, foreign countries, and global affairs.

I decided to focus on American studies, bolstered by my good fortune of landing a freshman seminar with Sacvan Bercovitch. As English professors go, he was famous; my father made it clear to me that studying with him was a big deal. Bercovitch had deeply impacted American studies by pointing out all the ways in which modern America owed its culture to the influence of the early Puritans.

Until then, I had considered the Puritan years to be the most boring period in all of American history, full of dour and interminable sermons by the likes of Cotton Mather. But to Bercovitch, the Puritans were the key to American identity. His seminal book *The American Jeremiad* described a distinctly American form of rhetoric that goes back to Puritan sermons and persists in our culture even now: a way of castigating society for failing to live up to its sacred covenant, while reinforcing the sense of promise in what we could become.

The threads of influence are easy to find, if you know what to look for. Ronald Reagan and John F. Kennedy each used the same phrase, "city upon a hill," to describe America's destiny among nations. In doing so, they used imagery that traces back to John Winthrop and the sermon he gave using that same phrase almost four hundred years ago, aboard the ship that would bring him and his followers to America. Bercovitch explained how Winthrop's image of America as a beacon of virtue would become the basis for an American exceptionalism that helps define our country to this day.

Bercovitch was an unlikely character for Harvard, a son of Canadian Jewish radicals (they had named him after the anarchist martyrs Sacco and Vanzetti) who began his career as a dairy farmer on a kibbutz in Israel. He described returning to Canada and becoming a manager at a grocery store, where his bosses funded him to attend night school out of embarrassment that someone in management lacked a degree. Though a giant in his field, in person he was unassuming, a little stooped, with big eyes and a permanent, mischievous smile. He was semi-retired by the time I got into his seminar, teaching just for the fun of it.

He took a liking to me, and hired me as a research assistant on his massive project of editing *The Cambridge History of American Literature*. I was happy to have the work, the pocket money, and the time around such an eminent scholar, though by now I was beginning to realize for certain that I would not become an English professor like him or my parents. Under his influence, I would write my thesis about another Puritan sermon, less famous than Winthrop's, a paean to the early missionaries' "errand into the wilderness."

A generation after Winthrop, in 1670, Samuel Danforth gave a classic jeremiad excoriating his followers and society for forgetting their purpose in coming to the New World:

> Now let us sadly consider whether our ancient and primitive affections to the Lord Jesus, his glorious Gospel, his pure and Spiritual Worship and the Order of his House, remain, abide and continue firm, constant, entire and inviolate. Our Saviour's reiteration of this Question, *What went ye out into the Wilderness to see?* is no idle repetition, but a sad conviction of our dullness and backwardness to this great duty, and a clear demonstration of the weight and necessity thereof.

If Winthrop saw America becoming a blessed example of godly living to which all others might turn, Danforth spoke of America's civilizing mission, to go out into wild and savage lands ("over the vast Ocean into this waste and howling Wilderness," he said) and make them more like the image of heaven on earth.

In my senior thesis, I drew a line from this thinking to America's Cold War insistence on invading Vietnam to "save" it from godless Communism, leading to a different and doomed errand into the jungle. I compared the American government's narrative about Vietnam with the views of outside commentators like the British novelist Graham Greene, whose novel *The Quiet American* bore out his skepticism of America's purposes. In Greene's novel, based partly on real events, an idealistic young American intelligence operative winds up contributing to a terrorist attack in Vietnam, all with the best of intentions. "Innocence," Greene observes in the novel, "is like a dumb leper that has lost his bell, wandering the world, meaning no harm." Greene's world-weary, English, Catholic outlook could not have been more different from the Puritan-inflected American understanding of its Cold War mission.

Though my focus was America, I also took courses in Arabic. In high school I had read the Sudanese novelist Tayeb Salih's masterpiece, *Season of Migration to the North*, which tells of an African graduate student's romantic conquest of several young British women in a sort of inverted version of the plot of *Heart of Darkness*. Just from the linguistic rhythm and the poetic richness of the translated language, I could sense how beautiful the Arabic prose must have been, and I wanted to learn the original. Plus, a bit vaguely, I figured that knowing Arabic would be useful for a future career in public service or journalism.

It was hard—much harder than the French and Spanish I had studied in high school, or even the Maltese (also a Semitic language) that I had picked up from my father. But it was also a highly rewarding language to learn. At first the English-speaking learner struggles to grab hold of something, since there are almost no similarities between our words and theirs. But after a year or two of learning, the structure of the language begins to unfold and reveal itself—and unlike almost any other language, you can derive most words you don't know by using the words you do know. After a while it's all prefixes, suffixes, and rearrangement of a few vowels to make whole families of words according to strict patterns. It all works by analogy: you can take the same changes you make to the word for "cooking" to get the word for "kitchen," and do it to the word for "writing" to get the word for "office."

When I showed up in late 2000, not many people were studying Arabic. I don't think there were more than a dozen of us in that first-year class my freshman fall. Most were Arab or Jewish students interested in getting in touch with personal roots. We knew the Middle East was important, but we had no idea that one year later the entire trajectory of America's relationship with the Muslim world would shift.

WHEN THE PLANES HIT, I was facedown on the bottom bunk, oblivious to the sunbeams angling in through the old windowpanes of my sophomore quarters in Leverett House. It was my dorm-mate, Uzo—rarely one to wake before I did—who knocked on the door, walked in, and said, "Hey, Peter, you might want to see this." Soon there were four or five of us gathered on the futon in the next room, watching the *Today Show* coverage as the idea that we had lived to see the End of History collapsed with the two towers.

That Tuesday happened to be registration day. At midday, not knowing what else to do, I walked to Harvard Yard to sign up for classes. Everyone seemed to be in a daze, and wide-eyed students everywhere, disproportionately from New York and Washington, were on their cell phones trying to call home, mostly without success. Standing at an interfaith prayer service hastily organized in Harvard Yard, I looked up and saw a lone fighter jet banking in the crisp and cloudless blue sky overhead, as if to advise all of us below that war was no longer going to be distant or theoretical for us.

After trying all day to call home, I finally got through in the evening and reassured my parents that I was all right. It now feels like an odd assurance to have had to make, since the attack happened hundreds of miles away, but that day it seemed as if we all had to check on each other for injury, as if anyone we cared about might have been harmed that morning just by being in the same world where this had happened. A few days earlier I had turned up at Logan Airport with my bags packed for school; this morning, some men had stepped on that same curb, walked through that same concourse, boarded a half-empty airplane, and murdered their way into a new chapter of world affairs. It was immediately clear that the project of my generation had just been reassigned in some way. The infinite peace of post–Cold War promise was in fact a mirage, and we would be dealing with matters we thought our grandparents' generation had settled, having to do with war, terror, and freedom. It was hard not to think of that wall in Memorial Hall, and wonder how many of my classmates would wind up among a new generation of war dead.

There was a few days' ellipsis in which politics seemed remote. As people were still being pulled out of the rubble and grief provoked us to say things like "We will never be the same," America felt more decent in mourning. Articles were written about the death of irony, and for a moment it felt as if the vengeful return of history would give us all the seriousness of historians, grappling with the complex forces that had brought us to this point. We seemed, for those few days, not just wounded but morally aware. Within days President Bush was visiting a mosque, eloquently distinguishing between Islamist terrorism and Islamic people. "Islam is peace," he said, in a speech largely forgotten today. "Women who cover their heads in this country must feel comfortable going outside their homes." Just weeks earlier, the nation had been obsessed with shark attacks and a philandering congressman; now we seemed to have matured overnight.

Perhaps inevitably, that sense didn't last for long. We might have lost our innocence and learned something about the world, but we did not suddenly become wise. Americans were facing the first case in a generation in which a chain of events that started overseas shook and changed all of our lives. It's impossible to expect that we would respond by leaping to a new moral plane, or that we would immediately grasp the complexity of the global forces that had just come to harm us. Nor were we remotely prepared for the idea of modern asymmetric warfare.

Scanning AOL Instant Messenger away messages (which in retrospect represented an early-2000s forecast of what Twitter would be
like), I saw a message from one friend that summed up how it looked to
many: "Doesn't Afghanistan know we have bombs?" It took a while to
catch on to the idea that this was an attack on the United States not by
the country of Afghanistan, but by Al-Qaeda, protected by the Taliban,
which governed most Afghans but was not exactly an administration.
We had been attacked by a transnational network, hosted by a rogue
regime presiding over a failed state.

The responses were largely knee-jerk; a PATRIOT Act that under-
cut the freedoms that define America, and several quick steps down the
slippery slope to torture. So slow were we to realize how fundamentally
different this was than wars we had studied in school or seen in movies that by October we were bargaining against our own values, moving
steadily and surely into the jaws of a trap that Al-Qaeda had laid for us.

IT WAS YEARS BEFORE I would get formal training in counterterrorism as a military officer, but it seemed clear even then as a history
student that the new national approach on terrorism was likely to be
self-defeating. The top priority of the terrorist—even more important
than killing you—is to make himself your top priority. This is why
protecting ourselves from terrorist violence is not enough to defeat
terrorism, especially if we try to achieve safety in ways that elevate
the importance of terrorists and wind up publicizing their causes. We
all want to avoid being harmed—but if the cost of doing so is making
the terrorist the thing you care about most, to the exclusion of the
other things that matter in your society, then you have handed him
exactly the kind of victory that makes terrorism such a frequent and
successful tactic.

A spectacle of murder and destruction, though it killed far fewer
people than ordinary gun violence, car accidents, or even cigarettes, had

the power to loosen our commitment to freedom at home and shatter our restraints on involvement abroad. It was clear enough why America had to do something to Al-Qaeda in Afghanistan, but it was not clear what American values the administration was willing to compromise in the context of what it was starting to call the Global War on Terror. Would our civil liberties be diminished in the name of protecting us? Would the longtime certainty that America does not torture people hold? Would America commit to supporting freedom and democracy in deed as well as word, or would we back any dictator who claimed to side with us in the new global war, ignoring what was happening in his own country?

The answers started to pour in, mostly discouraging. Soon our government was sending prisoners to third-party countries for torture. It was supporting a grotesque dictatorship in Uzbekistan abroad and checking on people's library usage at home, all in the name of fighting terrorism. At the same time, little was said about personal sacrifice at home for the purpose of winning a national conflict. Kids in World War II saved tinfoil from gum wrappers for the war effort, women reused nylon stockings as many times as possible, and everyone then knew why they were being asked to pay much higher taxes. This time around, it seemed that the war effort was wholly outsourced to those few Americans who served in uniform. America tripped over itself to salute them, without seeming to consider the possibility that civilians, too, could accept some risk or pay some contribution into the cause of freedom. I thought again of the names on that Civil War memorial wall as it became clear that this time, the task of dealing with this conflict would be assigned to a class of professional soldiers, not shared by all of our society on an all-hands-on-deck basis.

We might have had, in those years, a more serious conversation about what each of us owes to the country in a time of conflict. We might have been asked to weigh what risks we are willing to tolerate, personally, in order to remain certain that this is a free country. But after those first few seemingly enlightened days, the country's leadership showed little interest in helping us confront the choices we would have to make between safety and freedom.

Truly grasping and defeating the logic of suicide terrorism was too much for our Congress or administration, which lapsed instead into simplistic rhetoric. Emblematic of this was the sudden adoption, by administration spokespeople and Fox News anchors, of the bizarre term "homicide bomber" instead of "suicide bomber." It may have scratched an emotional itch, but the terminology was doubly useless, both belaboring the obvious fact that bombers are generally homicidal, and obscuring the tactically useful distinction between those murderers who are prepared to kill themselves in the process and those who are not.

Soon the president was telling us that "either you are with us, or you are with the terrorists," a dictum impossible for America to uphold or enforce in the case of Pakistan and many other states playing the three-dimensional chess game of geopolitics in the Islamic world. Next it was an "Axis of Evil," and so on. For the home front, the message was that we would be kept safe through the deployment of force and the acceptance of some encroachments on our freedom and privacy. And also, for some reason, we would need to invade Iraq.

As a student, I couldn't see for myself what this all was wreaking upon our politics until I went home for the summer of 2002 and volunteered on the campaign of Jill Long Thompson, who was running as a Democrat for the U.S. House seat in South Bend. The typical rule is that the president's party fares badly in a midterm election, but there was no indication that that would happen this year. Democrats, unsure of themselves, were afraid to sound like an opposition at all, and many carefully avoided opposing the Iraq War for fear of looking unpatriotic. (Some, particularly Hillary Clinton, would come to regret this posturing.) Instead they tried to change the subject, emphasizing Social Security and Medicare, even though global security was the dominant issue of our moment—even in Indiana.

One hot day that summer, I was sent to help with the Fulton County Democratic Party's entry in a rural small-town parade. As we prepared our little float with campaign signs and balloons, I did a double-take at the parade entry next to us, belonging to "Kountry Kidz Day Care." A group of cute, rambunctious ten-year-olds in red T-shirts proudly showed me their float, which consisted of a large, uneven pair of four-foot-high model skyscrapers made out of foam core. Around the top of the gray rectangular objects a loose wrap of fishnet and mesh suggested dark smoke, while flames made of orange construction paper shot out the side of one of the objects, surrounded by cotton balls representing more billowing smoke. A big American flag shared the flatbed that carried this strange scene, and a sign on the back read UNITED WE STAND. This was a rural Indiana kids' day-care craft project, circa July 2002: *they had made a little 9/11.*

BEFORE THE END OF THE DECADE I would see Iraq for myself, visiting Baghdad as a civilian economic adviser, but back then all I knew was what I learned in class and read in the paper. I saw our president declare that Saddam Hussein must disarm his chemical and biological weapons, and vow, "If he won't do so voluntarily we will disarm him."

The tough talk was rousing, but it made no strategic sense. Saddam was a notoriously sinister dictator whose top priority, as with all dictators, was his own survival. It followed that he viewed his arsenal of chemical and biological weapons (as most of us believed he had) as an insurance policy to keep him in power. He would only part with them voluntarily if it would benefit his personal security—an unlikely course for someone who did not trust America. But actually using them would almost certainly lead to his destruction, so he had every reason to sit on his weapons if he had them. The only scenario where he might use them would be if he had nothing to lose by doing so—and now, by invading, we were poised to create that very situation. Logically, this meant that an invasion would be very costly and bloody for American troops. Invited to represent the College Democrats at a rally outside the Science Center at Harvard, I spoke of the difference between necessary wars, like those memorialized in the church nearby, and unnecessary wars that could take young lives for no purpose at all.

It turns out that most of us, for and against the war, were wrong about the weapons. He didn't have any—and so they were not there to be used against American troops. Iraq fell quickly, and for a moment it seemed that the invasion was a vindication of American intervention abroad. Protesters like me looked foolish. Sure, the pretext for war was actually false, but who would quibble over that, as a brutal dictatorship was being turned into a model democracy at relatively little cost to America?

Then the suicide bombings began. We were not, as the administration had promised, "greeted as liberators." A well-functioning democracy did not emerge. And the ensuing chaos made it clear that the administration had not planned for the aftermath of the invasion, as Iraqi cities became a kill zone for our troops. We who were against the invasion had been wrong about the weapons, but right about the war. The administration had been wrong about both.

AS ALL THIS UNRAVELED, I was spending my senior year mostly absorbed in a different war—Vietnam, the focus of my thesis on the influence of Puritan thought. In an unused seminar room that a few of us had taken over, I sat surrounded by Dunkin' Donuts coffee cups and books, immersed in the recent past while its parallels with the present became impossible to ignore. I studied the way America's government in the 1970s told its people an increasingly improbable story of mission and moral clarity, trying to defy a reality on the ground that could no longer be denied amid a rising American body count.

I remember very little about Senior Week or graduation, other than that it rained, and that we had a sense of graduating into a darkening world where we would need to make ourselves useful. We had arrived on campus during the final months of the Clinton presidency, on the heels of the longest peacetime economic expansion in U.S. history. Now we were wartime graduates. It felt like a kind of memorial service for our vanishing college life as we filed in our black gowns into the expanse of the open quadrangle known as Tercentenary Theater and sat facing Memorial Church while the massive structure of Widener Library towered behind us under the warm rain clouds. I listened vaguely as the U.N. Secretary General, Kofi Annan, gave a speech about three simultaneous global crises of security, solidarity, and cultural division. Meanwhile, at William & Mary's commencement address, Jon Stewart treated the graduates to a cheeky but rueful commentary on the "real world," on behalf of the generation in charge: "I don't really know how to put this, so I'll be blunt. We broke it. . . . But here's the good news. You fix this thing, you're the next Greatest Generation, people."

3

Analytics

The education that began at Harvard continued in one form or another for the next ten years. First came Campaigns 101, for which my classroom was a cubicle in a windowless office in downtown Phoenix, where I did research and press work for the Kerry-Edwards presidential run of 2004. After that defeat I followed my boss, Doug Wilson, back to Washington, where he worked for the former defense secretary, William Cohen. The winter and spring amounted to Washington 101, an education in the mechanics of our capital, which I navigated as a sort of gofer for Doug, helping him to organize a conference of American and Muslim leaders. (This included an early lesson in the whims of political fortune after we invited the three Republicans then deemed most likely to become president: George Allen, Lindsey Graham, and Mark Sanford.) The summer of 2005 saw me back in an actual classroom, this time in Tunis, where a highly affordable language program gave me the chance to improve my Arabic.

Formal education continued that fall: a Rhodes Scholarship took me to Oxford for two years in large halls and small professors' rooms in the ancient colleges learning philosophy, politics, and economics. Back to the U.S. in 2007, I landed a job in Chicago at McKinsey & Company, and my classroom was everywhere—a conference room, a serene corporate office, the break room of a retail store, a safe house in Iraq, or an airplane seat—any place that could accommodate me and my laptop. The capstone on my decade of education was in 2010, when I left McKinsey for a tough but priceless year-long political crash course in which I challenged the state treasurer of Indiana, and was overwhelmingly defeated in my first experience on the ballot.

Geographically, the arc of these years was a sort of looped boomerang, a first departure from home that took me east, then farther west, then back east; then across the Atlantic; and then at last closer to home, to Chicago, less than a hundred miles from South Bend, and finally all the way back to the neighborhood where I grew up. In retrospect it was a homeward spiral all along: the more my worldly education grew with lessons from abroad, the clearer it became that this long and winding road was leading me back home, to find belonging by making myself useful there. Now it's obvious, but in the midst of that education it felt like just one step at a time. A Tunisian souk, an Oxford exam room, and a Great Lakes office park all had something to teach me, and each place nudged me closer to home.

EDUCATION CAN COME BY DRUDGERY or by adventure, and I had my share of both. Sometimes they're interwoven. In Washington, days spent mostly arranging other people's airline tickets were occasionally punctuated by the chance to tag along and meet some foreign ambassador as part of the conference preparations (adventure enough, for a twenty-two-year-old interested in policy). In Tunis, where air-conditioning was as rare as a summer day below a hundred degrees, mornings in the sweaty classroom gave way to afternoons walking through hookah smoke and perfume in the markets of the old city and trying, in vain, to get Tunisian acquaintances to reveal over coffee how they felt about living under a dictatorship. (A few years later, the Arab Spring would tell us things that the friendly yet circumspect young Tunisians would not discuss openly with foreign students, no matter how many prying and dangerous questions we naïvely asked.)

At Oxford, my chosen program was unforgiving. The watchword of the famous PPE (Philosophy, Politics, and Economics) program was rigor: any sloppy argument or imprecise claim would get picked apart politely by a skeptical professor or fellow student. It was the ideal prescription for someone like me, reared on a humanities curriculum in which a stirring phrase carried as much weight as a precise argument. The missing piece in my formal education had been the analytical side of things, which to my Oxford faculty was the element that mattered most.

I was forced to learn the British tradition of analytical philosophy, which breaks down the meaning of the words we throw around casually yet with conviction in debates about ethics and politics, sometimes without knowing what we are talking about. Under the gaze of the Oxford dons, every question was handled with the utmost precision, to get to the bottom of what was *really* intended by a term or an idea in the course of an argument.

For example, in a philosophical debate over the nature of free will, we were required to confront just how difficult it is to define what "free will" even means. We considered one definition: that a freely chosen act is one taken by someone who could have done otherwise. It felt intuitively like a good way of describing free will: if I did something, and could have done something else, then clearly I made this choice freely. But then, another philosopher pointed out, what if you chose to stay in a room all day because you wanted to, but without your knowing it the door was locked from the outside? It turns out you could not have done otherwise, but we also would believe this choice was a free one, so clearly a more precise definition had to be found . . . and the refinements and arguments would go from here.

I'm not sure I ever got to the bottom of free will, but these kinds of analyses and arguments cultivated a healthy sense of clarity. After years of painting, with broad verbal brushes, the kind of beautiful images that earn good grades in certain American college literature courses, I now had to make sure that every sentence and idea was precise, clearly defined, and airtight, in order to survive the skepticism of a British critic.

In the process, I learned more rigorous ways to explain the moral intuitions I already had about politics and society. Sitting in one of Oxford's ancient libraries, I learned the theories of John Rawls (who, ironically, taught at Harvard). Rawls became famous for creating a new definition of justice, which boils down to this: a society is fair if it looks like something we would design before knowing how we would come into the world. He imagined a fictional "original position," the position we would be in if we were told we were about to be born, but were not told about the circumstances we would be born into—how tall or short we would be, or of what race or nationality, or what resources or personal qualities we would have. This vision of justice is often compared to being asked how you would want a cake to be divided if you did not know which piece will be yours: equally, of course.

Like most good philosophy in the analytical tradition, it gave precise expression to something we already understand intuitively. For example, it gives us one way to explain why we know that racial equality is a feature of a just society: even a prejudiced group of people would probably all insist on a racially equal society if they were asked to design in advance a world into which they would soon be born, without knowing which race life's lottery would assign them at birth. It was a compelling way of thinking about fairness, and not hard to connect to debates about racial and income inequality in our politics back home. And, because nothing there was endorsed as "correct" but only as worth studying and picking apart, I was then led to Robert Nozick's impressive conservative critique of Rawls—followed by Gerald Cohen's equally impressive socialist critique of Nozick.

In ethics, I studied the debates between Kantians, who believe that your motivation is the most important thing in deciding whether you are doing good, and utilitarians, who look only to the outcome of your deeds, not your intent. Years later, in office, I would think of these debates often, knowing that government often requires you to think as a utilitarian—to try to bring about the "greatest good for the greatest number"—even if your personal philosophy is more Kantian, Christian, or otherwise grounded in something besides the cold math of utilitarian ethics. Meanwhile, studying international relations as part of the "Politics" leg of the PPE program, I learned to trace in detail what happened when a few colonial powers promised, to more than one group of people, the same small patches of Middle Eastern land. And I learned to debate the remarkable finding by political scientists that truly democratic countries almost never go to war with one another.

Most new and useful of all, perhaps, was a rigorous training in economics. I had taken an economics course in college, but had known nothing like the intensity of the tutorials at Pembroke College. These one-on-one or two-on-one sessions with faculty were the backbone of instruction at Oxford. In the case of my economics course, they felt less like the friendly and personalized instruction conjured up by the word "tutorial," and more like a weekly oral exam on whatever I had managed to teach myself in the preceding six days. But the system worked.

Racing to catch up to my second-year peers, I mastered the basics of supply and demand, utility, preferences, auction theory, and market equilibrium. I learned to admire the theoretical elegance of the free market under perfect conditions. Then I began to learn about all of the situations in which those perfect conditions break down, and all of the ways markets get skewed in the real world. One calculus equation at a time, I came to understand in thorough mathematical detail why supply and demand cannot be expected to deliver fair prices or efficient outcomes in many situations. Indeed, even the most orthodox economic theories showed that market failures were all but guaranteed to occur in situations, like health care and education delivery, where a seller has power over a buyer, or a buyer is seeking a service that can't easily be assigned a dollar value, or the seller and the buyer have different levels of information about the product.

The two years passed quickly, rushing toward the handful of days in June of 2007 when, in keeping with the Oxford tradition, I donned a white bow tie, suit, and gown to walk to the giant hall they call the Examination Schools. There, hundreds of students at a time would sit for each of the eight three-hour exams that would account for the entirety of our grades. Exiting the last exam, I received a pie in the face from a group of jubilant friends (also per tradition), and spent the next few days waiting for the results.

When they were finally posted, on a big sheet of paper with everyone's names on them outside the Exam Schools, I checked several times to make sure I wasn't misreading. I had finished with a "First," the highest grade in their remarkably simple (and very British) system of First, Second Upper, Second Lower, and Third Class degrees. To an English undergraduate, this single grade becomes a mark you carry for the rest of your life, shaping career opportunities for decades. Knowing I would head back to America meant that there was less at stake for me in the grade, but I took pride in it even while sensing that the time had come to learn what wasn't on the page and get an education in the real world, if there was such a thing. Which is why I went to McKinsey.

ANALYZING THE FINER POINTS of a profound question on the nature of freedom is one thing; analyzing a client's financial future and advising them on what to do about it is another. This is the specialty of McKinsey & Company, the dominant name in the field of management consulting. Since its product is, above all, the intellect of its employees, the firm (better known in consulting circles as the Firm) prides itself on hiring not just top business school graduates, but anyone it considers very bright and teachable, such as Rhodes Scholars.

To some, McKinsey is the pinnacle of smart and useful analysis in the business world. To others, it is the primary symbol of a trend that sees more and more graduates from prestigious programs go into the private sector when they could be committing themselves to public service, research, or some other worthy pursuit. When I decided to attend an informational session about McKinsey for graduate students, I felt ambivalent but more sympathetic to the latter camp. My education to date, and my hopes of making an impact in the world, pointed to public service, inquiry, and the arts, not business. But I also knew that I would have to understand business if I wanted to make myself useful in practice. Despite all my education, I felt ignorant about how the private sector really worked. I would leave Oxford with a degree in economics, but knew little firsthand about the functions—from logistics to finance— that made the private sector operate. And the firm known best for its expertise on how the private sector works was actually willing to give me an interview for a post-MBA job, taking a chance on the idea that if I was prepared to learn, they could teach me all the things about business I didn't know.

Also, crucially, they had a Chicago office. It was not the most glamorous office in the Firm—that title probably belonged in London, Dubai, New York, or Silicon Valley—but it was known for the diversity of industries it served, which would make it a good training ground. More importantly, it was a way for me to come back to the Midwest, a region whose role in shaping me had become more obvious the farther away I'd moved. When I finally saw the Chicago office for myself on the day of my final-round interview, I noticed not just the modern wood paneling, large abstract paintings, and big windows that signified an elegant corporate office space. I also saw, out the windows on the high floor of the Chase Tower where my interviewer received me, a view of

Lake Michigan's shoreline that you could trace, past Hyde Park and the South Side and the Skyway Bridge, all the way to the smokestacks marking the state line and the beginning of northern Indiana.

LET ME ASK YOU, for a moment, to imagine a list of the most interesting subjects in the world, ranked from one to infinity. The list is different for each of us. But some topics are fairly high on the list for almost everyone: topics such as television, religion, warfare, food, sports, space travel, the presidency, and sex. Now ask yourself where, on that list, you would put the subject on which I became an expert during the winter of 2010: North American grocery pricing.

Not in your top thousand? Me neither, at the time I was offered to join a team working on a client study on the subject. (For an associate, life at McKinsey mostly consists of months-long stints on a "team" of three or four people working on an engagement or "study" solving a problem for a client.) I was there because I had admired the partner in charge of the team since meeting him in the recruiting process. Jeff Helbling was low-key and clean-cut, with a sort of smart and unflappable discipline that melded the styles of his alma maters, West Point and Harvard Business School. A wise McKinsey alum had once told me that there were four things to think about when chasing assignments at the Firm: geography, industry, function, and people. Of these, she counseled, the most important is people. So when the chance came to work with Jeff, I jumped, even though I was uncertain how much professional fulfillment came from the prospect of commuting to Toronto every week to help a client in the grocery business figure out how to update its prices.

Soon I was spending my weekdays in a small, glass-walled conference room with three colleagues in a suburban office park, building models to compute how much it would cost to cut prices on various combinations of tens of thousands of items across hundreds of stores in every part of the country. The more I worked on the problem, the more complicated it seemed to become. Eventually the volume of data went beyond the capabilities of Microsoft Excel, and I began using a program called Microsoft Access. Access is designed to hold databases, but I was using it to do math, stretching its functionality to make it work partly like a computational spreadsheet on top of the data management program it was intended to be. As the data set grew to millions of lines, it started freezing my laptop computer. To make me more productive, the firm mailed a more powerful desktop computer to our team room. I hooked it up and spent the better part of many fourteen-hour days calculating at the machine, which my colleagues nicknamed Bertha.

Against all my expectations, it was fascinating. I wasn't just learning about the retail business or about computer programs—I was also learning about the nature of data. By manipulating millions of data points, I could weave stories about possible futures, and gather insights on which ideas were good or bad. I could simulate millions of shoppers going up and down the aisles of thousands of stores, and in my mind I pictured their habits shifting as a well-placed price cut subtly changed their perceptions of our client as a better place to shop.

Even more fulfilling, I became a useful part of a team that I liked. My manager, a young Englishwoman named Hannah Brooks with a varsity-level cricket career at Oxford under her belt, took good care of our team—checking on how we were doing and trying to protect our weekends from unnecessary encroachments of work—and I wanted to do a good job for her. Jeff came in every week or so to check on progress, and I felt motivated by the task of presenting him and Hannah with interesting results that he could share with the senior leadership of the client.

The problem grew ever more complex as we were asked to analyze the data more and more deeply. As the deadline for implementing the price cuts loomed, pressure grew—and so did the hours. Soon we were working sixty, seventy, eighty hours a week. At one point, a glitch in a computer pricing tool threatened to give every item the wrong UPC code by one digit, meaning the system could give dog food the price for olive oil, or price a snow shovel as a box of cereal. Everyone involved in the project had to do nothing else for days as we raced to manually correct the problem before the deadline for a round of price changes. One night I stopped work at four in the morning, only to toss and turn in my hotel bed, dreaming in spreadsheets. Friends became Excel formulas, fears were expressed as charts in PowerPoint.

Occasionally, I had worked that hard on a campaign or on my studies, but it felt strange to put in those kinds of hours not for a cause but for a client. I wanted to do a good job for my team, my firm, and my client—but this wasn't life-or-death stuff. And so it may have been inevitable that one afternoon, as I set Bertha to sleep mode to go out to the hallway for a cup of coffee, I realized with overwhelming clarity the reason this could not be a career for very long: I didn't care.

For purpose-driven people, this is the conundrum of client-service work: to perform at your best, you must learn how to care about something because you are hired to do so. For some, this is not a problem at all. A great lawyer or consultant can identify so closely with the client, or so strongly desire to be good at the job, or be so well compensated, that her purposes and interests and those of the client become one. But for others, work can only be meaningful if its fundamental purpose is in things that would matter even if no one would pay you to care about them. No matter how much I liked my clients and my colleagues, delivering for them could not furnish that deep level of purpose that I craved.

Once I understood this, I knew it was a matter of time before I had to find another career. I did find ways within the Firm to work more on issues that I considered intrinsically important, like energy efficiency research to help mitigate greenhouse gas emissions in the U.S., and war-zone economic development work to help grow private sector employment in Iraq and Afghanistan. But every few months the project and client changed, through the natural rhythm of the consulting business, and then it was time to study and care about something and someone new. The churn, which at first had been stimulating, now made me feel unmoored.

Not that I had ever truly expected management consulting to become my life's calling. I was in it for the education, and McKinsey had delivered on its promise as a place to learn—about industry, about project management, and about myself. Now it was time to seek work that linked whatever skills I had gained to the things that mattered most. Meanwhile, even before resolving what would come after life at the Firm, I began looking for ways to use personal time for causes I cared about, such as volunteering on campaigns. I also began researching military service, especially the possibility of being a reserve officer, which meant I could serve without necessarily making it a career. Unexpectedly, it was a campaign trip to Iowa that shifted my attitude on military service from curiosity to reality.

III

CAMPAIGNING

He must be . . . as aloof and incorruptible as the artist, yet sometimes as near the earth as the politician.

JOHN MAYNARD KEYNES

4

The Volunteers

"You boys are not dressed to be out in this cold," was how Farmer Daughton introduced himself as he stepped out of his truck and looked the three of us over.[1]

It was nearing midnight, and he did not appear to be in a very good mood, but we were as glad to see him as if he had been a long-lost friend. We had tried everything to get our little rental car out of the snow—pushing, pulling, rocking, revving. A clipboard from the back seat was used as a shovel, pick, and ramp, to no effect, until we finally gave up and decided to trudge toward the only light we could see, a farmhouse maybe a half mile away. So much for the shortcut.

The homeowner, an elderly lady in a nightgown, did not meet us with a smile and did not invite us in. Not that we were complaining— we felt pretty lucky that she hadn't greeted us with a shotgun, three

---

1 I think of him as Farmer Daughton, having gotten the impression he is a farmer, but I do not know his actual first name.

twenty-something men ringing her doorbell in the middle of the freezing January night. After we explained ourselves, she went to fetch a cordless phone and returned to the door, eyeing us as she reported to her son, "There's three fellas here say their car got stuck in the snow."

She listened for a minute, then looked at us and said, "He wants to know who you are."

I explained that we were campaign volunteers, not from around here, just trying to take a shortcut, and couldn't get our car unstuck. She studied us silently and then spoke back into the phone with her revised assessment: "It's three campaign fellas say they're stuck in the snow." She listened for a moment and hung up. He was on his way; we could wait outside.

So we were apprehensive but happy to see Farmer Daughton rumble up in his pickup truck and drive us back to the car. He didn't say much, other than that the temperature on the thermometer at his house read exactly zero and that we really should have had better gear for the cold weather. The Carhartt-type coveralls he was wearing seemed to do the trick for him; we did have winter coats on, but it wasn't much against the deep freeze. It was the kind of cold where you feel the hairs in your nostrils start to stand on end, the kind of cold where after ten minutes or so you don't feel cold at all, but just kind of woozy and weak-headed.

After a short drive we pulled up alongside our ditched car, its hazard lights still blinking, making me think of a half-sunken ship. He produced a towing chain and stood holding it for a moment; we weren't sure what was supposed to happen next. To clarify things, he asked a rhetorical question. "One of you boys gonna hook this up to your car, or am I going to get down on my hands and knees and do it for you?" Message received, we quickly got on all fours, racing to try to figure out how to attach it to our vehicle before he changed his mind about helping us at all.

I'd like to think that we won Farmer Daughton over, or at least that we parted on fairly good terms once the car was safely back on the main road, which is to say one that was actually paved, somewhere in the general vicinity of the town of Murray, Iowa. We thanked him profusely, even tried to pay him, but he would have none of that, and before leaving he had warmed up to the point that his grudging curiosity moved him to ask a question: Who we were campaigning for, anyway?

I think we were all dreading that question. This was as rural and white as any county in the Midwest: not Democratic territory in general, and if it was going to favor any Democrat at all, it would be John Edwards of North Carolina. Still, he had asked, and we weren't about to lie. After a moment studying our shoes, one of us finally coughed up that we were knocking on doors for Senator Obama. "Well . . ." He paused. "He's my second choice."

Turns out Farmer Daughton was a Bill Richardson man.

IN A WAY, MY MILITARY CAREER started that week, with my friends Ryan and Nathaniel, knocking on doors and canvassing local Dairy Queens in three of the lowest-income counties in the state of Iowa: Ringgold, Decatur, and Union.

Immersed in my business career at McKinsey but feeling like I couldn't just sit out the 2008 presidential campaign without being involved in some way, I had decided to take a little time off in January to do something to help the campaign of Barack Obama, who was still considered unlikely to overtake the juggernaut of Hillary Clinton but was showing increasing strength. I'd become aware of Obama when I was a senior in college and he was running for Senate in 2004; someone sent around a video clip of him speaking in a church, and it sounded different from any political rhetoric I'd heard before:

> If there's a child on the South Side of Chicago that can't read, that makes a difference in my life even if it's not my child. If there's a senior citizen on the West Side of Chicago who can't afford her

prescription medicine . . . that makes my life poorer even if it's not
my grandparent.

Inspired yet analytical, he seemed a welcome alternative to the bravado
of President Bush, and yet, unlike most running for Congress or Senate that year, he was able to campaign with very little reference to the
Republican side at all. Importantly, he had also opposed the Iraq War at
a time when most Democrats were afraid to say what they truly believed.

I started following his campaign, and as a graduating senior briefly
entertained a job offer from his race for Senate, before deciding to go to
Arizona instead for the Kerry campaign. My reasoning, idealistic if not
the most career-savvy, was that Obama was highly likely to win his race in
Illinois anyway, and so I could make more of a difference in a battleground
state on the presidential effort. It was there, on a thirteen-inch tube TV
in my office cubicle in Phoenix, that I watched the convention keynote
speech that made Obama famous. By 2008, it was clear to me that this
candidate was not like the others, and worth supporting for the presidency.

Many of my friends felt the same way, and three of us decided to
reach out to the campaign to see if we could be helpful by taking a few
days off to knock on doors. As a result, our trio spent the days around New
Year's 2008 in south-central Iowa, working in towns not very different
from the small communities I knew in rural areas around South Bend.

One thing I hadn't expected was how big a role the Iraq War was
playing in these one-stoplight towns with grain elevators for a skyline—
not as a political football but as a kind of local issue. The Iraq troop
surge was winding down but not yet over. Afghanistan, mostly out of
view, was simmering. Yellow ribbons were everywhere, and more than
once I would knock on a door and get into a conversation with a young
man who told me he would love to go to the caucus on Thursday and
vote, but couldn't because he was packing up for Basic Training.

In fact, it seemed like every other teenager I met was signing up
for the Army or the Guard. I was only twenty-five years old, but these

freckled young Iowan recruits looked like children to me. And I began asking myself how it could be that whole communities in this part of the country, just like those in rural Indiana, seemed to be emptying out their youth into the armed services, while so few people I knew had served at all. Warming up in a diner after a day's canvassing, Ryan and Nat and I tried to construct a list of people we'd known at Harvard who had gone into the military. You could count them on one hand.

It wasn't just us, and it wasn't just Harvard. In their book *AWOL: The Unexcused Absence of America's Upper Classes from Military Service— and How It Hurts Our Country*, Kathy Roth-Douquet and Frank Schaeffer examined the record and found that the Ivy League college with the most 2004 graduates going to the military was Princeton, with all of nine students going into service. Much had changed since the days when the names of over a hundred Harvard men made their way onto the wall in the transept of Memorial Hall. Some combination of social stratification, Cold War campus politics, and changing norms around elite universities meant that service had gone from standard to rare.

For my grandfather's generation, military service was a great equalizer—something that Americans (at least, American men) had in common across race, class, and geography. Indeed, for some prior generations the rate of loss in war may have been higher for the wealthy than for the working class, because service was so close to the heart of elite culture. There was nothing unusual about Lieutenant Junior Grade John F. Kennedy, scion of one of the most prominent and well-connected wealthy families in America, risking death aboard PT-109 in the South Pacific. The wealth and fame of JFK's father, Joseph Kennedy Sr., made it more, not less, natural that his sons would enter the service. Indeed, John F. Kennedy's path to the presidency was cleared only by the death of his older brother, Joe Jr., the one thought destined for high office until that naval airplane explosion in 1944.

The entire campus of the elite prep school Phillips Andover was in uniform throughout World War I, so it was hardly shocking that the outbreak of World War II would motivate a young George Herbert Walker Bush to enlist on his eighteenth birthday and find his own way to the Pacific. A year after Kennedy and the men of PT-109 were rescued from the island where they had washed up, another Navy operation would rescue young Bush out of the waters of Chichijima where he had been shot down during a daring strafing run.

NO LESS REMARKABLE, for men of such privilege, was the fact that they would have been interacting on more or less equal terms with people from other walks of life, regions, and backgrounds. As an enlistee Bush, whose father would soon be a senator, might have taken orders from the sons of farmers or laborers; Kennedy's fellow officers aboard PT-109 were from Ohio and Illinois.

In 1956, a majority of the graduating classes of Stanford, Harvard, and Princeton joined the military. But in the decades that followed, the once-diverse makeup of our military shifted dramatically. Especially after Vietnam, America saw a growing share of service members coming from places like Mount Ayr and Creston in Iowa, or Fulton County in Indiana—and far fewer from places like Harvard. The proportion of members of Congress who were veterans had fallen from 70 percent in 1969 to 25 in 2004, and fewer than 2 percent of members of Congress had a child who was serving.

As I reflected on it, I realized that my arrival at Harvard coincided with the near-disappearance of my own childhood interest in serving. At a younger age, when I had hoped to be an astronaut or a pilot, service in uniform was very much on the table. Indeed, on my mother's side, it was a family tradition.

One of my heroes growing up was a relative I had never met: my great-uncle Russell Montgomery, an Army Air Corps captain who died in a 1941 plane crash. My grandmother's house had a large painting of him on the wall, in the house where she and my grandfather settled after he retired from the Army at Fort Bliss in El Paso. In the painting Russell is seated, in uniform, his cap on one knee, a bookshelf behind him and a painting of a dog on the wall over one shoulder. Beneath a generous brow, he gazes forward with blue eyes that look commanding and serious, yet self-possessed and approachable.

After my grandmother died, the painting found a new home on the wall of our South Bend living room. Since we weren't a paintings-of-ancestors-on-the-wall kind of family, I once asked my mother how it came to exist. She explained that during World War II my grandfather, still grieving the loss of his brother, encountered a German officer in a prisoner-of-war camp in New Mexico who knew how to paint. Even in war, there was a gentlemanly understanding between officers of different countries. Using two photographs—one of Russell and one of his favorite dog—the young German officer was able to create the portrait, which my grandfather bought from him. It was the only painting in our house that hadn't been painted by my grandfather himself, or by my mother.

Besides the painting, the family had another treasure of Russell's: his logbook. The tiny, leather-bound notebook contained a log of his flight hours, but also little anecdotes about the life of an officer and pilot in those still-freewheeling days of early Army aviation. In it, he writes about hops across the Midwest to build up his flight hours, usually in the company of a fellow officer, and punctuated by football games and visits with girls. The entry for October 24, 1931, is characteristic:

Flew to Pittsburgh, Pa. with Lt. McAllister in BT-2B. Thru rain all the way but last 15 min. Left Dayton at 8:00 A.M. Arrived Pittsburgh at 10:05. Met some wonderful people. Saw Purdue wallop Carnegie Tech 13 to 6. Had lunch at Univ. Club. Went to Dance at Athletic Club with a very good blind date. Saw lots of

fraternity brothers. Flying time, 2 hrs 5 mins. Flew back next day
Oct 25 to Dayton. An awful head wind and air was terribly rough.
Was initiated into air-sickness, an awful feeling.

As far as we know, it was taken from his remains after the crash, and
I used to thumb through it with wonder as a child, a family relic even
more unique and special than the painting. The paragraph-long adventures were as engaging as a novel, but also may have added to my sense
that military service, like war in general, belonged to a different time
and place than my own.

These traces from my personal and family history had faded as
the adventures of Harvard, then Oxford, commanded my attention.
The question "Why aren't you wearing your country's uniform?" did
sometimes nag at me as I made, with the unique confidence of a college student, some lofty statement about public service or national
security. But it always seemed like there was something else for me to
focus on, and few of my peers were serving, either. Most of the role
models I would have had, military officers actually connected to me,
were relatives who had died before I was even born.

Back from Iowa and visiting my parents one day, I squared up to the
painting and looked at it closely. I put myself in Russell's place; I must
have been coming up on the age he had been when the original photo
was taken. For him and his generation, a college education and a military
career went hand in hand; for me, education had somehow made military
service seem more remote. Yet all around me, especially in small towns
and rural areas, men my age and much younger were making themselves
available for the defense of our country. The more I reflected on it, the
less it seemed I had any good excuse or reason not to serve.

THE FIRST TIME I TUGGED on the door of a recruiting office, I
found it closed. It was the first step toward realizing that getting into

the military was not as simple as I'd have thought. Later, a recruiter who called back from the 1-800 number I had dialed passed me to a cheerful NCO in the local office in South Bend, who routed me toward a lieutenant from somewhere in Michigan who would go silent for days, then suddenly pepper me with calls and emails, before going dark again. At one point I learned that when I'd told them my college coursework in Arabic might make me a good intelligence officer, they had recorded that my minor at Harvard had been in aerobics.

But the wheels of Big Navy did their slow work, one bubble test or triplicate form at a time, until one day an email directed me to check in at a Radisson in Des Plaines, Illinois, ahead of a physical exam at the Military Entrance Processing Station. Judging by the dos and don'ts in the email, the expectations seemed manageable. "Take a shower— be clean." Also, "No pants that shows exposed underwear." And body piercings "must now be removable and the pierced area must be free of inflammation or infection." I could handle this.

At 0415 over breakfast in the suburban hotel, it was hard to miss the fact that the vast majority of people entering the military were more like the teenage recruits I had seen in Iowa than anyone I'd known in college. As conversation around me focused on which girls were the hottest and how various parents had reacted to the news, I began to wonder if I was the only one old enough to drink among this group of seventy or so, preparing to be herded onto the bus to "MEPS."

The sensation of being an object on an assembly line began at the top of the stairs leading to the intake room, as a woman ran what looked like a marker across my forehead, leaving a moist imprint that I later learned had something to do with testing for swine flu. Then we were separated by service, with Army people going to the Army room, and so on. I took my seat on one of the chairs in the Navy room, warily eyeing a poster on the wall that staff used to identify tattoos containing hate group symbols. A TV was playing some action movie, which captivated most of the recruits around me.

My name was called. A very large woman with gray hair and purple sweatpants took my fingerprint on a computer and presented me with a folder and some papers to take to the "control desk," whatever that was. Soon I was in line for a vision test; I waited in rows of seats with the other recruits as people filed in, one-in-one-out, to the testing room. The girl behind me, a redhead looking about seventeen, struck up a conversation. "You're from a small town, aren't you?" Not wanting to correct her or weigh out loud whether South Bend qualified as a small town, I just asked how she could tell. "The cowboy boots." I looked down. In fact, they were shoes I had picked up at a Filene's Basement in Chicago, which slightly resembled cowboy boots if jeans were draped over them. I wasn't going to ruin our rapport, so I just nodded.

"I'm from a small town, too," she quickly volunteered. "Marseilles, Illinois."

I must have looked at her blankly, so she clarified: "It's close to Peru, Illinois." We had a Peru in Indiana, too, I offered a bit lamely. She hoped to work as a secretary in the military and had decided to join the Army because it would pay for college.

After the vision test came a color blindness test, a blood test, a pee test. Just as I began to feel a sense of momentum moving from station to station, the line for "urinalysis" came to a standstill. One kid, it seemed, was unable to produce—and, for reasons of security and integrity, pulling him out of sequence was out of the question. This was when I learned that there is a surefire way to make someone urinate: chug fifteen cups of warm water in quick succession. Regrettably, it may also induce vomiting. The unfortunate recruit dutifully did both, and the line began moving again.

There was a Breathalyzer, a doctor one-on-one, more waiting, more testing. The final exercise was in a room mysteriously called "ortho-neuro." Twenty-five at a time and stripped to our underwear, we were put through a number of exercises by a cheerful civilian and an ancient-looking, humorless doctor. Formed into two lines facing each other, we were told to swing our arms around, forward, backward, do something like jumping jacks, then something called a "duck walk" that involved squatting and walking at the same time, then walk on our knees, and so on through about twenty of these little routines. I began to feel like a preschooler, or like a recruit in newsreel footage from World War II, as they put us through our various motions and then told us to sit, in numbered seats on benches. All of our medical folders were placed in a row of little holders on the wall, each numbered, 1 through 25, just like our spots on the bench. Looking bored, the doctor examined them in no particular order, then in no particular order names were called.

"Winters! You're qualified." Winters gets up, is handed his folder, puts his clothes back on, and walks out of the room back into the hallway, looking like he just won the lottery. Macalester. You're qualified. Lopez. Tagatz. Bowman. Perez. Buttigieg. You're qualified. Ridiculously, you feel like you've accomplished something when they tell you you're medically qualified. For this, you get to go to another waiting room. Eventually you are called up. A man behind a desk, whom I recalled as an unpleasant presence during the vision test earlier, now seemed to be enjoying himself immensely. "Butti . . . wha? Hoo-hee, it's a good thing you're in the Navy. I just wish I had someone with your name in my unit. Ha-haah, the fun I could have. Damn, guy." Then, a little more quietly, confidential and approving, "You know how hard it is to get in for intel right now." Then another look at the stack of paper and, finally, "You're squared away."

OVER SUBSEQUENT WEEKS more paperwork followed, including the intense vetting for the background check that goes with a top-secret clearance. Screen by screen on a website belonging to the Office of Personnel Management, I carefully accounted for every foreign connection and trip: every commute to Canada for McKinsey, every Maltese cousin I kept in touch with, every penny of the fifty bucks or so that

I still had in a British bank account from Oxford. I ran down contact information for foreigners I had known, and told old high school and college friends not to be alarmed if someone approached them saying they were from the FBI and wanting to know how many times they had seen me smoke pot (not many, but more than zero). With a remarkably straight face, an investigator appeared in South Bend to meet with me, confirm some address information, and ask if I had ever attempted to overthrow the government.

At last, an email arrived in September 2009 affirming that everything was ready and it was time to take the oath. Even this process bore out the military mantra of hurry-up-and-wait, or in this case wait-and-hurry-up: after an excruciatingly slow process, the recruiting lieutenant insisted on getting the final signatures in by the end of the month. With my work travel schedule and her need to have me do the oath somewhere near her Detroit-area base, it wasn't easy to find a time and place. I had built up a certain mental image in mind for my commissioning—if not a stirring scene like the emotional swearing-in of Richard Gere's character at the end of *An Officer and a Gentleman*, then at least a photogenic moment with my right hand raised and maybe a few flags in the background, something worthy of a photo that I would frame and one day show my kids. I had assumed we would do the honors on the parade ground at Naval Station Great Lakes, the major Navy facility near Chicago. Instead, the lieutenant proposed we split the difference between South Bend and Detroit and meet at a Big Boy diner in Coldwater, Michigan. But the Big Boy was closed, so we wound up at a nearby coffee shop, where we went over the paperwork together one more time, and she showed me where to sign. Not big on ceremony, she added: "If you really want to raise your right hand, we can do that."

One minute later, I was a member of the military. A commissioned officer. Ensign, United States Navy Reserve.

5

"Meet Pete"

No one sits on his mother's knee and says he hopes one day to become a state treasurer. The truth is that I made it through my schooling and early adulthood without ever noticing the office existed, or giving any thought to what it meant. As a student, learning about the exploits of senators and governors and wondering if I might someday hold office myself, it never crossed my mind that "getting into politics" would mean running for an office that most people have never heard of. Yet by the time my twenty-eighth birthday approached in early 2010, I had decided to quit my job and spend the better part of the year, and my savings, seeking an obscure office that paid less than half of what I'd already been making.

It all happened because of a chance to stand up for the then-unpopular rescue of the American auto industry—and because I actually knew what an empty car factory looks like. It takes great imagination to look at the broken windows and falling bricks of a decaying Studebaker factory in South Bend, and picture the days when it was heaving with life and employing tens of thousands of people. It takes far less imagination to glance at today's enormous, well-kept Chrysler plants on the outskirts of Kokomo, Indiana, and picture what would happen if they were to fall silent. After about a year without maintenance, the walls would show disuse. Windows on the office side would be distressed or broken within a couple years, and by the end of the decade five-foot weeds would be pushing through the cracked asphalt of the massive parking lot.

ANYONE FROM SOUTH BEND KNOWS exactly what it looks like when an industry collapses. No one wants to see it happen to anyone else—which was why I followed the news closely when the 2008 economic crisis left Chrysler on life support. I was still at McKinsey, working out of borrowed office space and hotel rooms in San Francisco, Dubai, Seattle, or Stamford, depending on the day. On paper I was part of the Chicago office, but in practice I worked wherever the study took me. Traveling at least four days a week, by this point I'd realized that it didn't much matter to my employer where I actually lived, so I had moved home to South Bend. This cut my rent in half and gave me more time with my parents, who hadn't lived in the same state as me in almost a decade. And in those rare days at home, or when I needed a break from my spreadsheets, or on a plane from somewhere to somewhere, I would pull up news articles and follow the unfolding drama of the near-death and rescue of the American auto industry.

I hadn't spent much time in Kokomo, but like most people from South Bend who had occasion to visit Indianapolis, I'd been through it at least a dozen times. About half the size of South Bend, the city of Kokomo was the midpoint of the three-hour drive between home and the state capital. Every state band competition, soccer tournament, or family trip to Indy involved at least passing through the edge of town on Old U.S. 31. Coming southward, you know you're getting near the city limits when you see the Indiana Transmission Plant 2, or ITP2, on the left-hand side. From the highway, you wouldn't notice much about this white and blue building, other than its sheer mass. Decades newer than the Studebaker Main Assembly building I knew so well in South Bend, it was made of steel rather than brick, and was one story across sixty-one acres rather than six floors, but the overall proportions are similar, with over half a million square feet of space. ITP2 accounts for about two thousand jobs, and it's not even the biggest Chrysler facility in town. About three miles farther down the road, near the heart of the small city, you come to a stoplight and see two huge factories, one on either side. On the right is another transmission plant, with another thirty-five hundred jobs. Across from it is a plant that now belongs to GM Components Holdings with about a thousand more employees. The historic heart of Kokomo, with its quaint town square and the county courthouse, is about a mile west of the highway. Directly or indirectly, nearly everything in Howard County was fueled by the auto industry. In total, the town of fifty-six thousand had four Chrysler plants and one Delphi factory, and about one in five workers was in manufacturing.

So Kokomo had a lot to lose when the Great Recession struck our country and our state, with the auto companies hit hardest. As cable news told the story in stock market charts, workers at Chrysler and Delphi saw it in layoff notices. Thousands were suddenly out of a job, and with unemployment in Kokomo in double digits, there were not a lot of other options. At least layoffs meant the possibility of coming back; families hoped and waited for news of a callback before their savings ran out. The alternative, a total collapse of the companies, was unthinkable—it would take the whole city down, not just the factories. The area could see 40 percent unemployment. No business—from Applebee's to the Cone Palace, my favorite family-owned ice-cream shop—would stand much of a chance.

Nor would the disaster be confined to Kokomo. Even at rock bottom during the crisis, the auto industry employed sixty-nine thousand people in Indiana. South Bend's days of making Studebakers were long gone, but thousands of families in our city depended on good jobs at companies that made parts and supplies for the industry. At least we had our colleges and universities, and proximity to Chicago. If the auto industry went belly-up altogether, a city like South Bend would be wounded; a town like Kokomo would be devastated.

As Christmas approached, the news went from bad to worse. Having laid off twelve thousand workers in 2008, Chrysler announced in December that it would halt production at all thirty of its manufacturing plants. Dangerously low on cash and headed for bankruptcy, the company seemed unlikely to survive very far into 2009.

President Bush was preparing to leave office, but the emergency couldn't wait for the transition. In December he boldly initiated a $17.4 billion bailout loan package, saying, "Bankruptcy now would lead to a disorderly liquidation of American auto companies." To me, "disorderly liquidation" sounded like a cartoon whirlpool, with cars and workers waving their arms for help in the downward spiral toward the drain. A simpler way to put it was that millions of lives and hundreds of communities stood to be ruined. Yet the move to prevent this disaster was clearly not a political winner—something about the word "bailout" makes voters allergic—and the Senate was loath to vote for the package. When Congress refused to authorize funds, Bush acted unilaterally, rewiring money that Congress had authorized, with other purposes in mind, as part of the TARP bank rescue.

The new Democratic administration planned to continue the unpopular policy, but as President Obama took office in January 2009, it was clear that the funding was not enough to hold off a collapse. The new president faced an immediate choice about whether to put more cash into supporting the auto industry. The politics could not have been worse: one poll found that 72 percent of Americans were against further loans. Even in South Bend, many voters viewed the idea skeptically. The bank bailout had left a bad taste in our mouths, and some thought more cash into the auto rescue would just be throwing good money after bad. Bumper stickers began to appear around town with a sarcastic contribution to the debate: BAIL OUT STUDEBAKER. Within the White House, most of Obama's economic advisers were opposed. They didn't believe Chrysler could survive even with the additional loans. But Obama decided to proceed anyway, adding funding while helping to broker an alliance between Chrysler and Fiat to keep it in business.

And it worked. The newly formed, post-bankruptcy version of Chrysler was able to crawl, then walk, then run, and eventually the company exceeded expectations for sales and growth. And the auto industry comeback helped lead the overall economic recovery of the country. By the fall of 2010, all of the laid-off workers had been called back, and unemployment started moving back to normal levels. And with remarkable speed, the government had recovered most of the taxpayer money that had gone into the deal.

By 2012, this once-unpopular policy had come to be seen as a clear win. Obama used it as a cudgel against his opponent, Mitt Romney, who had opined against the bailout in a 2008 op-ed entitled "Let Detroit Go Bankrupt." In 2008, that had clearly been the safe position to take, but by 2012 voters understood that bold action had been needed. The tables had turned, and now Romney was left trying to explain away his previous view. When it came to health care, Romney refused to admit that he was the true father of what came to be known as Obamacare. But when it came to the auto industry, the reverse was true: his campaign actually tried to take credit for the bailout he had once opposed. A campaign spokesman said of the structured bankruptcy: "Mitt Romney had the idea first." To be fair, Romney was making some nuanced and sensible points in his article about the need for Detroit to modernize, but events had disproven his bottom-line 2008 prediction: "If General Motors, Ford and Chrysler get the bailout that their chief executives asked for yesterday, you can kiss the American automotive industry goodbye."

I knew what South Bend had to deal with after losing just one car company. Even now I shudder to think of what would have happened to the industrial Midwest if the entire American auto sector had been allowed to fall apart. South Bend's current renaissance would have been impossible; in fact, it's doubtful that the Great Recession would have been reversed at all.

MY CAREER IN ELECTED POLITICS, as I mentioned earlier, began in the midst of this American economic drama. What pulled me in was a weird subplot to the remarkable rescue: a lawsuit that almost stopped the Chrysler bankruptcy dead in its tracks. At work one day in the spring of 2009, I was calculating the effects of energy efficiency policies on utility balance sheets when I needed a break. The spread-sheet went into the background and I flicked through the news. An article caught my eye: "Indiana Pensioners Object to Chrysler Sale." I clicked and read the unbelievable news that the state treasurer of Indiana, Richard Mourdock, was going to sue, demanding that a judge block the bankruptcy and liquidate Chrysler instead. In other words, an elected official in Indiana was attempting to stop the president from saving the livelihoods of thousands of Indiana families.

Mourdock was no household name even in Indiana, but if you fol-lowed our state's politics closely, then you could see him doing this sort of thing. There was something genial and earnest about him, but you could also read in his eyes the fixations of a fierce ideologue. Trained as a geologist, he had become a coal company executive and then a peren-nial candidate, trying three times unsuccessfully to win southwest Indi-ana's congressional seat. He finally landed a commissioner position in Vanderburgh County, and, after a couple other unsuccessful campaigns for different offices, managed to become treasurer in 2006. Through his many races, he established the reputation of a strong conservative, mak-ing it clear that bipartisanship was not his thing. He once told a cable news host that "bipartisanship ought to consist of Democrats coming to the Republican point of view," adding that "to me, the highlight of politics, frankly, is to inflict my opinion on someone else."

You might wonder how such partisanship could possibly play into a job as technical and non-ideological as state treasurer, whose main role is to manage the state's pension funds for government employees and teachers. But someone with a deep enough ideological worldview, coupled with strong ambitions to run for something bigger, can always find a way to use an office—any office—to make a name for himself.

Mourdock was a purist when it came to free markets, and therefore was totally against the idea of government playing a role in the economy. The auto bailout was a Bush-initiated program designed to hold off a possible depression, but that didn't make it any more acceptable in Mourdock's view. Even worse, the terms of the negotiated bankruptcy were favorable to the United Auto Workers, anathema to a dyed-in-the-wool conservative who viewed organized labor with contempt.

Cleverly, Mourdock realized that Indiana's pension funds owned some Chrysler bonds, and reasoned that this might give him standing in court to challenge the deal. When else would an obscure state treasurer get a chance not only to assert free-market principles and deal a blow to labor, but also to provoke a showdown with the hated Obama administration over a major policy priority? The temptation was irresistible, and so Mourdock went to court.

The theory of his lawsuit was that the pension funds were secured creditors, and should have been given better treatment when they took a loss on their holdings as part of the bankruptcy and restructuring of Chrysler. The Chrysler bonds represented less than 1 percent of the pensions' holdings—about $17 million—but that was the legal toehold Mourdock needed in order to intervene. He hired a New York–based law firm for about $2 million and filed a lawsuit asking that the bankruptcy be halted. The stakes were enormous: If he succeeded, the entire rescue might have been prevented, pushing the company into liquidation. The company, its assets—and, most importantly, the jobs—would be gone forever.

On Friday, May 29, 2009, New York's federal bankruptcy court rejected the motion. Mourdock appealed. On June 5, the appeals court also affirmed the sale, leaving Mourdock heading into the weekend with nowhere to go but all the way to the Supreme Court. He filed a request for an emergency stay on Sunday, June 7, and the next day the court granted a temporary stay while reviewing whether to intervene. To his original argument, Mourdock added a constitutional challenge, arguing that it was not legal to use funds from the Troubled Asset Relief Program for this purpose. Using the TARP money this way was Bush's work-around after the Senate refused to fund the auto bailout in late 2008; if found unconstitutional, it would push the entire matter back into the hands of a Congress incapable of doing anything unpopular.

Until the Supreme Court could decide whether to take the case, the sale was on hold. But it couldn't wait long: the entire bailout deal had a June 15 deadline. Meanwhile, the unemployment rate in Howard County had soared to 20 percent. Kokomo's mayor, Greg Goodnight, braced his employees and community for the possibility that their biggest employer might never get back on its feet. Services would have to be cut, families would have to reconsider plans to send their kids to college, and the entire population of the town would begin to drain away.

Obscure bankruptcy proceedings don't generally get much notice outside of the business world, but over that weekend the country began to take notice. Mourdock was making the rounds of the cable shows, and in the process became a hero in what was just beginning to be known as the Tea Party for standing up to government, labor, and Obama all at once.

By now Chrysler was estimated to be losing $100 million a day. One industry expert told CNN that "if the case drags on for even a few weeks and Chrysler is unable to restart its plants by the end of the month as planned, it could spell doom for Chrysler." Its suppliers would be next—and the simultaneous rescue of GM might fall apart, too.

In a filing on Monday the eighth, Solicitor General Elena Kagan, soon to be named to the Supreme Court herself, responded for the administration, reminding the Supreme Court and the country of what was at stake. "The liquidation of Chrysler would have very severe effects on the American and Canadian economies. . . . More than 38,000 Chrysler employees would lose their jobs; 23 manufacturing facilities and 20 parts depots will be shuttered; more than 3,000 Chrysler dealers would suffer significant and possibly fatal harm to their businesses; and billions of dollars in health and pension benefits for current and former Chrysler workers would be wiped out."

In addition to the economic gravity of the situation, there were serious legal flaws in Mourdock's case. The biggest was that the holdings he represented would actually be worth less under liquidation than in the proposed bailout deal. In other words, if the pensions won the lawsuit, they would actually lose money compared to the plan they were suing to stop. In general, American case law does not allow you to go to court and sue to make yourself worse off.

On Tuesday, the Supreme Court denied the stay and declined to hear the case. The sale could go forward—as it did, the next day. The sense of relief was still tentative. It would be years before we would know that the rescue was a success, with the companies and jobs saved and the government paid back. But the Indiana communities that rely on the auto industry—and possibly the American economy as a whole—had dodged a bullet.

Mourdock himself was no worse off for his courtroom rejection. He had made a name for himself, and in his own mind he had stood on principle by defying Washington and the auto workers who had pushed so hard to save their jobs. Gripped by ideology, Mourdock simply could not accept that government getting involved could be a good thing, even if it prevented the destruction of thousands of lives. But I wonder, sometimes, whether he talked to any of the families whose livelihoods could have been wrecked by his legal adventure. Did he think about the stakes for them, or was it just numbers on a page to him?

To Mourdock, it seems, the most important issue at stake in the auto rescue was that investors on the bond market would have to take a haircut. To the rest of us, the most important issue was that families' lives could be ruined by the same kind of economic disaster that had nearly killed my hometown half a century earlier.

To me, the whole episode was about what happens when a public official becomes obsessed with ideology and forgets that the chessboard on which he is playing out his strategy is, to a great many people, their own life story. Good policy, like good literature, takes personal lived experience as its starting point. At its best, the practice of politics is about taking steps that support people in daily life—or tearing down obstacles that get in their way. Much of the confusion and complication of ideological battles might be washed away if we held our focus on the lives that will be made better, or worse, by political decisions, rather than on the theoretical elegance of the policies or the character of the politicians themselves.

RICHARD MOURDOCK WAS UP FOR REELECTION in 2010, and when I investigated who was looking to run against him from the Democratic side, the answer was no one. I was surprised. I knew down-ticket races, especially for Democrats in Indiana, were thankless, difficult, and hard to recruit for. But a candidate as extreme as Mourdock seemed beatable—at least if there were a favorable national atmosphere, a flawless campaign, and a little bit of luck. Surely someone would take him on, in the name of the people and communities who could have been devastated by his adventure. And if no one else was going to step up, why not me?

In American political culture, you are not supposed to admit you have any interest in running for office until the moment you declare. I didn't even realize this was a particularly American quality until studying in England, where I would often meet students who made it clear they would stand for Parliament at the earliest opportunity, and then did exactly that. It's hard to say where this norm of ours comes from; I'd like to think it has something to do with the premium we place on humility. There is something jarring about the idea that anyone thinks himself truly fit to perform the tremendously difficult and sensitive tasks of public office, and so putting yourself forward to do so seems immodest.

Partly for this reason, a politician's account of how he or she first came to run for office is supposed to begin with a ritual mention of having been urged to do so by others, being flattered, demurring, and eventually feeling called to step forward. Later, for other offices, something like this really would happen to me. But not this time. No one was pleading with a twenty-seven-year-old management consultant to run for statewide office in Indiana as a Democrat. I just started to think about it and felt like it could make sense.

Of course, I knew that this might or might not be a good idea, and that I would need to consult people who knew this world better than I. I needed to figure out how to explore the waters, before giving up my job and income in order to run for statewide office. What would I have to consider? How would I gauge the odds? What steps do you even take to get prepared and under way? I contacted Jeff Harris, whom I had gotten to know while helping our nominee for governor in 2008, to get his advice. Jeff had worked for years in and around campaigns and the labor movement, and understood the state's press corps, legislature, and Democratic Party as well as anyone. I thought he might be put off by the idea that I, in my mid-twenties, wanted him to help me pursue something you would normally work your way up to for years. Still, over soup at a favorite diner, I worked up the nerve to tell him what I had in mind. "After watching what went on in that office, I was thinking that maybe someone like me could—"

"Do it," he interrupted. "You should do it. I'll help you." He offered not only to help me think about it but also to bring me to events where I would meet the kind of party and community leaders I would need to know in order to mount a serious campaign.

Campaigning for office is enormously difficult, but in a way, it's not very complicated. You have to persuade voters to vote for you, raise money so you can reach more voters, and get other people to help you do those two things. Half the battle is name recognition, and my biggest problem was that no one had any idea who I was. My name was unfamiliar and unpronounceable. (Jeff and I spent half a day just figuring out how to render it phonetically, settling on the breakdown "Budda-judge," which was close enough and easier to remember than any other way we could think to write down.) Plus I was twenty-seven years old, and baby-faced enough to pass for a college student. In a campaign office, I would be more likely to be taken for an intern or perhaps a young organizer than an actual candidate. My family had no Indiana political connections, and neither did my employer—McKinsey didn't even have an office in the state.

Jeff quickly devised a way to deal with the name recognition problem, at least among party regulars. He spotted a perfect opportunity at a traditional statewide gathering of Democratic activists at the old French Lick Resort in southern Indiana, held every year in late August. Party faithful from every corner of the state, from longtime county committee officers to young volunteers, would come together for a little bit of party business and a lot of socializing. It was a captive audience; with the right strategy, we could become known to the entire party base over the course of a single weekend.

Jeff prepared by printing hundreds of stickers and spray-painting dozens of old yard signs from other campaigns with a simple, stenciled, two-word message: MEET PETE. The first day of the gathering, he arrived early. Leaning on old friendships, he convinced anyone he could to wear one of the stickers. And he installed a lawn sign every few hundred feet along all the country roads, winding through rolling hills and cornfields, that led to the tiny town and the big hotel. It was impossible for anyone attending the event to miss the low-budget advertising.

By the time I stepped across the porch of the old restored hotel and into the bright, big lobby with its old-fashioned chandeliers and mosaic floors, there was a buzz about the signs. Enough people were asking, "Who the hell is Pete?" that I had an instant conversation-starter when I introduced myself to the various county party chairs, labor leaders, students, state legislators, and assorted other characters who milled about the lobby and corridors. And while I may have been an unfamiliar figure, I convinced people that my business background and education could qualify me to challenge an opponent who had just made a name for himself in the worst way.

Buoyed by the response at French Lick and encouragement from the state party chairman, Dan Parker (who was probably relieved that a somewhat qualified candidate was willing to try this at all), I took my message to the chicken dinners of as many county parties as we could find. If a dozen Ball State College Democrats were willing to meet, so was I. If a friend of my parents was willing to organize a house party in South Bend, I was there. A church basement in Sullivan or a one-room Farm Bureau office among the mint fields of Starke County would do fine—anyplace that would let me introduce myself and talk about how important the office was. I also went around union halls, hearing firsthand what was happening to communities that had relied on auto jobs, and sensing the anger and frustration of workers who felt that their own elected officials could not be trusted to support their livelihoods. Over rubber chicken, ham and beans, chili, or sweet potato pie, I listened to stories in one town after another coming to terms with the kind of devastation that had ripped through my own city a generation before.

Technically I was still "just thinking about it," but the reception at these events made me feel that I could hold my own as a candidate, and that there was a path to victory, however uphill. True, no Democrat had held this office since the 1970s, but an underfunded candidate in 2006 had come remarkably close, and Mourdock's track record meant it might be the hottest-ever race for treasurer, if there was such a thing. All I had to do was quit my job.

I WAS READY FOR A CAREER CHANGE; still, it wasn't an easy leap. Moving home to South Bend had worked wonders for my cost of living, but I still felt uneasy about living without an income for a year so that I could campaign full-time. And if I actually won, I could look forward to getting paid a fraction of what I'd be making if I stuck around the Firm. But seeking this office was a chance to do something uniquely important—and something no one else seemed prepared to do.

It also meant finally ignoring what the script says a well-credentialed young professional ought to do. Up to that moment, at virtually every juncture in my life there was a powerful brand name associated with whatever I was doing. Harvard. Rhodes. McKinsey. United States Navy. When you are connected to an institution with that strong a name, people use it as a shortcut for understanding who you are. And if you're not careful, you use it as a shortcut, too, taking on the shape of that name yourself over time.

Contrary to every unspoken rule of my education, running for office now meant trading a stable and prestigious role for an unlikely and unheard-of effort. It was time to step out of the warm embrace of well-branded institutions known for both nurturing and defining their people, and exchange it for the chance to build—and become— something new.

As a single person, I had lived simply during my time at McKinsey, and had saved enough to get me through one year. So, other than Navy Reserve drill weekends, I was a full-time candidate for most of 2010. Jeff and I set up a simple office in the basement of the Building Trades Union Hall in South Bend, next door to the Insulators and across from the Painters. Like my high school, the interior of the place had a distinct feel of the 1950s—dark brown tile on the floor and what looked like asbestos panels on the ceiling. It was also functional, close to home, and filled with likeable and jocular labor organizers—and the price was right. We moved in and got to work.

As with any other job, there is no better way to learn political candidacy than by doing it. An introvert by nature, I slowly became comfortable with the outgoing disciplines of campaigning. Each day brought a new lesson. Up at dawn to shake hands at a manufacturing plant gate when the shift changed, you learned that the people coming into work were a much better audience than the ones who were leaving, tired and ready to go home. Crossing the state in a hurry to get from a parade in one county to a lunchtime function in another, you learned that car time can and should also be call time, your best chance to reach potential donors and allies during the day. Watching faces rise and fall during a dinnertime speech to, say, the Dearborn County Democratic Party at an Elks Lodge, you learned which stories would resonate where, how long to make your speech, when you had an audience in your hands, and when you were about to lose them. Sticking out your hand to introduce yourself to a stranger enjoying his pork tenderloin at a county fair, you learned that it was a lot better to start a conversation by asking about his goals than launching right into yours.

The call time was the hardest. It meant reaching out to everyone you had ever known to ask if they would send you money. You have two minutes' small talk, a quick windup about the state of the race, and the inevitable hard ask: "Sooo, I was hoping I could count on you for a two-hundred-fifty-dollar contribution." Eventually I came to prefer calling strangers to calling acquaintances, since they took less time to realize why you were calling and were more comfortable giving a yes or a no. I spent hours on this daily, and often wonder if most Americans realize this is how many elected officials spend most of their time. It's not unusual for a member of Congress to spend twenty hours a week doing this, and you have to wonder whether, like spending too much time typing or sunbathing, it does something unhealthy to you over the long run. In the car or at a desk in headquarters, I would go through page after page of calls that our finance director had prepared for me, based on lists of people who had a history of giving to Democrats. And just when I was losing hope, after an hour spent leaving ten voice mails that I knew would never get returned and having three conversations that all ended in "Okay, let me think about it" or "I'd have to talk to my wife," someone would actually help.

"Is this Charles?"

"Yeah, I go by Charlie, but yeah."

"Well, my name's Pete Buttigieg, and I'm running for state treasurer. Have you followed the race much?"

"Not really."

"Okay, well, I'm the Democratic candidate, and we're putting together a campaign to stand up for a better way to handle our state's finances. Did you know that the Republican incumbent—"

"I'm actually a Republican."

"Oh. Um . . ."

"But all my friends are Democrats. John says you're a good guy, so I'll write you a check."

I think, *Really?* but I say, "That's great, here's the address. . . ."

In fact, more strangers said yes than I'd have expected, and friends were extraordinarily supportive once I got over the awkwardness of asking for their help. And as with everything else, I got better at it with practice.

Compared to fundraising, retail politics was a simple pleasure. Indiana has ninety-two counties, and we visited nearly all of them. A typical Saturday that summer would involve three or so parades, perhaps a county fair or two mixed in, and one or more appearances at a Jefferson-Jackson dinner, each event usually at least an hour's drive from the next.

The Jefferson-Jackson dinners, or "JJ's," were the central ritual of campaigning within the party. (A decade later, Democratic organizations would reconsider naming their annual events after these two morally problematic men, but that trend is only now penetrating throughout Indiana.) Jeff and I would appear at the Elks Lodge, Legion Hall, community center, or, in the very biggest counties, a hotel ballroom. If I was lucky, a county chair would recognize me and show me in, but usually I started at the check-in table, where a volunteer asked my name and then furrowed her eyebrows, studying a printed list as she tried to figure out how to spell my name without asking me again to say it. I'd buy a few tear-off tickets for the fifty-fifty raffle, go into the hall with the tables, and introduce myself to every single person. The faces would be skeptical but polite, and eventually we would all settle in over chicken and beans as the program began: the pledge, the prayer, and the speeches. The custom of working your way up to the most distinguished speaker is often reversed at a rural JJ dinner: if a congressman was present, he would usually go first, so he could leave for another event. The down-ticket statewide races typically came late in the program, somewhere after the state representatives and before the auction.

I could write a book just about the food we ate. A street fair comes to mind, one summer night in Evansville, a city about the size of South Bend but on the opposite end of the state, across the river from Kentucky. At the unforgettable West Side Nut Club Fall Festival, I was met with a mostly delicious range of offerings that amounted to a cardiological nightmare. That night in my journal I copied just a portion of the "C" section of a two-page guide in six-point font that spelled out, alphabetically, all the sins available by booth: "Caramel Puffs, Catfish Filet Sandwich, Catfish Nuggets, Chai Tea, Cheese Balls, Cheese Soup, Cheese Sticks, Cheese Quesadillas, Cheeseburgers (about a dozen booths listed for this one), Cheesecake, Cheesecake on a Stick, Cheesey Fries . . ." Walking among the booths, I don't remember seeing any Chai Tea, but there was certainly an abundance of cheese. I somehow avoided the featured delicacy that year, Deep Fried Turkey

Testicles, as well as the festival's well-known tradition of brain sandwiches. But you have to eat something, and I ended up sampling candied jalapeños (of which the guy from the church selling them said, "All I can tell you is they've been in this here jar since the last festival a year ago"), and something called Pig in the Mud, which is a sort of peanut-butter-and-bacon sandwich covered in powdered sugar.

That summer I played a small part in setting a world record: most fried chicken ever prepared in a single serving. A little geographic background is in order. There is an invisible line that goes on a northeasterly slant across the northern third of our state. North of it, the preferred fair food is pork burgers; south, it's chicken. Cross another line into the southern third of the state and the fare is typically schnitzel, only you call it pork tenderloin. (If you are going to use ethnic meat names, you'd better know what you're doing—once in South Bend, I saw a visiting politician from a German-settled downstate city take the mic at a sausage-intensive Polish festival and make the mistake of praising the "bratwurst" instead of the "kielbasa," and the air went out of the room for a second.)

I'll spare you the deeper nuances to this fair-food geography; the important thing is that Franklin County is in chicken territory, and the people there had been looking for a way to make the Canoe Festival more exciting that year. So they decided to get their community into the record books by filling a canoe with the most chicken ever placed into a single container. The previous world record was held by some KFC distributor in the Persian Gulf who had put twelve hundred pounds of chicken on a giant hummus plate a few years earlier.

In the glint of the evening summer sun, we gathered near the county seat, Brookville, population 2,596. The atmosphere was somewhere between jolly and crazed. I met a Colonel Sanders impersonator who pointed out that the Colonel had actually been born in Indiana, not Kentucky. Signs saying things like MAKE CHICKEN NOT WAR and BEAT KUWAIT ringed the canoe, while people streamed in from every corner of town, bearing Styrofoam coolers full of fried chicken from restaurants and family kitchens. Eager to please, I tried to make myself useful by carrying a few coolers from a staging area to the boat, where the chicken was promptly dumped in. When the president of the Canoefest Fryers Club announced the official weight of the chicken—1,645 pounds—the applause heralded an authentically achieved moment in the life of the community. Then, of course, we ate it all.

Some of the rural counties blurred together; others you can't forget, like Crawford County, where a faithful intern and I pulled up to what we thought was the county courthouse in a town called English and found no one there at all. Nolan, the intern, was as confused as I was; after dutifully following the GPS device, we stepped out of my tungsten-green Taurus into steamy air and overgrown grass and looked, blinking, through the midday glare at the brick-and-cinder-block courthouse. The parking lot was empty. The building was locked and, on closer inspection, definitely abandoned. We looked for signs of life nearby, and found no one. Not only was the courthouse empty, but the whole town was literally deserted.

It turns out that was the old courthouse, before a series of floods prompted the town council to relocate not just the courthouse but the entire town. Thus there was Old English and New English, and we were in the wrong English. By the time we sorted it out and got uphill to New English, we had missed our appointment with Jerry Brewer, the local Democratic chair who was supposed to meet me there.

Crawford County being pretty small, the lady in the clerk's office who saw me looking for him told me we could just call him at home. She dialed the phone on her desk and held out the handset for me to take as it rang. When he answered, he told me he wasn't going to be able to leave his farm that day anyway, because the harvest was coming early and they had to pull up the corn as quickly as possible. Assuming this meant our meeting was canceled, I was about to say goodbye when he explained that we could still meet—as long as I didn't mind taking the meeting in the cab of his tractor while we did a few rows of corn. So that's where we met.

In the middle of the field under an August sun, it felt in the air-conditioned cab like we were in some kind of vessel, gliding over the top of the corn as though sailing in an infinite sea of tasseled ears and husks. In front of us, the machinery calmly devoured six, maybe twelve rows at a time. At one point, we came to a sort of clearing in the vast corn-field and stopped to talk to the farmhand, a bearded, tattooed, burly man whose eyes looked somehow too young to belong to someone as bearded, tattooed, and burly as he was. He was fresh back from serving in Iraq, Jerry said, and was helping in the fields for the summer. We got out of the tractor while Jerry and his employee did something involving a trailer hitch that I did not fully understand, and then we were back on our way, leaving the young man doing whatever he was doing out there as we kept on a straight path along the rows toward the tree line in the distance.

YOU CAN READ THE PROGRESS of the campaign calendar in the condition of the corn. After you announce and begin campaigning in the early spring, you drive between great squares of rich black soil, freshly turned up, with innocent two-leaf sprigs ornamenting the earth geometrically with dots of green. Then the stalks grow into fair and parade season, well past "knee-high by Fourth of July" if all goes well. When you can't see over the top of the corn, such things as corn mazes become possible, and it's almost back to school. Harvest means it's right around Labor Day, and by now you also have at least a rough sense of what kind of year it's going to be for your party.

You're in the home stretch when the harvest is over and you can again see across the fields over the tops of the chopped-off stalks. Rumbling through them in the passenger seat of Jeff's hybrid Saturn SUV,

I would think of the nineteenth century Hoosier dialect poet James Whitcomb Riley:

> *The stubble in the furries—kindo' lonesome-like, but still*
> *A-preachin' sermuns to us of the barns they growed to fill.*

If it was too early or late to call someone, I might listen to Lyle Lovett's "Up in Indiana" and thumb through news stories on my iPhone, seeing more and more evidence that this would not be a good year for Democrats in our state or anywhere else.

Democratic members of Congress were still licking their wounds from the tongue-lashings they got in town halls across America over the summer of Tea Party rage, heaped with abuse from voters who had been led to believe that the health care bill amounted to red socialism, complete with "death panels" and all manner of evil. Conservatives were energized in ways not seen since the early Bill Clinton administration, and the makings of a wave were under way. This was not good news for me. In a state like ours, a down-ticket Democrat stood a chance of winning only under the best of circumstances, and these were clearly not going to be the best of circumstances.

In the final days, the obscurity of our race added to a sense of doom. We had gotten some good press coverage, and my fundraising events and phone calls had even yielded enough money to do a few TV ads, rare for a campaign like this. But outside of party activists, organized auto workers, and public finance wonks, most voters had still never heard of me. On November 1, the day before the election, I woke early in South Bend and headed down to Indianapolis to campaign at an early-voting site, hoping to catch the occasional voter near their County-City Building. It was humbling, a reminder that campaigning for office often resembles nothing so much as your first experience handing out flyers for something. In 2008 there would have been a line around the block as Obama drew record-breaking numbers of early voters, but this

November morning in 2010 felt like the sorriest, quietest Monday that plaza had ever seen. A lone intern joined me, having driven me down from South Bend, holding a MEET PETE sign duct-taped to a stake as I looked vainly for someone to shake hands with. At one point the police stopped by to make sure the two of us did not constitute an unauthorized demonstration.

I perked up when one person came over and said he recognized me from my commercial, but then he explained that he was not able to vote because of his felony convictions. At one point there was no one at all to talk to but a man walking up and down the block in a sandwich board from Paddy's Legal Beagle Pub advertising a $5.99 lunch "speacil." Figuring he was a voter, I introduced myself, drawing breath and winding myself up for one more, "Hi, my name's Pete, and I'm running for—"

But he interrupted: "I'm not big on elections, I'm a monarchist myself."

I must have stared dumbly at him for a minute, so he clarified that he was awaiting the King of Kings, and therefore not particularly interested in the democratic process.

The road home went through Kokomo, and past those big Chrysler and Delphi plants one more time. I stopped at the ITP2 for a last round of handshakes with the UAW guys before returning to headquarters in South Bend to work on two speeches, one for each outcome, and a bunch of thank-you notes that I would need either way. At seven in the evening, I excused myself to go to Saint James for the All Saints' Day service, then headed back to the office, where my next-door neighbors had dropped off sandwiches for me and the small team. Finally there was nothing to do but go home and go to bed. At home, I asked myself in my journal: "Are we walking into a buzz saw, or does a phenomenal surprise await?"

At least a buzz saw is quick. But Election Day itself is torture for candidates. You've made the arguments, raised the money, and shaken the hands, and there's not much left to do but tell reporters you're confident of victory and go make phone calls or knock on doors like everyone else. Other than that, you are powerless. In Indiana the polls close at six in the evening, a terrible policy when it comes to voter participation but a small mercy for candidates who find Election Days interminable.

It didn't take long after that for me to officially find out which one of my two prepared speeches I'd be giving. I had worked harder on the concession speech anyway. By eight p.m. it was clearly over, and I called my opponent to congratulate him. I offered my well-wishes and anything I could do to help the state. Mourdock was gracious, and I was exhausted. Together with volunteers around the state, dedicated interns, and a paid staff that peaked at three people, we had treated this race as though it were the tightest and most closely watched campaign in the country. I had crisscrossed the state for months, generated almost exclusively positive press coverage, made friends in every corner of Indiana, and raised more money than any candidate for this office had in years. And yet we had finished with less than 40 percent of the vote. Technically, I can claim that I led the Democratic downstate ticket, since I got slightly more votes than my running mates for secretary of state and state auditor. But that did little to take the edge off the fact that the very first time I put my name on a ballot for office, fully one million people had voted for the other guy.

Taking the stage at the West Side Democratic Club in South Bend, I faced a hall full of friendly faces, festooned with campaign signs and banners. It was my chance to thank supporters for everything they had done to help. I had been clobbered and so had many other Democratic candidates that night, but the atmosphere was far from grim. Joe Donnelly, our member of Congress, had managed to survive the Republican wave—one of a tiny handful of endangered congressional Democrats to get reelected that night.

After congratulating Joe and talking to everyone who was at the watch party, there suddenly nothing left to do. My team and I finished the night at Club 23, a dive bar named for its address on State Road 23.

Unpretentious and friendly, it was the kind of place where your shoes would stick to the floor a little bit, a mostly dark and quiet space brightened by the orange pleather chairs, the dartboard, the pool table, and a few neon signs. Behind the bar, Mo (yes, Mo), the owner and bartender, presided with a sharp gaze and a tight grin. I planted myself at a stool, trying not to look at the TV mounted off to the side where the local news was reviewing the election results.

"How's it going?" Mo asked.

"I lost."

"I know," he answered, as he glanced at the TV and reached for the tap.

ALMOST IMMEDIATELY AFTER BEATING ME, Mourdock got to work on his true objective: running for Senate in 2012. Using the treasurer's office as a platform, he challenged the Republican incumbent, Dick Lugar. Lugar, a towering statesman who had had the misfortune of announcing his candidacy for president in 1995 on the same morning as the Oklahoma City bombing, was a moderate best known for brokering strategic nuclear arms reduction treaties with the post-Soviet countries in the aftermath of the Cold War. Helped by his far-right credentials and loyal Tea Party base, Mourdock won the primary, ending Lugar's thirty-six years of Senate service.

In the general election Mourdock faced Donnelly, who had entered the Senate race after his House district got redrawn unfavorably by the now very Republican state legislature. During the final debate in the last days of the election, Mourdock made another national splash—this time by saying he believed pregnancies resulting from rape were an expression of the will of God. An outcry followed and national Republicans distanced themselves from him, allowing Donnelly to beat the odds and win the seat.

We didn't know any of that would happen on that November night in 2010, but I did know better than to feel bitter or pessimistic. Buoyed by the support of friends and strangers, I had learned how to leave a comfortable world to take a big risk in defense of the people and ideas I cared about. Even in total defeat, I was proud of the campaign and the people who had been part of it. Old friends had dug deep to send donations. The nine- and eleven-year-old children of the Montgomery County party chair had marched at my side in countless parades, distributing flyers and toting the MEET PETE sign, expecting no reward beyond a visit to Dairy Queen later. My neighbors in the union hall had become friends and allies. Everyone who had been involved became a new kind of community, one that I knew I would be able to turn to in the future. Most of all, I had received a priceless if humbling course of education, a fitting conclusion to a decade of learning.

6

A Fresh Start for South Bend

Ten weeks after my statewide political defeat, on January 21, 2011, *Newsweek* ran a story called "America's Dying Cities." The authors analyzed demographic data, especially declines in the population of young people, to arrive at the conclusion that ten communities in particular epitomized urban decay and were on their way out. Most were in the Midwest; South Bend was number eight. The short commentary concluded with this: "What is particularly troubling for this small city is that the number of young people declined by 2.5% during the previous decade, casting further doubt on whether this city will ever be able to recover." I had just turned twenty-nine.

South Bend reacted intensely. A Facebook thread from the time captured the range of opinion. "Doesn't surprise me a bit," one resident said, summing up a general pessimism among many who had seen employers, jobs, and stores disappear. "The demographic, the workforce, even the economy is all going downhill," said another. But in the comments and coverage of the time, you could also see the stirrings of a resistance to the doom-and-gloom narrative—especially among young people. On the same thread, a classmate of mine commented: "If you live here, quit complaining and do something to fix this town."

THROUGHOUT THE PREVIOUS DECADE, the fate of South Bend had already been a constant topic whenever I was with people I had grown up with, inside or outside the city limits. Most of my friends had left if they had the opportunity—heading to Chicago, Indianapolis, or New York for a good job and a more appealing lifestyle—and those who stayed were restless. We would often gather over beer when we returned home for the holidays, swapping stories and news from mutual friends at Club 23 or the South Bend Chocolate Café. Inevitably, conversation would turn to the question of how South Bend could get moving again: What would it take for there to be more good jobs, and more places to hang out here? Did a city like South Bend have a future?

The sentiment wasn't just generational. Many people older than my parents sensed a need for our city to get its groove back with youthful leadership. "What our city suffers from is a lack of *imagination*," my mother would say from time to time. A retired business leader and a professor teamed up to put the sense of malaise into numbers, issuing a report called "Benchmarking South Bend" that showed numerically how South Bend was falling behind our peers on all the key economic measures that determined growth.

In the business community, the discomfort showed signs of ripening into rebellion. As 2010 drew to a close and the 2011 mayoral election approached, there had been rumblings of recruiting someone to challenge the mayor, though it wasn't obvious who that challenger would be. One prominent attorney organized a major fundraiser for Henry Davis, Jr., an outspoken administration critic on the city council. It was a signal that Henry might be readying for a challenge to Mayor Steve Luecke from within the Democratic Party, but most doubted that he was ready for prime time. Others began to call me, but I was not inclined to blame the mayor for our city's problems, and I was already running for a different office—state treasurer. But the latter excuse died with my campaign on November 2, 2010, and then the conversations changed.

IN THE FIRST FEW DAYS after I was defeated, there was plenty to think about besides my near-term professional future. I had a thousand-page-high pile of thank-you letters to sign, a campaign headquarters to clean out, and a lot of grateful phone calls to make, not to mention a personal need to recover from the total exhaustion of a year's statewide campaigning. Running for a down-ticket statewide office entails the same geographic scope as running for governor or U.S. Senate but with a tiny fraction of the resources. Joining the Navy Reserve had compelled me to get into the best physical shape of my life, and the campaign had still all but burned me out.

But signing one thank-you letter after the other, calling everyone who had lent a hand, and carting lawn signs and boxes out of the office was quicker work than I had thought—even the sleep deficit didn't need long to take care of. And then there was the inescapable question of what to do next. It might be possible to go back to the Firm, but I knew by then that consulting was not for me in the long run. I could try to take up active duty orders with the Navy, but I was still only an ensign in the Reserve, relatively early in my training and unlikely to be found useful enough to deploy for at least a couple more years.

Meanwhile, talk around town focused on a handful of prospective candidates for mayor—including me. The filing deadline wouldn't be for a couple of months and so I didn't feel much pressure to look into it too quickly, until the doorbell rang one day while I was puttering around the messy domain of my dining room, sorting through piles of mail I had ignored while campaigning. I opened the door and stood on the porch blinking for a moment as I faced a TV camera and a local reporter clutching a wand microphone, wanting to know if I was planning to run. I don't remember exactly how I said no, but hopefully it was polite.

In all honesty, it's not like it hadn't crossed my mind. I was one of those impatient millennial products of South Bend who cared about the city and wanted it to do more. But Mayor Luecke had not decided if he was going to run again—and, while I shared the general sense of impatience, I was unsure how much of the city's malaise ought to be laid at his feet. In fact, I liked him a great deal. Tall, pastoral, and infinitely gentle, he had in his fifteen years as mayor held the city together through a punishing recession, keeping its finances afloat even through state-mandated property tax cuts that had forced savage cuts in the local budget. Business leaders were impatient, but under the circumstances, any one of the developments that did take place was miraculous. At the very least, he had earned the opportunity to decide whether to seek another term before others came rushing onto the scene.

Meanwhile, I wasn't just tired—I was also getting near the bottom of my savings account. I had health insurance and a little income from Reserve duty, but that came to about $400 a month, just shy of enough to cover my mortgage—and half of that seemed to go to military expenses like uniforms and gas money for getting to my monthly drill duty at Great Lakes, Illinois. Another campaign would wipe out what cash I had left and leave me reliant on credit card debt to keep going.

But I also felt strongly about how the city could be run differently. Well trained at the Firm in performance management and economic development, I could envision an administration that ran on business principles without abandoning its public character. I felt that I understood our city's problems, not just as a resident but also as a professional; the overlap and balkanization of our city's economic development efforts reminded me of what I had seen on my trips to Afghanistan as a consultant dealing with the bewildering array of development agencies on the ground there. I couldn't yet picture myself as mayor, but I could picture how the city might run differently if I were in charge.

Meanwhile, people I respected wanted me to look at it—and not just young people. It was one thing for a high school friend to prod me about it over a beer (though some of them, like Mike Schmuhl, had become accomplished political staffers and their words carried weight). But there were also people who had noticed me during my statewide run, people like John Stancati, a compact, energetic man old enough to be my grandfather who had once run the South Bend Water Works, and who asked me to get breakfast with him before I had even lost the treasurer race so he could urge me to run. I'd have thought the old-timers would be content to work through the party machinery, but they seemed as eager as the rest of us to see something completely different.

So I became a regular in the Main Street Coffee House, a drafty corner hangout where I could ask different figures around the community what they thought, one cup of coffee at a time. In between camped-out students and businesspeople having meetings, I sat listening to anyone who would give me time—the redevelopment commission president, the head of the local community foundation, the most respected black pastors on the West Side—to see what they thought of the city's future, and to gauge what they might think of me.

I sought out former Mayor and Governor Joe Kernan, who still lived in town and had taken a liking to me during my doomed run for treasurer, perhaps out of affection for me as a fellow Navy man. If I were a serious contender for a job like mayor, I should be able to look a former mayor in the eye and tell him I was thinking about it—and his reaction would tell me a lot about whether my candidacy might be taken seriously. I asked him to lunch, and he agreed to meet me at Joe's Tavern, a smoky neighborhood dive bar on the West Side not far from the minor-league baseball stadium.

Governor Kernan is a picky eater. He likes green peppers on his pizza, but prefers to add them himself at the last minute, so their moisture doesn't make it soggy. ("It droops, Pete," he once explained, holding up a slice to demonstrate and staring intently yet warmly at me from under his thick white eyebrows.) The governor also does not care for pumpkin, for the understandable reason that he ate little else during his eleven months as a POW in Vietnam.

Now he was retired from politics, but his name was inseparable from South Bend. He'd been city controller, then got elected mayor in 1987, before being offered a slot as Frank O'Bannon's running mate when O'Bannon ran for governor in 1996. Loving the job of mayor, he first refused the offer but then reluctantly accepted, and then won. In his second term as lieutenant governor, Joe faced a decision about whether to run for governor himself. He weighed the decision with friends, family, and allies, before making his decision: he would not run. Party faithful were shocked, since he was expected to be a shoo-in for the nomination if he wanted it. But he and his wife, Maggie, were ready to go back to life in South Bend. Throughout 2003, other candidates began preparing to run the following year, raising money and competing for endorsements.

Then a death changed his plans. While visiting a trade conference in Chicago in September of 2003, Governor Frank O'Bannon suffered a massive stroke, and died a few days later. Unexpectedly and immediately, Kernan went from being a lieutenant governor, preparing to retire from politics, to a sitting governor called to lead the state in the wake of a tragedy. And serving as governor changed his outlook. It was no longer a decision about whether to compete for an open seat; it was a reelection, and he decided to run and seek a full term. But he had missed crucial time to build up a campaign organization, while the Republican Party had been rallying around Mitch Daniels, a former White House official and a senior executive at Eli Lilly and Company, perhaps the most influential firm in the state. Daniels defeated him soundly.

Maybe this history explains why, after I worked up the nerve to ask him whether he thought it made sense for me to run for mayor, he stared at his basket of french fries in silence for several seconds before taking a breath and saying, "So much, in politics, is outside of your control."

He didn't tell me I should or shouldn't, but described his love of the city and of the job. In fact, he said, "It's the best job I ever had." That was impressive, coming from someone who not only had held the top job in state government, but also went on to live out the boyhood fantasy of being president of his hometown baseball team. After his defeat, Joe had organized the purchase and rescue of the floundering single-A South Bend Silver Hawks, and divided his time between presiding in a memorabilia-filled office at the stadium, teaching a course on leadership in a seminar room under the Golden Dome, and traveling the world with Maggie and his Notre Dame Class of '68 golfing buddies. It seemed like a pretty good life to me. Yet even now he looked on his days as mayor—not governor or lieutenant governor or baseball team owner or naval aviator—as the best job he'd ever had.

Lunch by lunch, coffee by coffee, I gathered advice around town—and began to realize that my own certainty about a run was growing. My friend Mike Schmuhl, architect of Joe Donnelly's unlikely 2010 reelection, promised to run my campaign if I decided to go for it, and many of the community leaders I respected most were offering not only to support me if I ran but also to help raise enough money to get me started.

All eyes were on the incumbent, the longest-serving mayor in history. Steve Luecke had taken over for Joe when he became lieutenant governor in 1997, and Joe himself had been our city's longest-ever serving mayor at that time—which meant the city hadn't seen an open seat for mayor in twenty-four years. The small-city rumor mill had Mayor Steve announcing his intentions by Thanksgiving, but the holiday came and went with no word. Finally, on December 8, local TV stations showed him standing by the flags in the mayor's office, flanked by tearful staff, announcing that he would not seek another term. The seat was open; the race was on.

By this point there were two credible candidates in the Democratic primary, neither of whom was me. Easygoing and relatively young himself, Ryan Dvorak had been a state representative since 2002, when he was in his late twenties. His father, Mike Dvorak, had held the same state house seat for sixteen years before Ryan, and was now the county prosecutor. The Dvoraks were almost a political party unto themselves, operating phone banks for fellow Democrats from a stand-alone head-quarters separate from the party office. Thanks to his statehouse career, Ryan had the support of some labor groups, and a healthy campaign account. Lobbyists with business in Indianapolis were reluctant to cross him, as were lawyers in the area who wanted to stay in his father's good graces. But many in the community were skeptical that he was the right choice for mayor. Some viewed him as a bit too partisan, while others remembered with displeasure his father's legislation to prevent South Bend from annexing the suburbs around it, a bill that was popular in the unincorporated community of Granger but perceived as anti-city by South Bend residents. Awkwardly, Ryan lived on my block, and the back of his house faced that of my parents, so we crossed paths even more than normal as I explored a run.

Ryan's rival for the nomination would be Mike Hamann. With salt-and-pepper hair combed in a sensible part, he looked like the coach and family man that he was. A well-liked teacher at Saint Joe High, Mike had been county commissioner as a Republican, then switched to the Democratic Party and was now on the county council. Like Ryan, he had the benefit of an enormous Catholic family—not only his own kids, but, by marriage, the well-liked Murphy family, which seemed to be one degree of separation from just about everyone in town. More conservative than Ryan, he was especially appreciated in pro-life Dem-ocratic circles, and he was the choice of the local Democratic Party chairman, Butch Morgan.

Asked to describe his opinion of a troublesome politician, Butch once said, "If I ever write a book, he's going to be a chapter." Butch would rate his own political biography, if someone wanted to write about how politics worked in South Bend when I was growing up. He once wielded influence in our county in the tradition of the urban Midwestern party boss, an enormous man with a baby face behind huge aviator glasses who more or less personally directed all aspects of the local party (except for the rebellious Dvorak wing) for years. From behind a desk heaped with walk sheets, clipboards, tote bags, chocolate wrappers, flyers, and campaign swag, he ran things mostly through the old touch-tone phone on his desk. If you went to see him in his office, he would receive and place several phone calls during the meeting, without breaking his train of thought. If someone's name came up in conversation, he would call them on speakerphone for a ninety-second conversation, as if he were hollering to them in the next room. If his phone rang, he would take the call, give some instructions, hang up, and resume midsentence. An embodiment of the old school, he had lately taken to using email as well, but typed laboriously, with one finger, this, too, in the middle of a conversation. He was known sometimes to sleep on a couch by the phone bank; politics was his life.

Butch was deeply religious, and had become a teetotaler at some point long before we met. ("If I could get rid of three things in this world," he once said to me, "it would be alcohol, abortion, and racism.") He specialized in retail politics of the sort that had driven local office-holders for years—chicken and spaghetti dinners, lawn signs and nail files bearing candidates' names, parade entries, and puckish charm. His shtick on being introduced to someone for the first time had become a well-worn routine:

YOU: "Hi, I'm so-and-so, nice to meet you."
BUTCH: "Do I owe you money?"
YOU: "Um, no?"
BUTCH: "Then I'm very glad to meet you, too!"

When he showed up at an event, his face was usually obscured behind an enormous gift basket he was bearing from the South Bend Chocolate Company to be auctioned off or given out as a door prize. He was so unassuming, genially disheveled, and absorbed in old-fashioned retail politics that it was easy to underestimate him. But, while closely managing the local politics around him (he seemed obsessed with getting the right candidate for County Council District H), he was also one of the most powerful figures on the Indiana State Central Committee, close with most of the state's top Democratic officials.

Butch was also capable of various kinds of political mischief in order to get the outcomes he wanted. When a candidate named Cheri Schuster ran against Phil Dotson for county recorder without the blessing of the machine, Butch persuaded a loyal party volunteer with the surname of Schafer to enter the race as well. She conducted no campaign activities, but the names were similar enough that voters were confused about whether they had meant to vote for Schafer or Schuster, splitting Cheri's support and helping ensure victory for Phil.

Butch had been very encouraging during my race for treasurer. But now, from behind his heaped desk, Butch affably made it clear that he was not going to support me for mayor if I got in. "I'm concerned about your age," he began, before ticking off a number of other reasons why he didn't think I was the right pick. And Butch had done his homework on the local landscape to see where I might get support. At one point, I mistakenly told him I had a shot at earning the backing of Karl King, the influential coauthor of the "Benchmarking South Bend" study, whom I had come to think of as a mentor. Butch called Karl on the spot, on that indestructible speakerphone, and got Karl to make it clear he was backing Hamann, while I looked on awkwardly. Not that I had expected Butch to weigh in for me—I had gone to see him more as a courtesy than as an attempt to win his support—but it was clear as I left headquarters that we would have to outmaneuver the party in order to win.

At least I knew the Schuster/Schafer trick wouldn't work on me. With a name like Buttigieg, I'd be hard to miss on the ballot. I figured the name might even help me. Needless to say, the Maltese vote was sparse: I knew of four total Maltese-American voters in South Bend, including my dad and myself. But an unpronounceable, ethnically ambiguous name is practically an asset in northern Indiana politics. Depending on their own background, people could assume it was Hungarian, Polish, Serbian, Czech, or Belgian—all of which carried their own tribal loyalties in the area. The roster of local elected candidates around here is like a tour of Eastern Europe: Niezgodski, Zakas, Kovach, Wesolowski. For every black, German, or Irish candidate with a name like Morton, Davis, Dieter, Bauer, or O'Brien, there was a Kubsch, Kruczynski, Kostielney, or Grzegorek. Most illustrative of all was the former County Councilman Randy Przybysz, pronounced something like "sheepish" and spelled without the involvement of a single vowel.

THE STAKES OF RUNNING FOR MAYOR of my hometown would be a lot higher than they had been in a long-shot race for a state office few had heard of. Lose once in an uphill race your first time out of the gate, and you can still impress people by running respectably. Lose twice in less than a year, and you're probably done with politics, at least for a while. But this was home. I cared about this race even more than I had cared about Chrysler when I challenged Mourdock.

The reason to run—the ideal reason to seek any job—was clear: the city's needs matched what I had to offer. The city was fearful of losing its educated youth, and I was a young person who had chosen to come home and could encourage others to do the same. Its politics were mired in the struggle between two factions of the Democratic Party, each with its own candidate in the race; I belonged to no faction, and could arrive without strings attached. And as the administration struggled to generate economic growth and maintain confidence in the business community, I had a professional background in economic development and was fluent in the language of business—even while having fought and bled politically for organized labor in the auto industry. This didn't just feel like an opportunity; it felt like a calling.

It would come down to whether that match looked as clear to the voters as it did to me. Once again, I began to go through the motions of laying groundwork for a campaign. I enlisted Mike to organize a team, and he started recruiting local talent and colleagues from his last campaign. We got a booster of my potential run to donate some office space that he owned. I signed the paperwork to set up a new committee, and bought a couple new dress shirts. On Saturday, January 29, 2011, about a week after that *Newsweek* article said South Bend was dying, I officially announced that I was a candidate for mayor.

SATURDAY MORNINGS IN JANUARY in South Bend don't exactly invite you to leave the house, and my campaign staff of three was not sure how many people would materialize for our campaign announcement in the empty downtown storefront, next door to a small Thai restaurant, that would be our headquarters. With neither the Dvorak family nor the local party organization behind us, it was vital that we pack the room in order to show this was kicking off as a serious campaign. Luckily, the phone calls and cups of coffee over the preceding weeks had paid off. By the time I took the podium, the windows facing Main Street were fogged up with the breath of over a hundred supporters.

Standing behind the podium in the better of the two suits I owned, I gave a speech that ran headlong into the issues surrounding the campaign. I opened by talking about that "dying cities" article, saying, "This is not an occasion for denial, it is a call to action." I took up the age issue, too, reminding the audience that our city was founded by a thirty-three-year-old fur trader named Pierre Navarre and that the University of Notre Dame was the creation of a twenty-eight-year-old frontier priest, Father Edward Sorin. I promised to grow jobs by simplifying business process, to set up a 311 line for customer service, and to deal with the hundreds of boarded-up vacant homes in our neighborhoods.

As soon as the speech was over, volunteers settled into folding chairs at plastic tables to hit the phones, and I went out to trudge up snow-covered porch steps to knock on doors, just as we had in Iowa three years earlier. This time the campaign was for the future of my home-town, and the name on the flyers and buttons was my own.

ONE ADVANTAGE OF RUNNING for office statewide is that people generally understand you can't be everywhere. If someone invites you to a rubber-chicken dinner in Terre Haute and you've already promised to be at a fish fry in Evansville, then that's that. But in local politics, people know you're in town. If they invite you to a chili cook-off, and you choose to go to someone else's corn and sausage roast, they will find out whom you favored at their expense, and they will remember. And so we did our level best never to say no to an invitation or miss an event if possible, even if it meant arriving late or cutting out early to get to the next one. My record, set during Lent, was four church-hall fish fries and a Polish dinner in less than three hours—including a few minutes' unscheduled pause to change clothes after a pierogi malfunction sent globs of cheese and cabbage onto the front of my blue shirt.

Another feature of local politics is that there are a lot of people in charge of their particular spheres of influence, and it is important to pay them every courtesy. Some were very clear whom they were for or against. Others were more canny and subtle. James Harris Jr. pre-sided over a shack of a liquor store in a lower-income neighborhood near campus, on land slated for a road to go through as part of a project backed by the university. A precinct chairman, he knew how everyone in his area was going to vote—with a stack of voter registration cards on the counter, he had personally registered any customer who stopped by from the neighborhood, if they weren't voters already.

Every once in a while I would stop in to visit and try to see how he was leaning, but Mr. Harris remained permanently cryptic. I would lean over the counter as the occasional regular came in, usually for a forty from one of his buzzing refrigerator units or a fifth of whiskey from off his plywood shelves. Under the fluorescent lights, Mr. Harris would hold court, unless his wife was minding the store for him. Getting up in years, he would look up past his glasses at me and smile a little mischievously, as if we were both in on the same joke, as I began our ritual conversation:

"Hello, Mr. Harris, it's good to see you."

"Well, I'd rather you be seeing me than viewing me."

"Have you thought any more about the election?"

"Oh, yes. I like what you're doing. I hear you saying a lot of good things."

"Does that mean I can count on your support?"

"Now, I like the other guys, too, of course. All I know is, I've got my store, got my wife, got my house. Notre Dame says they want my store. But what they really want is the *dirt*. Huh? Bullshit!"

If he was trying to get me to take a position on the upcoming road development, he never made it clear what question he was asking—or what answer he was hoping to hear. It was an infinite loop. We'd go around and around, and I never did get a clear expression of preference over whom he would back, but I'd like to think I won his vote in the end. In any case, Notre Dame must have paid handsomely for that shop with the house on top, because there's no trace of the liquor store, and yet whenever I see him in town these days, Mr. Harris is in a very good mood.

ORGANIZED LABOR WAS DIVIDED. Many of the rank and file appreciated my stand for auto workers during the treasurer fight, but they also felt loyal to Dvorak because of his stances in the statehouse. I courted the ones that hadn't already promised to support him. The Sheet Metal Workers came through quickly, and the Fire Fighters signaled they were open to a conversation, so Mike and I, fresh-faced and clean-cut, went to meet them at their hall. Sitting with his fellow union officers at a big round table opposite Mike and me, Kenny Marks, the president, heard me out. A big man who was also a deacon at Mount Carmel, the fastest-growing black church in town, he leaned back in his seat and shifted between knowing glances at his fellow firefighters and piercing stares at us. He seemed interested but skeptical. "I like what I'm seeing, and I like what you're saying. But how do I know you're not just another sweet-talking devil trying to get my pants off?"

It was hard to think of a good answer to that, so I kept on with the pitch. "I don't know about that, but you'll be able to hold me accountable for what we achieve from day one. . . ."

You could never be sure, but I felt that our case was convincing—and that the groups we sat down with were responsive. Indeed, the Fire Fighters Local 362 came through with an endorsement, complete with T-shirts. Then came the Chamber of Commerce, and eventually the *South Bend Tribune*. It was hard to tell if any of these would be decisive, but at the very least they showed that our candidacy was serious. It was starting to feel like we had a real shot. And one day in March, as Mike and I walked out of a lunch event with Latino leaders, he looked at his phone, started grinning, and put his hand on my shoulder.

"What? What happened?"

"I got the poll. My friend, you're tied."

Until then we had no actual research showing we could win. But we had raised enough money to do a poll, and the poll showed me and Ryan each with about thirty points, Mike Hamann in low double-digits. For reluctant supporters who said they liked me but weren't sure I could win, this could be the tipping point.

In the detailed demographic "cross-tabs" at the back of the book of results that came back from the pollsters, there was a curious detail: the older the voter was, the more likely he or she said it was a "positive" that I was twenty-nine years old. To this day, I wonder why. Is it that senior voters are less likely to see distinctions between twenties, thirties, and forties? Did I remind them of their children? Whatever the reason, we took the data as a reminder that you should never assume who will or won't support you.

Soon Dvorak released his own poll, saying he was ahead by seven. We knew we were competitive, but there was no infallible way to gauge where we stood—especially since an off-year race like this, with no federal or state elections sharing the ballot, would depend heavily not just on how residents felt, but on which campaign could turn out the most voters on Election Day. My two main rivals had been turning out voters in South Bend since I was a student; our team would have to outwork and outwit them in order to succeed.

THE VIBRANCY OF A CAMPAIGN headquarters grows exponentially in the late weeks of a race. At first there is nothing going on but a candidate fundraising and a staff member or two—the space is quiet, almost grotesquely empty as its floor awaits tables, chairs, and volunteers. Then, imperceptibly, it begins to feel like a small community. Volunteers begin to populate the place, supporters drop off food, strangers pop in, and soon it is a hive of activity.

Looking into the main room from the window of my small office—the "tank," as we called it—I watched the energy of my campaign change from that of a lonely project to something resembling a movement. By mid-April there were a dozen staff members, mostly focused on organizing our volunteers. Racing to fund their paychecks, my call time intensified. Sitting across from Kathryn Roos, a talented young architect fresh off a stint in London, I ground out hour after hour of calls. Kathryn had expected to be home in South Bend only for a few weeks and was busy applying to graduate school, when a chance encounter in the soup aisle at Martin's with our mutual high school teacher, Mrs. Chismar, led her to a different path. Nearly all careers in campaigning and politics are either long-planned or unexpected, and hers was the latter. At Mrs. Chismar's urging, she had stopped by head-quarters to introduce herself; a week later, she was the second full-time staff member of my campaign team, working as operations and finance director as the rest of the team grew around her, Mike, and me. Under her command we raised over $300,000, enough not only to pay our staff but also to launch a substantial mail and television ad campaign.

ONE AFTERNOON AT HEADQUARTERS, I plopped down at a desk, loosened my tie, and picked up a sheaf of papers, scrutinizing them intently yet quickly, as a mayor would.

"Okay, that was good. But this time loosen your tie a little quicker. This whole scene is only going to be three seconds in the ad."

Again.

"Okay, not bad. Try to look up a little more when you're looking at the papers."

Again. Then the ice-cream shop, and the living room. The spot opened with a shot of me jogging in my neighborhood, and then had all the scenes you would expect in a campaign ad: me with seniors, me with kids, me at a factory. But because this was local politics, I actually knew the seniors, the kids, and the factory—and voters would, too. I thought it was a good commercial, and had raised enough funds to put it all over television for the final days of the race. But there was no way to be sure of its effect; a second poll wasn't in the budget.

One evening, I was at my parents' house for a rare family meal, when I glanced at the muted television and saw myself—the same clip of me jogging that we had used, but in black-and-white. I grabbed the remote, turned it up, and heard the dark voice-over. "What is twenty-nine-year-old Pete Buttigieg running from? Maybe it's the facts!" The ad went on to say I lacked "the real experience for elected office." The ad had come from the Dvorak campaign. My mother was displeased, but I was delighted; going negative on me was a clear sign that our competition was worried—and that I was now the candidate to beat.

Back at headquarters, nervous volunteers asked how we would respond. By the standards of modern negative television advertising, it was pretty tame stuff. My campaign staff was almost gleeful that we were doing well enough to be worth attacking on television. It meant that our poll was not a fluke, though the ad might soften up our numbers if people found it convincing. But thanks to our poll, I knew what Ryan's team didn't: reminding people of my age would only help. Rather than respond in kind, I decided to stick to our plan, focus on the economy, and stay positive. The penalty for negative advertising, I suspected, was greater in a local race where people know each other. In a community like ours, there might even be a political upside to the high road.

EASTER WEEKEND CAME JUST TEN DAYS before Election Day. I was sitting at a passion play at Washington High School when my campaign staffer Isaac Goldberg started looking anxiously at his phone in the seat next to me. He stepped out, then came back to his seat looking shell-shocked and whispered to me that Mike Hamann's wife had suddenly passed away. She was traveling with family in Paraguay, and experienced a massive hemorrhage after a hike on Good Friday. So, as Easter approached and the campaign was in its final days, Mike and his family were left not only grieving but having to figure out how to get her home to the United States.

Hundreds of us packed the funeral at Holy Cross Church on the Near West Side. As at almost every Catholic funeral in South Bend, we sang from our hymnals the haunting refrain, "Shepherd me, O God, beyond my wants, beyond my fears, from death into life." People mingled after the service, exchanging words of admiration and appreciation for Mary's life and Mike's commitment to his family. The tragedy had achieved what might otherwise have been impossible: a gathering of hundreds of active community members, just days before the election for mayor, with not a word spoken about the ups and downs of the campaign. With the heat of campaigning cut, at least for that one day, everyone could pause and remember that this was not a fight but a competition, among people who all wanted South Bend to be a good place to live in, for us and for those we loved.

ON EASTER MONDAY, BETTER KNOWN in South Bend as Dyngus Day, the campaign had just one week to go. It is difficult to convey to an outsider the importance of Dyngus Day, funny as it may sound. The holiday originated in Eastern Europe, where it was customary by the thirteenth century for boys to sneak into girls' homes at dawn and douse them with water as a sign of their affection; the girls would respond by giving the boys eggs, and/or striking them with pussy willow branches. (If you think this is absurd, envision what a European historian eight hundred years from now will think about photos of us celebrating the Resurrection of Christ by placing terrified children on the laps of man-sized Easter bunnies in late twentieth century American shopping malls.)

There's a lot more to the medieval East European tradition, but it's taken on a very American life in cities with large Polish and Hungarian populations like Buffalo, Cleveland, and South Bend. The day has traditionally been marked with parties at union halls, social clubs, and bars, serving copious quantities of Polish sausage and beer. Since the early 1900s, this was also an irresistible occasion for meeting voters, and thus became a fixture on the calendar of retail politics in places like South Bend. When Bobby Kennedy came to South Bend for Dyngus Day celebrations in the spring of 1968, it helped pave the way for the first primary victory of his presidential campaign, just a month before its tragic end.

These days, Dyngus Day for politicians begins before dawn, where we help (or attempt to help) boil sausage, noodles, and cabbage in the kitchen of the oldest and largest Polish-American establishment in town, the West Side Democratic & Civic Club. Local TV crews are there with live reports, and if the timing is right they catch the arrival of several hundred pounds of kielbasa from Jaworski's Market. The most senior politician present, usually me or Senator Donnelly, has the honor of ceremonially signing for the sausage order.

What follows is best described as a politics crawl, each location having its known slot on the rounds of the office-seekers. There's breakfast at the UAW Hall, then a visit to the Crumstown Conservation Club, where beer is flowing and people are dancing the polka by about nine in the morning. It is also customary to visit the African-American Elks #235 Lodge on Western Avenue, where a "Solidarity Day" party is held that is just like Dyngus Day, but with barbecued ribs and chicken taking the place of the kielbasa and kluski. Keep moving, and eating, and by noon you're back at the West Side Club for the largest event, complete with a blessing from a Polish priest and some short speeches. Afternoon campaigning is not for the faint of heart; it's best to stick to churches, and more senior-oriented clubs, where the beer hasn't flowed quite as liberally.

THIS YEAR, DYNGUS DAY FELL just one week before the primary, and by lunchtime the West Side Club was packed. As the smell of sausages and cabbage wafted to the ceiling, the candidates made our final case. I talked about the need for a fresh start for the city. Ryan Dvorak stressed his experience. Mike Hamann, through a surrogate, thanked everyone for the support for his family and made clear he was still in the race. Barrett Berry, running a distant fourth, spoke of his South Bend roots and time as a staffer in the Clinton administration; the fifth candidate on the ballot had dropped out altogether.

I voted before dawn, in a brightly lit lobby at the Notre Dame basketball stadium, the polling place for my neighborhood. Next came a ritual Election Day breakfast with my parents at Nick's Patio, and a visit to the Grotto on campus, to light a candle. What followed was as interminable as my last Election Day, but more excruciating because I felt this one was mine to lose. Once again, I had written two speeches, a concession and a victory speech. To blow off steam I went to a park with my friend Nat, who flew in at the urging of my staff to keep me company (and keep me sane), to toss a football around. In the sunlight outside Jefferson School I did another round of interviews on how I felt confident but not complacent, and, with nothing else to do as a candidate, headed back to headquarters to make campaign calls with the others.

"*Les agradezco de su voto*," said Benito Salazar into the telephone, and moved on to the next name on his list. Cordell, our volunteer coordinator, checked on walkers headed to African-American neighborhoods on the West Side, while my high school teachers Mrs. Chismar and Mrs. Lightcap sat at a folding table and called through the voter lists one last time.

There were dozens of people helping to get out the vote. With every seat taken, my sixty-six-year-old mother was sitting on the floor, a cell phone in one hand and pen in the other, marking down responses on a clipboard propped on her knees. People from every corner of my life filled the once-empty storefront. There was Jody Freid, the self-described universal Jewish mom of the campaign, next to a friend of mine from Harvard who had come in to help for the final days. There were high school kids that our intern, Tyler, had recruited, next to neighborhood leaders and sheet metal workers. An elderly homeless veteran, whom we had nicknamed "Jimmy Carter" because of his resemblance to the former president, made calls next to a Notre Dame student taking a day off from class.

"How's it look?" I asked one staff member or another every ten

minutes or so, peering over their shoulders in the boiler room at headquarters as they obsessively refreshed the spreadsheets on their laptops. Trackers at key precincts sent back reports on turnout, showing
our strongest precincts coming in very strong. We wouldn't know how
people voted until six, but the places where I was most popular were
voting off the charts.

I retreated to my house by the time the polls closed, wanting to be
out of the team's hair and needing a little quiet before preparing, win
or lose, to face my supporters and the cameras. I climbed out through
an attic window onto the small balcony overlooking the river, and
was watching its mesmerizing flow when the phone rang. Dvorak was
politely conceding and pledging his help in the general election; soon
Hamann called to do the same.

Mike drove me back to headquarters, and Kathryn met us as we
came in the back door. It felt as if everyone I had ever known was in
there. It took about fifteen minutes to get to the other corner where a
podium was set up for me to give a speech, working across the room in
a blur of handshakes and hugs. We had won a majority in the five-way
race, decisively securing the party's nomination in our Democratic city.
The Republicans had not found a strong nominee on their side; indeed,
many Republicans had crossed over to vote for me in the Democratic
primary, knowing that a Democrat would likely win in November and
hoping that it could at least be someone with a business and military
background. Almost certainly, this was the ball game.

In my speech I thanked each staff member, down to the interns,
and the campaign volunteers. I reminded them the real work was
ahead, then insisted as we had at the campaign's outset that South Bend
had everything we needed to succeed and grow. But I knew now that
the challenge ahead would be different in nature. It was one thing to
pull together a coalition for a campaign; another to keep a community
unified through momentous changes. After the speech, as the applause
grew to a roar, I turned to Mike: "Let's be sure to enjoy this. Pretty soon

we'll have to start making decisions, so tonight may be the most popular we'll ever be."

WITH MOST COMPETITIONS, YOU SLEEP in after the big day and begin to recover your energies. But for political candidates, the day after a win at the polls usually starts even earlier than Election Day itself, making the rounds of the morning TV shows. Determined to cover all the local stations in the morning-show window, I raced through the green rooms and studios of all four, in one case going on right after the puppies from the animal shelter. On television, you typically get two or three minutes to boil down whatever you have to say—and in my case, the hardest part was doing so while seeming lucid before dawn. It felt like one last challenge to cap off the months of phone calls, debates, and fundraisers. But I knew as I faced the studio lights and camera lenses that this was going to be the comparatively easy part. Going from campaigning to governing meant there would be plenty of interest in what I had to say, but far more attention on what I was actually going to do.

IV

GOVERNING

When you are writing laws you are testing words to find their utmost power. Like spells, they have to make things happen in the real world, and like spells, they only work if people believe in them.

HILARY MANTEL

7

Monday Morning: A Tour

Waking up comes hard. I've never been a morning person, and nothing can take the edge off a 5:30 cell phone alarm tunneling into the sweet haze of sleep. Strategically placed, the phone sits in the next room so that I can't snooze or silence it without first getting out of bed. That four-second-long walk will bring just enough alertness to remember my promises. I must stay in motion, and not slide back into the warmth of my dreams.

I try not to wake Chasten as I slip out from under the covers and walk to the small table where the phone sits. Truman is indifferent, curled up into a brown fur oval on a bench two feet from the bed. I lumber across the floorboards of the landing toward the bathroom to brush my teeth. The one-inch white hexagonal tile, cold on my feet, is the same kind as in the foursquare house where I grew up, some five hundred feet away. In the mirror, I make eye contact with an unshaven, bleary-eyed man in his mid-thirties, looking harmless but not thrilled to see me at this hour. I'll just never be a morning person.

If it were a Tuesday, I would have about half an hour to create the impression of being a morning person, for the benefit of a local TV or radio audience. Though I'm hours away from my best level of functioning, coffee and professional necessity can make me just lucid enough to coherently answer the questions of the hosts on my near-weekly round of morning news appearances. It's one of my best opportunities to make the case for a new idea or make the public aware of a new development in the accelerating growth of our city.

But this is Monday; no media today, and no early event, which means it's a run day. It's cold out, but there is no ice on the ground. Ice will deter us, and sometimes rain gets us down, but if it's more than zero degrees out and not slippery, then Joe and Tim and I can do our morning run. I pull on track pants over long underwear, a U.S. Navy hoodie over a long-sleeve T-shirt, and think about the saying I heard once during a delegation to Scandinavia: there is no such thing as bad weather, only bad clothing. (It rhymes in Danish: *ikke dårlig vær, bare dårlig klær.*) In other words, put on enough layers and you'll be fine.

Even the stairs are grouchy; they creak no matter how softly I tread. Everything in this 1905 house moves a bit, breathes a bit, especially in the wintertime. When I step out onto the porch to fetch the *South Bend Tribune*, I can see my breath, just as I could see it indoors when the real estate agent showed me the house in 2008. It had been vacant for nearly two years; most of the pipes had burst, and an irregular chorus of low-battery beeps came from a half dozen smoke detectors upstairs. The porch was in near-collapse; some of the small columns holding up the second-floor veranda were split in two, yet somehow still in place. Two big columns held up a small balcony outside the attic, one with a hole in its base so big you could put your hand through it. Carpenter ants and termites had undermined the pillars. Inside, every room had either cracked plaster or strange and peeling wallpaper, or both.

Yet the house drew me in. There was a fireplace, not working but salvageable. No one had painted most of the wood inside, including paneling in the hall. Its beauty was faded but not destroyed, and even the textures of its decay were appealing, like the irregular painted flooring of the small back porch. Every few days I'd check the asking price online, and watch it dip by a few thousand dollars each month as the bank that had foreclosed on it grew more realistic. Half a year after I first noticed it being advertised, it finally fell to where I could afford it. The mortgage, insurance, and taxes all together would be about eight hundred bucks a month, about half of the rent for my Chicago place and considerably less than I used to pay in Washington for a basement studio apartment accessible by a door facing an alley behind U Street.

This house had good bones, as they say, and just needed a little work. Specifically, rebuilding the porch, tuck-pointing the chimneys, and replacing the broken pipes and collapsed floor in the bathroom. And then there was the rotted wooden framework holding up the third-floor balcony, and the small columns, and the bases of the big columns, and the wiring, and everything in the basement, which had flooded at some point during its vacant period, and the termite-ridden baseboards, and the unmoored light fixture dangling only by an electrical cord. . . . Friends kept asking me if I had seen the film *The Money Pit*.

It will never truly be finished, but we've got it looking good now. It's home. From the porch I can see the lights of Memorial Hospital and the Chase Tower downtown, across the swift and steady river embanked alongside our street. The *Tribune* now in hand, I step back off the porch into the hall, stuff the paper into my briefcase, fold a suit over one arm, sling a gym bag over my shoulder, and try not to close the back door too loudly. I pull the back gate shut, step onto the concrete slab in the alley, and begin scraping the windshield of the Jeep. At 5:50, it is totally dark. But by now both Joe and Tim have taken leave of their wives and children and are also headed toward the gym. They'll be ready to go at 6:00 sharp, and so will I.

The Jeep warms up quickly. It's more car than I need, but the brutal winter of 2013, along with a transmission problem, motivated me to part ways with the old light green Taurus I'd bought when I moved home, known to interns and staff members as "the Chick Magnet." The Jeep is better for transporting a bike, a visiting reporter, or a small contingent of staff. Its interior enjoyed fifteen minutes of fame when Mark Zuckerberg visited South Bend for a mayoral tour and decided to go live from an iPhone mounted by suction cup to the dashboard, inviting in hundreds of thousands of viewers. And, crucially, it has seat warmers.

The Jeep and I are nearly alone on the small bridge over the St. Joseph River, pulling up to a roundabout with WELCOME TO SOUTH BEND spread across it in big, illuminated white letters. This roundabout, and a second one afterward, are not the most popular thing I've done, but they've improved traffic flow and the look and feel of our entrance to downtown. Through the second one and down Main Street, I turn onto the cross street and pull into a parking garage. I drop my suit and car keys off in the locker and put on a hat and gloves. Tim will be waiting in the lobby of the gym, a carpeted area with a big-screen TV where retirees sip coffee before or after their lengthy morning fitness routines, while young professionals and working mothers stride purposefully across the carpeted floor toward the aerobics classroom or the weight and treadmill area upstairs.

Tim is a lawyer, formerly an accountant, taller and slightly older than me. Raised in Argos, about forty-five minutes south of here in Marshall County, he is judicious and conservative both politically and personally. The day I came out, via an op-ed that hit early in the morning, he was one of the first to text me something encouraging. Partly this was because he is a good friend and the kind of person to make sure to reach out. But it was also partly because his farm family upbringing never left him, which means he gets up ridiculously early, and so was among the first to read the paper that day.

Joe, by contrast, is nearly ten years younger than I am, a college track team miler who had interned in my office during my first summer as mayor. He was one of a handful who had humored me by joining the early Wednesday morning outdoor workouts that I organized that summer for staff and interns, during a particularly zealous and short-lived CrossFit phase. We'd go up to the track by the former Saint Joe High School and flip two-hundred-pound tractor tires that had been left there in the grass by the football team, do sets of push-ups between laps around the track, heave bags of water softener salt, and swing sledge-hammers, that sort of thing. The interns called it CrossPete. That regimen didn't outlast the summer. But Joe and I kept in touch, and he took up running with Tim and me after he finished college in Fort Wayne and moved home.

One reason we get along so well is the three of us don't talk too much. Chatting is optional, depending on collective mood and energy level. A companionable silence governs the first few minutes as our trio gathers by the mouth of the parking garage in our sweats and hoodies and we trot, still in darkness, east on Jefferson across the two lanes (formerly four lanes) of Martin Luther King Jr. Boulevard (formerly Saint Joseph Street) and across the parking lot of the Century Center toward the sweep of the river.

From the Jefferson Boulevard Bridge, you can see the man-made rapids in the river and the River Lights, a permanent legacy of our 2015 anniversary celebrations. We raised over $700,000 to have an artist install a dynamic light feature to illuminate the cascades of the river in sweeping and shifting colors. Rob Shakespeare and his wife, Marie, moved to South Bend and spent three months in town perfecting the design. The International Brotherhood of Electrical Workers Local 153 volunteered the labor to set up the lights, some of which had to be mounted under the arches of the bridge. Like all good public art, the "Bean" in Chicago being the best example nearby, it has a charismatic quality that invites people to come up close to it, and to mix with others not like them. On summer evenings you will see clusters of people, clearly from different neighborhoods and lifestyles, walking in the park overlooking the cascades among lighted towers that respond to motion with patterns matching the lights on the water below. The colors of the light sculpture make up a universal language; very different faces light up in the same way, responding to its hues, when it surprises them with a burst of gold or pink. At this hour, no one is in the park to take in its kaleidoscopic glow, but we are treated to the red, then blue, lights striking the mist from the cascade and the fog from the comparatively warm river in the cold air, as we continue east toward Howard Park.

Careful not to slip on some remaining clumps of snow, we run on tiptoe down the concrete stairs connecting Jefferson above to the park below. The stairs bring us to a river walk, leading to a path originally built by the WPA during the Great Depression. Farther downstream the river roils with eddies and whirlpools, but here above the cascade it is wide and slow, almost glassy in the morning dark.

Monday is for long slow runs. The ideal running week (not that I claim that this happens often, but you have to work from an ideal) involves a long slow run on Monday, an interval workout at the track Wednesday, and a fast-tempo run on Thursday or Friday. Depending on the month, and the year, and things like whether one of us has a new baby or a pressing deadline these days, the Monday run is five, seven, or nine miles. To show you more glimpses of the city, we'll say that today's run will be all nine, a full figure eight.[2]

TWILIGHT TECHNICALLY HAS THREE PHASES, each brighter than the last: astronomical, nautical, and civil. The vague and doubtful suggestion of blue now must be somewhere between astronomical and

---

2   For the purposes of this chapter, I have created a sort of composite Monday morning. Some of these features of my mornings change from month to month or year to year. The Jeep has given way to a Chevy, for example, and at one point over a year passed without us managing nine miles. Still, this is as representative and honest an account of our long runs as I can offer. This would be closest to a typical run in February or March of 2016.

nautical, as we round a succession of curves on the riverbank beginning with the path by the boathouse, where squads of lean rowers from Notre Dame will appear in a few months when it gets warmer, walking from the building down to the dock holding the sleek boat over their heads.

The twilight will unfold, unhurried, across the St. Joseph Valley. There is soon just enough to make out the heron, if we are lucky, stalking cautiously on the opposite bank. To some he is a villain, guilty of helping himself to fresh protein from neighbors' koi ponds, but to me he is an elegant bird.

Down past the campus of IU South Bend and on across the bridge, we are for a few seconds outside the city limits of South Bend and instead in Mishawaka, our smaller twinned city to the east. But turning right, heading back west with the dawn's early light at our backs, we almost immediately come back onto South Bend territory. Along the way, geese hiss and rearrange themselves while we proceed on a wide, well-lit sidewalk, perfect for running except for the minefield of goose shit.

Some say that these were once migratory Canada geese that, as a result of habitat shifts, or climate change, or perhaps sheer laziness, decided to split the difference between Canada and Mexico and just hang out all year on the banks of the St. Joe. Whether that's true or not, they are certainly abundant. With goslings around, they are warier and meaner than usual, flapping their wings at us as we cut through a group of them dominating the bank and the sidewalk. Mayors in South Bend and Mishawaka have tried to abate the goose situation over the years, but none has solved it yet. Efforts to scare them off have been ineffective; the occasional move to cull them met fierce opposition from animal rights activists, even a "vigil to honor slain geese" organized on Facebook in response to a particularly aggressive effort in Mishawaka once. With all respect for those who care for animals, the response to that situation displayed a loss of perspective worthy of TV satire, or beyond it: even the writers of *Parks and Recreation* would probably have stopped short of dreaming up the sign someone held up that day, reading QUACK LIVES MATTER. In any case, leaving the geese alone has proved to be the least bad option so far, and so joggers and geese will have to coexist.

Back across the footbridge to the north side of the river and running back the way we came, light gathers around us and brings the trees along the banks into relief. Across the water from us is the Crooked Ewe, once a VFW hall and now one of the best restaurants and breweries in town. Where Vietnam veterans once hosted fish fries, the Ewe now offers nitro coffee and ramen with smoke shiitake, glace au poulet, kombu, scallion, and one-hour sous vide egg, with your choice of brisket, pork belly, shrimp, turkey, or andouille.

On this side of the river it's a little more old-fashioned, as you pick up the scent of bacon from the diner in the middle of the Farmer's Market, whose red walls have stood on this ground for nearly a hundred years. As farm-fresh food has come in and out of fashion, the place has hosted its butcher, Polish baker, fruit and veggie offerings, cheese shop, knickknack dealer, and lunch counter as always. Now you can also find coffee roasted by a start-up in an old factory nearby and arugula from a community garden network, but the place has never lost its heartland style. Its feel is still homey, and jars of pickled eggs and strawberry preserves outnumber those of salsa and kombucha. Under its roof on a Saturday morning, it is as if American society never fractured after World War II. Korea vets in flannel shirts down from Michigan, accompanied by ruddy grandsons in Under Armour camo jackets, coexist peacefully with Montessori moms navigating strollers between clumps of grandparents eyeing big baskets of apples and small ones of plums. Trucker hats are worn without irony here; the hipsters are welcome but not in charge.

We pass under the Grand Trunk Western railroad bridge, and hear the rumble of a train advancing overhead. There is no horn, thank God.

I think of the painful summer that once followed a miscommunication involving a letter sent by the Federal Rail Administration. The letter went to a city attorney, who never opened it, for the understandable reason that he had passed away six years earlier, and the consequence was a suspension of this neighborhood's designation as a Quiet Zone. Horns from a hundred trains a day blared at all hours, and an entire side of town began to lose its mind and told me so, one email and phone call at a time. My public works staff worked aggressively to make sure all of our railroad crossings met the guidelines to be safe enough that passing trains don't have to sound their horns, then waited powerlessly for the FRA to respond—all while my inbox filled with messages, and sometimes recordings, from frazzled neighbors desperate for a good night's sleep. They were not interested in hearing that this was out of our hands and with the federal government, or that the railroad companies were deciding on their own how long they would take to comply with the reinstated Quiet Zone. I was the one they knew how to reach, and I had better explain what we were doing to fix it. It took months, but at last the horns were silenced.

We pass under a bridge, part of a structure that I've begun calling the On-Ramp to Nowhere. A highway-style cloverleaf here governs an intersection that could easily be handled by a stoplight or a roundabout. It was completed in the 1960s after years of planning, designed to handle the flow of tens of thousands of workers leaving the Studebaker zone at the same time every day—and finished shortly after the plants went quiet forever. Someday it could be redeveloped into a small park, a residential block, or, who knows, maybe a flying garden after the fashion of the High Line in New York or an on-ramp-to-park project now in the works in Buenos Aires. But that's not in the budget just yet.

Off to the right rises the stately facade of Jefferson Intermediate Center, the finest piece of architecture in the South Bend public school system. It seems too big to be a middle school. Chasten taught here, as a long-term sub while he was in graduate school, after he moved in with me. The kids here range from middle-class families in the well-off neighborhood nearby, to residents of the homeless center downtown.

Back through Howard Park, we stay low along the water and come to the East Race, the best symbol of our city's knack for finding new value in what is already ours. The East Race began life as a canal for powering sawmills, typical of the 1840s, when canal-building became such a craze that it led to the bankruptcy of the entire state of Indiana and a provision in the state Constitution to prohibit the state from going into debt. This canal seemed to have worked out fairly well in its day, but by the 1970s it had fallen out of use and was filled in, a sort of industrial scar across the east side of the downtown. Mayor Roger Parent saw value in it and, controversially, invested heavily in restoring it until it was opened in 1987 as America's first man-made whitewater rapids. Today it's part of our parks system, and for a few bucks you can raft or kayak down its thousand-foot run. We can raise or lower the speed of the water through three large gates at the top, adjusting the difficulty level of the rapids.

The East Race embodies our community's style of development: a healthy city can take things that seem like liabilities and turn them into treasure. Looking across to the left as we run, I can see Stephenson Mills, a once-shuttered underwear factory now back to life as trendy lofts overlooking the East Race; one adaptive reuse supporting another. Behind it sits the Commerce Center, once a coal-fired power plant and now an office space slated for further development. One summer, the owner allowed eleven artists to set up installations in its basement, which includes an abandoned pool that once served as the central amenity of a fitness center there after a prior repurposing in the 1980s.

That's not even the most creative use of an old swimming pool in the city. Farther downtown, the former Central High School, where John Wooden once coached basketball, is full of people even though its bell rang for the last time in 1968. It, too, was reopened as apartments in the 1990s. Around the time I became mayor, a Navy lieutenant named Gus Bennett took up residence in an apartment made out of what used to be the school swimming pool. Though it was potentially the least usable space in the building, Gus and his roommate, Dena Woods, saw a way to give it new life, hosting bands that would play in the deep end and filling the rest of the former pool with sofas where people could take in the concerts while others watched from around the railings above. Good local acts and traveling bands played there, a testament to the fact that a good eye can see future value where others see disuse. In many ways, that's the story of the city itself.

To our right is the headquarters of AM General, the company best known for making Humvees used by the military, a continuation of the tradition of military vehicle–making in our city that dates back through World War II trucks to Civil War–era Studebaker wagons. It's about 6:45, but we already see one person sitting at a desk in the office, probably servicing a Middle Eastern or European account. In Mishawaka, the day shift has been under way since five a.m. On the commercial side of the plant, workers have been assembling Mercedes-Benz R-Class sport-utility vehicles for sale to the Asian market. Now that that contract has ended, the facility is being retooled to make electric vehicles for SF Motors, a Silicon Valley–based firm backed by Chinese investors.

We come to where the East Race is reunited with the main course of the St. Joseph River. Here, the river is a rebellious churn of swirls and eddies, in a hurry to get somewhere. Trotting up a flight of concrete stairs, we pick up the East Bank Trail, which incorporates a former railway and will take us all the way up to the edge of the Notre Dame campus. The asphalt is smooth and wide, and the daylight is now peeking through between leaves under a canopy of trees that arches over us, as if the city were nowhere near. From my office on the fourteenth floor, most of the city looks like a forest, and in the summertime you would never guess that whole neighborhoods sit below the dark green carpet of treetops.

We cross over U.S. 933, the north-south spine of the city, on a footbridge adapted from its original use as a railroad. I used to hate that bridge. Walking under it every day to get to school, I remember dreading the approach. Cars rushed by with nothing to buffer the sidewalk, which was then barely above street level, and the concrete support of the bridge held up an ugly green iron mass, while an inch-high ridge of pigeon droppings marked the beginning and the end of the passage under. A few years ago, a local artist decided the bridge could be a lot more. With city support, he recruited volunteers—over nine hundred of them, from local grade school kids to me and my mother—to paint the concrete and the bridge itself in a sort of giant paint-by-numbers project.

At the bottom of the hill we turn left at Stink Corner. It smells fine now, but for years I knew it as Stink Corner because of the sewer outfall there. Fixing the sewer so that it doesn't overflow into the river as often is the goal of a twenty-year, near-billion-dollar project I have inherited known as the Long-Term Control Plan. Judging by the fresh air at this corner, the project has been helpful.

Our house comes into view, hard to miss with the white, blue, and yellow of the South Bend flag hanging over the reconstructed porch. The Michigan Street Bridge that I crossed alone in my Jeep an hour earlier is now full of rush-hour traffic. Crossing the street and back up the hill toward the East Bank Trail again, we are mostly silent on mile eight, falling into the runner's trance. I become aware of feeling a little cold and a little hungry. The trail leads us downhill, back toward downtown. We return to the East Race, on the other side now, and come to Seitz Park.

As we cross back over the Jefferson Bridge, I glance at the contagion of potholes and make a mental note to check whether it's still on the list for repaving this year. Across MLK, we look to the right through the windows of the Chicory Café, where lawyers are fetching coffee and a couple graduate students are settling in for a long morning. A couple years ago the owner knocked out a wall and doubled the size of the café, partly because of revenue from selling beer after we used a state law to allow any business within a thousand feet of the river to get a deeply discounted three-way liquor license, helping the number of restaurants downtown double. One beer at a time, downtown has come back to life.

We kick it up for the last couple blocks, a sprint to mark the end of the run. Everything hurts, and I lose my breath for a beat, but now the hardest part of the day is over, at least physically. I suddenly realize how cold it is, covered in sweat on the street corner. Joe peels off to go home, while Tim and I walk up the stairs of the parking garage to get to the gym. I shower and shave in the locker room, and make small talk with the others, mostly downtown professionals and retirees my parents' age. One of them asks how much longer it will take to get those potholes on Jefferson taken care of, and as I stand there with a razor in my hand and a towel around my waist, I share my official views on the progress of the road-funding bill in Indianapolis while fighting the urge to insist on a rule that I believe should be understood implicitly: anyone not wearing pants should not have to talk about work.

Soon I'm in my mayor's uniform; dress slacks and a tie, or a suit if I'm doing something formal later. No breakfast meeting today, so I can head to the South Bend Chocolate Café and take my customary booth in the back. I shovel in scrambled eggs and ham, fruit on the side, washed down with coffee while I check the *Tribune* for surprises, examine the emails on my phone, and thumb through Twitter. Fed, hydrated, and caffeinated, I am ready to get to work. On the way out, I pass by the triceratops skull in the back room—the eccentric owner of the Chocolate Café is also a dinosaur enthusiast with a sort of ad hoc museum on the premises of the shop—and head back out into the cold air and toward the County-City Building.

THE COUNTY-CITY BUILDING IS NOT a beautiful structure. It is fourteen stories of steel and glass, with mostly tile floor and drab walls that proclaim its 1960s origins, yet it has a certain appeal. I pass the concrete pylons toward the glass doors, walk up to the metal detector, empty my pockets, and lay my briefcase on the belt of the X-ray machine. Under Indiana law, the only reason you can be prevented from bringing a gun into the building—or even into my office—is because the building is connected by tunnel to a courthouse complex.

Curtis is working security today. In his brown county police uniform, sitting in his usual spot beside the X-ray and glancing at the monitor, he reaches out for our customary handshake.

"What do you know, Curtis?"

"Not much," he replies.

False modesty. He's retired from the city police, and seems to know half the city. His annual August birthday party brings hundreds of people to the yard of his ranch house on the West Side's curving Lombardy Street a stone's throw from Washington High School. Every year he stays up the night before, slow-cooking his celebrated ribs.

Once, during one of these morning hellos, he signaled that he was going to share the secret to his ribs with me. For days, maybe weeks, he strung me along. It turned into a game. "I'm going to tell you the secret, but not yet." What was it? I'd ask. Molasses? Beer? Some kind of pepper in the dry rub? I enjoyed the game but was also genuinely curious, because his ribs were just right—tender, sweet, and juicy. "I'll tell you one day."

I assumed the game would go on forever, but the day really did come. "You want to know what the secret to my ribs is?" Smiling, mostly with his eyes, he disclosed the secret ingredient: "Patience."

AT THIS HOUR, THE ELEVATOR will be crowded, and usually I'll know where someone is headed the moment they step in.

Homeowner with a tax bill in hand: treasurer's office on two.

Slightly angrier-looking homeowner with a letter in hand: assessor's office on three.

Sweatpants plus neck tattoos plus nervousness equals a trip to the fourth floor for adult probation.

A gentler anxiety, mixed with resignation, in the expression of a low-income male in his twenties usually signals a visit to child support on the sixth floor.

A mom with a toddler is probably headed for immunizations at the county health department on nine—or, if she looks like she's in the middle of a divorce, vital records on eight.

Sherriff's deputy with a red folder, probably a subpoena, is headed to the prosecutor's office on ten.

Those are the county floors. The top three floors are ours, the city's—legal, admin and finance, public works. Code enforcement on thirteen has a soda fridge worth visiting from time to time; it's also notable because it used to be impossible to see across the room because of the stacked files, before we maneuvered the department and its masses of paperwork into the digital age.

I STEP OUT FROM THE ELEVATOR on fourteen and look to the right, where my name appears in black letters on the glass door to the Office of the Mayor. In this corner of the floor are six full-time staff and as many interns as we have room for, guiding an administration of up to thirteen hundred employees, serving a community of a hundred thousand.

A narrow corridor leads me to the desk of Yesenia, my scheduler and the first one in today. After greeting her, I step into my own office, walk across the carpet, and take a seat behind the big desk angled to look out through the windows onto the west and north sides of the city.

At eye-level out the window, a peregrine falcon swoops into view, angles toward my corner of the building, spreads its wings, and slows to alight on the roof, like a fighter landing on an aircraft carrier. Part of a mating pair living in a box right above my office, she patrols the downtown constantly, sometimes pausing to survey the realm from a nearby radio tower or a building across the street. A dive-bombing falcon is the fastest-moving animal on earth, capable of moving at two hundred miles per hour. Occasionally she gets a pigeon, making it difficult for me to concentrate as I look past an unsuspecting visitor, over their shoulder, at the shower of pigeon feathers drifting past the window.

In Egypt, falcons were considered to be symbols of the rising sun. Now, at last, the sun is up, shining on the American flag flying over the Tower Building across the way. I take a breath, pick up the phone, and begin to learn what kind of day this will be.

8

The Celebrant and
the Mourner

Civic ceremony, to put it mildly, was not my forte at first. Shaped by my consulting background, I arrived in office wanting to get concrete, measurable things done. My intentions focused on erasing inefficiencies and producing results. I took office eager to redesign the organization of local government and guide the course of our local economy, to see collapsing houses removed and urban infill built. The more concrete and countable my work product, the better. As for what you might call the symbolic functions of a mayor—sitting on a dais at a charity lunch or standing smiling next to a congressman or governor amid an endless sequence of speeches prior to a ribbon-cutting—to me this was a cost of doing business, an irritation to be dealt with as quickly as possible so I could get back to work.

A college classmate, elected to local office in another state, once surprised me with the comment, "Sometimes I wish we still had a royal family in America." I asked what he was talking about, and he explained: it would be nice if a royal family were available to handle things like cutting ribbons and waving to people in parades, so that elected policymakers like us could focus on the real work of legislation and administration. I thought of him often while standing alongside other officials at some event where I had no substantive role but to be present, and imagined what it would be like to just outsource that part of the job to some municipal prince or princess, or perhaps a "lord mayor" in the English tradition, so I could stay at the office and work on a way to improve trash pickup or eliminate some duplicative paperwork from our tax abatement applications. It seemed like standing there blinking in my suit, which required no real skill or intention, was a waste of time. Plus, the mental picture of a local official consumed with photo ops evoked the image of mayoring that I liked least—that cartoon concept of the sash-wearing, cigar-chomping petty official, with a puffed-out chest and a shit-eating grin, like Mayor Quimby from *The Simpsons*.

BY THE TIME I STOOD at an outdoor podium one warm May evening in 2015 and raised a glass to the city of South Bend in honor of her 150th birthday, I had gone through a full transformation in my regard for ceremony. By then, my old attitude seemed narrow. Growing into the job of mayor entailed grasping that the symbolic role given to me was no less substantive than the power of policy—if deployed wisely. It was a gradual conversion that began, like most important growth, in a moment of pain: the aftermath of a murder.

My first year in office, 2012, was our city's deadliest year of gun violence in a decade. By the end of 2012, there would be eighteen homicides, double the previous year. In 2013, I would assemble community leaders, engage experts, and initiate a new evidence-based strategy for dealing with the gang-related violence that had been driving this spike in crime. But in my first weeks and months of office we didn't have a clear sense of how to deal with the increase, and each violent incident made me feel powerless. Every time my phone vibrated with a new alert, I asked myself how we had failed to prevent the latest shooting.

Amid all the bad news of early 2012, one murder got my attention even more than the others. It was the first double homicide we'd seen in years, and both of the victims were only nineteen. Then, a few months later, an eighteen-year-old was killed in an unrelated incident *at the same address.* I wondered what could possibly be going on at this residential corner to make it so violent. So, on the quiet Saturday morning after that crime, I drove to the location, a few blocks from my boyhood home on College Street. Stepping out of my Taurus and standing alone on the lawn of the house, I tried to imbibe the energy of the place, seeking some kind of insight or understanding by virtue of being there. But the scene seemed totally ordinary. There was no sinister aura hanging in the air—just a regular house with white vinyl siding on a small corner lot.

A tired-looking man wearing a football sweatshirt walked toward me on the sidewalk, and then stopped next to me. I think he recognized me. I explained what I was doing there, not that it was really explainable, and he said that he was a relative of the victim. Then a couple more people appeared on the sidewalk, and a few more stepped out of two cars. Family, friends, and neighbors were converging, and soon it was clear that I had inadvertently crashed a kind of impromptu wake. I joined the neighbors in the headshaking, muttered condolences, and tried to think of something meaningful to say. Then one of the men pointed toward a car pulling up on the cross street. It was the mother of the victim, he said, and he asked if I wanted to go speak to her.

Honestly, I didn't.

It's not that I didn't wish to comfort her or be helpful, it was just that I didn't know how. I had expected to be here alone—and being among these mourners already felt like intruding. Besides, I had no relevant skills for this situation; nothing from my McKinsey training or college education was going to be useful here. I had no knowledge of grief counseling, no qualification for dealing with victims of this kind of trauma.

The grieving mother stepped out of the car, composed but devastated, leaning on a relative for support as she walked up the slight slope of the small lawn, not because she wasn't physically able but in case she became overwhelmed with sorrow and unable to stand. And I realized then that, of course, I was going to have to go talk to her.

I approached her, and she recognized me. I shook her hand, which seemed like an absurd thing to do. I tried to think of something comforting to say, something about how the whole community was holding her in our hearts.

"I know you," she said. Then, out of nowhere:

"Didn't you go to Saint Joe?"

"Yes, I did."

"I went to Saint Joe, too. So we have something in common!"

Small talk felt unnatural in the midst of grief—but isn't that what we need, sometimes, when grieving? Just someone to talk to, about nothing in particular. Nothing profound. Just being there.

I don't remember the particulars of the conversation. I'm sure it was awkward, and consisted mostly of generalities and obvious expressions of sympathy, a pitter-patter that I would have thought of as inappropriate for the situation before I became more practiced in consolation and mourning.

Yet later, occasionally, I would run into her or another relative who would let me know how much that conversation had meant. It was humbling, since I had not said anything memorable or used any particular skill. But this was the point: you do not necessarily console through the wisdom of your words, especially as a public official. It was a powerful, if grim, early lesson in the fact that as an elected official, I had become a symbol. What mattered to her was that I showed up. In contrast to my student or consulting days, the value was not in the cleverness of what I had to say, but simply the fact of my being there. Not that I, Pete, was there, but the *mayor* was there—a walking symbol of the city, and therefore a signifier of the fact that the city cared about her loss.

CARING, OF COURSE, is not enough. As the count of shootings rose, I became more practiced and capable at consoling bereaved mothers, and utterly sick of doing so. Every time, there were the usual cathartic statements about how we as a community won't tolerate this kind of violence, "never again," and so forth. But what would it actually take? Attending the funeral of a teenager whose mother worked as a secretary for the city, I asked myself what would have to happen for us to change the trajectory of violent crime in the community. The police were policing, preachers were preaching, the politicians were condemning, and yet here I was at a funeral for a fifteen-year-old boy, and I knew he likely wouldn't be the last teenager we would lose that year.

Somewhere in the course of my search for answers, I learned of the Boston Miracle. In the late 1990s, during a similar crisis, community leaders tried a new approach to dealing with the gang-related violence that was causing an epidemic of youth homicide. Using rigorous analysis to map group associations, a team of researchers joined with prosecutors, law enforcement, social service providers, and faith leaders to identify and contact the people most likely to kill or be victimized. The young men (nearly always men) were gathered, in person, for a "call-in." Here, officials and community members would promise to concentrate all law enforcement attention on anyone involved in the next group or gang to be involved in a killing—and also offer social services for those prepared to make a change before it came to that. Sometimes misunderstood from the right as an amnesty or from the left as a crackdown, the strategy's true core is in recognizing that would-be shooters are also people. Leaving aside the handful of people who are actually pathological, most of them just make decisions based on incentives and influences around them.

The overall message was, "We'll help you if you let us and we'll stop you if you make us," and it was backed by agencies committed to keeping their promises on both enforcement and support. Reading David Kennedy's book *Don't Shoot*, which explains the approach in detail, I learned of the dramatic drop in violent crime in some cities that successfully executed the strategy.

Under various names including "Operation Ceasefire" and "Group Violence Intervention," versions of this approach were being used more and more widely around America, and I decided to apply it in South Bend. Controversially, I hired an outsider from Massachusetts to fill a vacancy in the position of police chief, and with him convened an Anti-Violence Commission consisting of relevant players from around South Bend. Mixing the symbolic and the substantive, we sat around a big square table at the West Side's Martin Luther King Center, on public display acknowledging the problem and committing to the strategy. Over a period of months, one working-group session after another honed the plan. The "call-in" was arranged, set for precisely one hour, the speakers carefully chosen and rehearsed. A mother, a pastor, a prosecutor, an ex-offender, and so on. I couldn't be there for the evening of the first call-in, on military duty half a world away. All I could do was watch the numbers, as a violent spring of 2014 gave way to a period of relative peace after the event.

It worked. At least, it seems to have worked. Like economic development, our understanding of violence prevention remains primitive, partly because so many overlapping causes are at play. It almost resembles the state of medicine in the nineteenth century: finally advanced enough to do more good than harm, but only barely and not always. Still, I believe that it has made a difference. Shootings began to rise again in 2016 and 2017, but data from the program suggested it might have been higher otherwise. And the whole thing would have been worth it just to get the relationships built among the working group that still meets quarterly to oversee the strategy's implementation. At countless tense moments for the community, we've been well served by having that team—a federal prosecutor, a minority pastor, a young analyst, an ex-offender specializing in street outreach, and a dozen others—accustomed to working together, with each other's cell phone numbers when we need them.

We had hit on a policy that I believed in. But finding an approach as a policymaker did not relieve me of my duties as a symbol. What I saw, beginning on that sad summer morning, is that policy and symbolism cannot be decoupled. As a manager, a mayor must focus on what can be measured and proven, difficult decisions, and the use of new and old tools to solve important problems. But as a leader, sometimes the most important thing is simply to show up, or to gather the right people together, to send a certain kind of message. And while the mayor is the chief executive for the city as an administration, it is no less important to be, as the legendary Indianapolis mayor Bill Hudnut once said, "the celebrator, and sometimes the mourner, to the city as community."

PERHAPS THE DEPTH OF SORROW we sometimes feel as mourners is what makes us best appreciate the value of celebration. When you inhale the spirit of a city on both its best and worst days, you find yourself swelling up with joy at events that a younger self might have found banal—the first pitch of a baseball game, the turn of a ceremonial shovel at a groundbreaking, the handing out of an award plaque. Introvert that I am, I even came to love a good parade.

In a way, a parade more than anything symbolizes this mode of mayorcraft. My parade style is to begin alongside the "City of South Bend" entry, with as many city employees and interns as we can muster carrying a banner and passing out candy, but then I inevitably fall behind them as I go along the curb to shake as many hands as possible—and then sprint to catch up to my group before doing the whole thing again. I will meet hundreds of people but have no actual conversations. The younger me would have dreaded the idea of so many interactions without substance. As I trot by and stick out my hand, I have little to say beyond, "Good morning!" or "Happy St. Patrick's Day!" or "Nice work finding this spot to sit in the shade!"

Even though it is superficial and brief, there is meaning to each encounter. The purpose of the contact is not to persuade, problem-solve, or convey information. That can wait for a Mayor's Night Out, a State of the City speech, a council meeting, or an exchange of letters. This is about being present, on behalf of the city, not as an individual who may have something in particular to offer, but as a mayor whose role is to embody the community.

CEREMONIES AND SYMBOLS ALSO SERVE to express the values of a community, and perhaps this is why I should not have been so surprised by the degree of controversy aroused by the naming of things. The renaming of a post office is sometimes used as a stock example of how Congress wastes its time when it could be doing something more important. But I learned through experience that the renaming of a street could be as significant as any piece of legislation.

For as long as I could remember—but in reality, only since 2005—our city had a street on the West Side named after Dr. Martin Luther King Jr. This drive bearing his name extended less than a mile, and some residents pointed out that not one building actually had MLK Drive as its address. From time to time, someone would come to the open-mic portion of a council meeting and argue that the naming ought to be extended to a longer stretch of the road, or applied to a different and more prominent street. It made sense to me; especially compelling was the idea of making sure it was a street with a bus route, given the significance of the Montgomery Bus Boycott, so that a bus could be seen in South Bend with Dr. King's name over its windshield.

It turns out that one of the few unilateral, unchecked powers that an Indiana mayor has is to rename a street through a city Board of Public Works, so it seemed like I could just uncap my blue pen and take care of the issue. But I also knew to make sure that the choice had some community support, so I worked with our council to set up a volunteer committee of respected local residents to gather feedback and make suggestions. Then came the opposition, surprisingly fierce on the part of some. A remarkable number of reasons were presented to the committee why it couldn't be this street, or that street. Some complained about the loss of history if an old name was removed to make room for MLK. Others spoke of the cost to businesses of changing their addresses. Some warned of a loss in land values.

Of course, racial tension lurked near the surface of almost all these conversations. But it was always offstage, something you could feel but not point out, shading the discussion through vague allusions to "desirability" or "history." Looking for guidance and precedent, I learned that thousands of pages have been written on the topic, ranging from books with titles as straightforward as *Along Martin Luther King: Travels on Black America's Main Street* to academic articles as esoteric as "Street Naming and the Politics of Belonging: Spatial Injustices in the Toponymic Commemoration of Martin Luther King, Jr."

Every idea I floated for such "toponymic commemoration" met a new angle of resistance. Lincoln Way West drew opposition because it was a historic highway. Extending the existing route along Chapin Street was opposed out of regard for the historic neighborhood and the city father, Horatio Chapin, for whom it was named. (The *Tribune* recounted a 1995 debate on the same topic: "One lady said, 'Martin Luther King Jr. is dead.' And we said, 'Well, we're pretty sure Mr. Chapin is dead, too.'") People living in that area hired a lawyer who went so far as to say that it would be illegal for me to rename the street there on the advice of the committee, because the city clerk had forgotten to advertise a couple of the committee meetings as required. A lady from that area came to a Mayor's Night Out event and suggested, fire in her eyes, that North Shore Drive, where I lived, should be considered. I was about to tell her that that was fine by me, though I didn't think the community activists would find it prominent enough; but by the time I had the sentence formed in my head, I was looking at her backside as she stomped off, apparently satisfied that she had proven her point with an outrageous suggestion.

There turned out to be a natural alternative: Saint Joseph Street. There were enough places already named after our area's patron saint of nearly everything (a church, a hospital, a middle school, a high school, the river, and the county, to take a few) that I didn't think he would mind. And with a major downtown streets initiative wrapping up, it would be one of the finest streetscapes in the city. It was prominent— right in the middle of downtown—and had major addresses on it, including the Century Center and the School Corporation. The com- mittee members seemed to like it, though they had made the more modest recommendation of extending the existing road. I announced it, arranged for the street signs to be made, and made it official on Dr. King's birthday in 2017.

Achieving this took us four years (or over twenty, depending how you start the clock). And now, along Dr. Martin Luther King Jr. Boule- vard, there has been no cause for regret. The street looks good, and so do the buses bearing Dr. King's name that run along it. Land values are only rising there, and I've heard nothing about any impact on whether the area is "desirable." Instead, it is a statement of our city's belief in racial and social justice and a measure of pride in the diversity of our past and present. It stands among the other ways my administration has found to honor Dr. King, like adding it to the calendar of city holidays, and unveiling a statue of the moment in which he stood arm in arm with Notre Dame's president, Father Ted Hesburgh, in Chicago in 1964, all part of a symbolic texture revealing what is important to our city. Along- side more direct expressions of the lessons of civil rights—like the lec- tures and exhibits at our Civil Rights Heritage Center, built under my predecessor from the remains of a once-segregated natatorium—it signals to us the value that a city can place on the struggle for justice. And it forces us to acknowledge that the struggle is still under way.

On issue after issue—safety, neighborhoods, growth, race relations, and traffic—I learned this lesson: symbols and ceremonies very much matter because they establish the tone for all of the work we come to do in the public square. And so, one May evening in 2015—some three years after wishing that we had a royal family to do things like this so I wouldn't have to—I smiled with sincere pleasure with a glass of champagne in my hand. From a stage on the concrete island behind the Century Center, amid the rushing waters of the St. Joseph River, I addressed a crowd of thousands and led a toast to the city's 150th birthday.

THE IDEA OF A MAJOR CELEBRATION in 2015 had begun during my campaign, four years earlier. Zoned out from too much call time one day, I was staring blankly at an image of the city seal on some document on my cluttered desk. The seal features a rising sun amid a field of puffy clouds, an American flag, and the word PEACE. I'd never really paid much attention to it, but now I wondered why the city fathers had chosen this imagery for our seal—nothing to do with corn, or machinery, or the river, or anything else native to our city. Then my eye fell on the bottom of the seal, where it read: 1865. I went to look up the precise date of the city's incorporation, and found that the city was given its present legal form in May of that year—just six weeks after Lee's surrender at Appomattox.[3]

---

3 A historically minded reader may note that South Bend must have existed in some official form prior to this date. It is true that the community went through more than one early form of incorporation, reaching back as early as 1835, but 1865 seems to be the consensus "official" foundation date because it was then that South Bend incorporated as a "second-class city" under Indiana law, taking its present form. Of course, the Pokagon Band of Potawatomi Indians had a presence here long before any European-style municipal administration at all.

Now the seal made a lot more sense. The American flag was not some generic symbol of nationalism—it was the flag of a republic whose very existence had just been gravely threatened and freshly vindicated by the grievous and mortal test of the Civil War. The word "peace" was not a vague blessing or pleasantry then, it was the fond desire of a population traumatized by its opposite. What a hopeful act it would have been, to draw up paperwork and formalize the presence of a city in the aftermath of that dreadful conflict, deep in prairie land that was, in those days, still considered the West.

And then, instinctively, I did the math. Incorporated in 1865. That meant the city was 146 years old. It followed that the winner of the 2011 campaign would be in office to preside over the 150th anniversary of the city in 2015. Remembering this while on my journey toward recognizing the power of the ceremonial, I came to realize that a major celebration of this date would offer the perfect occasion for something badly needed: a chance to consolidate and celebrate the psychological gains of our present comeback, and to offer a decisive reply to the decades of gloom that had culminated in the stinging mention of our hometown in *Newsweek*'s "Dying Cities" article.

I asked my staff to organize a committee, and we began raising private funds to help mount a sweeping celebration of the city's past, present, and future. Everyone was invited to celebrate in their own way, from a restaurant creating a special dish for the occasion to the library hosting a "scan-a-thon" for historic family photos. We decided the celebrations should last all year, but the events would hinge on the actual birthday of the city, which happened to fall on Memorial Day weekend. We would close major streets downtown, create a citywide festival with everything from a technology expo and food trucks to a three-on-three basketball tournament and zip lines installed over the river. It would all kick off with a party and fireworks show downtown.

Of course, if the city hadn't actually been coming back, none of this would have worked. Like an anniversary party for an obviously failing marriage, it would have drawn half-hearted crowds and murmuring behind the scenes. Responses would have been tepid or even sarcastic. Thus, the celebration would function not just to assert, but also to test, my claim that the city was on a roll once again. For any of this to work, the contention that South Bend's decline had ended would actually have to be true.

But by 2015 there was no denying the real comeback under way. When I had taken office in 2012, the aftereffects of the Great Recession had compounded our half-century-long economic slump and brought us to a miserable unemployment rate of 11.8 percent, three full points above the national average. Now unemployment was down to 5.6 percent, a mere half point from the U.S. rate. We had cleared or fixed most of the thousand vacant and abandoned houses at the center of our neighborhood redevelopment strategy. The number of restaurants opening in our once-quiet downtown had doubled, deals were under way to add two major hotels to the city center, and investment was up in our industrial areas. Safety was improving, and at last the national coverage of our city was more likely to be about innovation than post-industrial ruin. Whether by statistics or intuition, you could feel that South Bend was trending in the right direction.

And so the banners and fireworks of this birthday party for the city, just the type of civic ceremony I had once dreaded, embodied a kind of propulsive civic energy that was self-fulfilling. Though the effect was beyond quantification, we all sensed that evening an advance in the psyche of our city, which would unlock further investment and growth to come. As I raised the glass and said, "South Bend is back," the roar of the crowd at once reflected, certified, and caused it to be so.

9

A Plan, and Not Quite Enough Time

Only later did I grasp the connection between two hundred hours of piano practice and those thousand vacant houses in South Bend. Some things like this only become visible with the benefit of hindsight—along with a paper coffee cup with a quote by Leonard Bernstein printed on its side: "To achieve great things, two things are needed: a plan, and not quite enough time."

It was Bernstein who conducted the authoritative recording of Gershwin's *Rhapsody in Blue*, and he was on my mind as I took a bow, exhilarated and relieved, on the stage of the Morris Performing Arts Center, in front of about two thousand people on a February-evening in 2013. I'd been a mayor for thirteen months, and a concert pianist for twenty minutes. By briefly becoming both, I had found a way to support the arts and to demonstrate how our city can punch above its weight class—all thanks to a chain of events that began with a Soviet defector, a Chinese maestro, and an ambitious music school dean.

Indiana University has long boasted a very strong music program, and so does its South Bend campus. At its center is Professor Alexander Toradze, a Georgian pianist who defected from the Soviet Union in 1983 while on tour with the Bolshoi Symphony Orchestra—and somehow wound up in the Hoosier State. The circle of professionals and students who grew around him, known as the Toradze Piano Studio, perform around the world and win prestigious competitions. As if a prerequisite to study with him, his students have magnificently complicated names, like Vakhtang Kodanashvili, one of Toradze's star students who also plays with the South Bend Symphony Orchestra, or Maxim Mogilevsky, whom I once saw attack a piano with such vigor during a performance of Mussorgsky that they had to give it a quick retuning at intermission.

The presence of so many gifted graduate students meant that South Bend had an abundance of talented and willing piano teachers. They were available at very reasonable rates to parents like my mother, who figured out quickly that I was not destined to be a Division I athlete, and instead developed the hope that I might fund my college education with a music scholarship. She lined up piano teachers starting when I was five, and continued patiently taking me to lessons every week for years. After my childhood teacher, Kayo Tatebe, moved out of town, Mom began to deliver me every Friday to a basement practice room in IUSB's Northside Hall for lessons from a Singaporean student, May Lin Ding, whose name was a rare exception to the polysyllabic norm around the department.

When May Lin moved on, my mother started taking me half an hour up the road to Berrien Springs in Michigan, where Dr. Sandra Camp lived and practiced her twin passions of music education and cat showmanship—her split-level home containing both a piano studio and a breeding operation. As I became a teenager, the weekly commute ensured a little quality time with one or the other of my parents. We might talk, or not, as we crossed the state line, either in Mom's giant blue Buick LeSabre listening to NPR news, or Dad's two-door Chevy Cavalier listening to what might have been his sole cassette, the

Creedence Clearwater Revival masterpiece *Cosmo's Factory*, looping permanently in the tape player for about as long he owned the car.

In a wall-to-wall carpeted room at Dr. Camp's house, full of sheet music and Persian longhair cats, I labored under her no-nonsense gaze, which in retrospect was itself a little cat-like. She taught me technique and theory, tempo and musicianship, until I became a pretty good pianist, skilled enough to play Rachmaninoff's C-sharp minor prelude in competitions.

Good, not great. I rated honorable mentions here and there, but by the time I was a teenager I was practicing less faithfully and getting more interested in guitar, teaching myself those Creedence songs, then graduating to Jimi Hendrix solos and Dave Matthews acoustic licks. A capable guitarist, I wound up occasionally gigging with a garage band that we called "Turkish Delight" for some reason I can't remember. While a scholarship wasn't going to happen, music would stay with me as a discipline and a retreat.

When I left for college, the "Peter 2000," a Stratocaster-type guitar I'd built from a Carvin self-assembly kit, joined me on the trip to Boston. The piano, of course, did not. I stopped playing almost completely, until I moved back to South Bend in 2008. Not yet having bought a home, I was renting a carriage house out back of a professor's house farther down the river when my mother—ever the champion of my fleeting music career—overheard a stranger on a bus in Chicago lamenting that he couldn't get rid of his old piano. Having once heard me say something about wanting a keyboard, she sidled up to him and asked if he was selling a piano.

"No, I'm trying to give it away! No one wants it. I'm about ready to put it in a Glad bag and drop it out the window," he told her.

What did my mother say to him next? Who knows? But soon after that, I found myself standing among knickknacks in this gentleman's carpeted apartment in Chicago, looking at a rather neglected antique grand piano. The pianist in the household had been his wife; she had passed away years ago. The instrument was not in great shape. It hadn't been tuned for years; some keys were broken and others didn't move at all. But it looked like something that could be repaired. So I called Steve Merriman, a neighbor of my parents who seems to embody one of South Bend's defining characteristics: a knack for salvage and reuse.

Some years ago Steve and his wife, Mary, launched a piano-tuning business, which developed into piano reconditioning and more. Over time, the business escalated into a kind of mission. Whenever Steve hears of a piano on its way to the landfill—someone passing away, a church moving, a school upgrading its instruments—he intervenes and commences a rescue. He recently moved his operations into a disused dry-cleaning facility with all the space he needed both to store and fix them. But back then, he was constantly negotiating with someone to get more space to park the pianos he had caught and saved, unwanted and unplayable. At his pleading, someone's garage or storeroom would become a foster home for his wayward instruments until he could get them repaired.

Like a devoted volunteer at an animal rescue shelter, he is always on the lookout for potential owners, anyone who will fund him to fix an instrument. He's not really looking to sell or "flip" the pianos, just seeking someone to cover the cost of his time to restore them. In fact, he's not even a pianist—he's a jazz drummer—but he has a compelling vision that a good instrument belongs in every home. As he once told me in his gravelly voice, his eyes at once smiling and piercing, "I just believe that every house oughta have a furnace, it oughta have a toilet, and it oughta have a piano."

So, standing in the living room of a bemused elderly gentleman in Chicago preparing to leave his wife's possessions behind and go to a second retirement somewhere in Mexico, we called Steve back in South Bend, describing the piano to him and asking if he thought he could fix it. A couple weeks later, the living room of my modest quarters had been converted into a sort of piano workshop. The black hulk of an instrument now dominated the room, surrounded by little pieces of wood, scraps of felt, and a mysterious arsenal of tools as Steve took the piano apart and put it back together. And soon after that, for about as much money as I had saved to spend on a good keyboard, I was the proud new owner of a working 1920s Conover grand.

I noodled on it every now and then but didn't play that much, until one day in 2012 when I heard from Dr. Marvin Curtis, dean of the School of the Arts at IU South Bend. He was looking for me to do something with the symphony orchestra, some gimmick to show my support for the arts and help drive up ticket sales. Occasionally, for example, they arranged for a community leader to guest-conduct a piece. Would I be up for something like that? Sure, I said. Anything to support the symphony. Then I thought, aloud, what if I actually played something? Could I perform a serious piece of music with the South Bend Symphony Orchestra?

Marvin embraced the idea so readily that I now think he hatched the idea before I did. Maybe he had heard from someone around town that I used to play. He promptly sent me to meet the orchestra's maestro, Tsung Yeh, at his house for what began as a social cup of coffee but ended up more like an audition. The maestro had presided over our South Bend Symphony Orchestra for more than twenty years—I could remember school trips to see him conduct educational concerts—and was known for squaring a genial demeanor with an exacting command of a symphony several notches above what you might expect for a mid-sized city in Indiana.

I hadn't played consistently in more than a decade, and never with an orchestra. But after hearing me play some things I could still remember, the maestro concluded I might be up to it. What better way to send a message that the arts were vital to the city than for the mayor to perform with the local orchestra?

I thought of the blue-jacketed solo arrangement of Gershwin's *Rhapsody in Blue*, which came into my underused sheet music collection when my grandmother, herself a piano teacher, had passed away. Even when she was still living, I used to find it on her bookshelf and try to tap out Gershwin's familiar passages. My hands not yet big enough, I tried to reach the octaves of its soaring final theme, known to a generation of commercial-watchers and frequent fliers as the official music of United Airlines. Considered by many to be Gershwin's masterpiece, *Rhapsody* is a rollicking ecstasy of jazzy piano and symphonic interplay. To me, it is the most American piece of orchestral music ever written. I'd always loved it, but never actually learned it properly—nor even reached the skill level needed to play it.

But Marvin had a plan. "We just have to get some Russian in you." And by Russian, in this case, he meant Georgian. He arranged a course of lessons with Edisher Savitski, one of Toradze's star graduate students. A genial man with a cloud of wavy dark hair, Edisher would spend an hour with me every week, patiently coaching me into becoming a concert pianist—with not quite enough time.

We had six months. I practiced every day, usually early in the morning, on my old grand piano, which probably hadn't been played two days in a row since Ronald Reagan was in office. On this ambitious time line, daily practice was a must. A famous pianist (the Internet can't agree which one) once said: "If I miss one day of practice, I notice it. If I miss two days, the critics notice it. If I miss three days, the audience notices it."

The quotation became my mantra. If I was traveling, I found some way to get access to a piano—at the home of an acquaintance, perhaps, or an unsecured hotel ballroom where the night maintenance staff could be relied on to look the other way. Once, around five-thirty in the morning, I found myself in O'Hare Airport on my way to Miami to see Notre Dame play for the BCS title, aware that I might not see a piano for three days. I found one by Gate C16, alongside a deserted bar, a discreet rope around it, no bench. The concourse was almost empty. I gingerly moved the rope, and wheeled up my roll-aboard bag to sit on. And I began to play. Pretty soon I had a couple listeners, then a small audience, and at the end there was applause—and, awkwardly, a couple of dollar tips.

If I was running with Tim and Joe in the morning, then I'd fight exhaustion and practice before bed. Once, after a near-all-nighter coming home from the Democratic Convention in Charlotte in time to host Mitch Daniels, our Republican governor, for a lunch with business leaders, I hurried home for a lesson in between the airport and the restaurant. Standing as Edisher demonstrated a passage for me, I felt my knees go out from under me and grabbed the side of the piano. He looked over, alarmed, and asked if I was all right; I had fallen asleep standing up.

As I got to know Edisher I learned more of his story. He had come from the Republic of Georgia at Toradze's invitation, with no money and no English. He was already emerging as a world-class pianist—he once won a grand piano at an international competition—but had to start from zero financially. While enrolled at IUSB, he got a job making submarine sandwiches at a Blimpie in a strip mall on South Bend Avenue—he described to me once covering a sandwich in garlic powder after misunderstanding a customer's emphatic and repeated demands to have no garlic on his sandwich. He's since become a professor, a fitting outcome for a classically American story of opportunity, but when I think about his journey I can't get past the thought that it was a crime to allow such talented fingers so near to a meat slicer.

Each week for one hour, he would sit in my living room and hone my technique. I'd play a passage for him, and he would lean back thoughtfully, bring his hands together, and say, "Okay, lots of beautiful things. Now . . ." And here he'd begin deconstructing my performance and putting it back together. He would say things that sounded strange at first, like, "Don't play the notes—just play the music." Explaining how to make one passage twinkle, he described the first time he saw an American Disney cartoon and asked me to evoke its characters. It seemed cryptic at first but began to make sense over time. After a couple of months I was dreaming *Rhapsody in Blue*. I could close my eyes, start at any point, and play the rest of the piece in my mind.

After two rehearsals with the orchestra, which were my first and second times ever playing piano with an orchestra, it was time for the performance. The whole program was Gershwin, with two talented vocalists teed up to do *Porgy and Bess* for the second half. My part would be before intermission. The date was February 16, the show called "A Valentine from Gershwin." I did my best to stay calm in the dressing room as the maestro warmed up the orchestra and the audience with "Strike Up the Band," then I hovered offstage as they turned to "An American in Paris."

Finally, it was time. Wearing a suit instead of a tux (a concession to the reality that at the end of the day I was a mayor, not a professional pianist), I stepped out onto the blond wood of the stage at the Morris Performing Arts Center, a space that started as a grand vaudeville house in the 1920s and became a movie theater before the city took it over and renovated it. Through the glare of the spotlights I could just barely make out a sea of over two thousand faces. It was more than I'd ever seen for a symphony performance. I wondered if they were there because they loved Gershwin, or to cheer me on. Some part of me sensed that many had in fact come to see if I would succeed or not; beyond the unlikeliness of the spectacle, it was above all the possibility of failure that created the suspense.

I exhaled, took a bow, and walked toward the piano. I had decided at the last minute not to bring sheet music. It was just me and the instrument, the orchestra to one side and the audience to the other. I had given speeches to crowds this size with no discomfort, but this was terrifying. Lose your place in a speech, you can take a breath and resume. Lose the orchestra in a fast-moving passage, and you might never find your place again. But I had practiced this thing into the deepest furrows of my brain. I was ready. I settled onto the bench, breathed again, looked at the maestro, and gave a little nod.

The clarinet began with that famous trill, turning into a scale that bends into a high note, sounding just enough like a siren to suggest that the piece is in some way about the American city. The horns join in as the clarinet swingily pipes out the main theme, then the other sections begin joining in. I enter with the low notes on the piano, raising the tension in a slow crescendo up to the big moment when the orchestra arrives in full force. At first the piano is doing little more than punctuation, but then the powerful chords come, and the thrilling sequence of flying fingerwork, urgent yet disciplined, fast and precise, one passage supposedly inspired by the rhythm of an accelerating train as a panicking Gershwin sat on board and scrambled to compose the piece in time for the deadline of his composer's commission.

I kept time with the maestro out of the corner of my eye, alternately working the piano and hanging back during the passages of rest, until the final, lyrical flight known to anyone who has ever seen a United commercial or Woody Allen's *Manhattan*. The review in the *Tribune* later would say that "technique sometimes took precedence over expressiveness." Still, "Although it looked like stunt casting . . . Buttigieg acquitted himself well," the critic concluded. I muddled a couple runs but felt the thrill of nailing most of the hardest parts, all the while sensing the audience following intensely as the piece soared to its emphatic and muscular finale.

And when it was over, the crowd sprang onto its feet. Through the glare of the stage lights I made out a few familiar faces but saw mostly strangers, cheering, delighted. I'll never know if it was the music that moved them most, or the spectacle, like the end of a tightrope act, of seeing someone succeed who might have fallen at any moment.

THE EXPERIENCE BROUGHT TO MIND a comment I had recently heard from former Baltimore Mayor and then-Governor

Martin O'Malley about being a good mayor: *that leaders make themselves vulnerable.* It was an odd thing to hear from a mayor best known for data-driven performance management, not for emotional resonance. But that was precisely the point: using data in a transparent way exposes leaders to the vulnerability of letting people see them succeed or fail. Being vulnerable, in this sense, isn't about displaying your emotional life. It has to do with attaching your reputation to a project when there is a risk of it failing publicly. The more a policy initiative resembles a performance where people are eager to see if the performer will succeed, the more vulnerable—and effective—an elected leader can be.

The possibility of highly visible failure has an exceptional power to propel us to want to succeed, and that power can be harnessed to motivate a team or even a community to do something difficult.

TWO WEEKS AFTER that Gershwin performance, I committed publicly to a more widely consequential effort: to confront a thousand vacant and abandoned houses in a thousand days. It would become one of the defining projects of my administration, but it also had the potential, like the symphony performance, to be my most visible disappointment. Previous administrations had torn down hundreds, but never seemed to get ahead of the contagion of blight. By the time I was campaigning for mayor, it was the number-one issue we heard about when knocking on doors and making phone calls. Despite years of work and millions of dollars, there always seemed to be more vacant houses than the city could deal with—so many that when I first took office, no one could confirm how many we even had.

It was clear that we would need to do something different, with more resources and an intense approach. Soon after taking office I convened a task force, which spent a year analyzing the problem. Mayor's office interns were handed over to code enforcement to help count and classify properties. County, state, federal, private, and nonprofit partners came to the table. We debated the use of land banks, explored novel applications of federal funding, and explored the role of utility disconnections in speeding or slowing progress.

The result was an extensive report explaining the various conditions and issues to take into account. The sophistication of the analysis was at a level South Bend had never seen before. But I was also fearful that we had just done one more exercise in describing the problem, without actually solving it. And I knew the residents of our city had no use for a data-obsessed mayor who didn't know how to turn analysis into action.

Without a different level of motivation, our administration and community might never get ahead of the issue, no matter how well we had assessed it. Worse, knowing the many nuances of the issue could actually make it harder; anyone who has sat on a big committee with lots of experts knows the feeling when people around the table display their expertise by mentioning one complication after another, admiring the dimensions of the problem in an ever-deepening discussion that cries out for some modicum of simplicity so that there can be action.

So, after a session sitting with my team over a draft of the report and talking through ways to announce our findings and begin moving toward an approach to actually fix the problem, I leaned back in my chair and took a breath before proposing that we use the richness of the report to back a goal of childlike simplicity: "Let's promise to deal with a thousand houses in a thousand days."

The faces of my staff immediately tightened with worry; they, after all, would have to do most of the implementation.

"It's a little more complicated than that, Mayor," someone piped up.

They were right, but it was also clear that a simple (or even simplistic) goal would create the kind of risks, and rewards, that could cut through the problem of analysis paralysis. When I added that we should create a real-time online scoreboard to update how many houses we had fixed, demolished, or failed to deal with, the staff members looked simultaneously excited and terrified.

The announcement certainly made us vulnerable, even more so than when I had stepped out onto the stage at the Morris. The public would know if we succeeded or not, and would hold us—that is, hold me—accountable if we failed. But with that vulnerability came a kind of energy, too. People would be watching closely, keen to pick up on mistakes, looking to see if we could really achieve this audacious goal. And inside the administration, the team would have a sense of urgency and focus motivated by a desire to deliver for the public. Just as I couldn't miss more than a day of practice, we couldn't miss any opportunities to raise funds, prod bureaucracies, or persuade residents to help us meet the goal. The very difficulty of meeting the deadline would provide its own propulsion, making good on Bernstein's adage.

It was through this effort that I began to understand the difference between my job and everyone else's. The experts on the task force could evaluate the market conditions in the various neighborhoods and identify the legal tools for addressing neglected property. The council could allocate funds for dealing with the problem. The code enforcement staff could press landlords to address the condition of the houses. But only a mayor could furnish the political capital to get the project done, by publicly committing to a goal and owning the risk of missing it. I began to realize that the job was not about how much I knew, but how much I was willing to put on the line. The application of political capital, not necessarily any kind of personal expertise, was how I would earn my paycheck as a mayor.

The scorecard went online, along with a map, updated continuously so that it was easy to know whether we were succeeding. Checking our website on Day 500, you would have seen that we were nowhere near having five hundred houses addressed. Repairs were moving slowly, and the gas utility was taking its time in disconnecting houses set to be demolished. Environmental rules required us to inspect homes for asbestos at a more rigorous level than before, and inspectors qualified to do the work were expensive, threatening to increase the cost of the program beyond our budget. But being behind was energizing, rather than demoralizing. I didn't have to give a locker-room talk at halftime; the team saw the same numbers that I did, and knew what they meant. Facing this pressure, the staff got creative—for example, the asbestos inspector issue was resolved by getting our own code enforcement staff certified as asbestos inspectors. Creative lawyering led to a partnership with the U.S. Treasury Department to use federal dollars, originally earmarked for mortgage workouts but now at risk of being sent back unspent to Washington, to help with blight elimination instead. And numerous community forums helped take in feedback from residents in areas from LaSalle Park to the Southeast Side on how their neighborhoods could be impacted.

Two months before the deadline, on a sunny September morning in 2015, I stood with the Jara family on the porch of their newly repaired home on Clemens Street. The gray ranch-style house had been on the affirmed demolition list when they bought it, but the family was repairing it with their own hands, and we celebrated their work as the one-thousandth home to be removed from the vacant and abandoned list, a reminder that repair was as important as demolition. By the thousandth day, our community had addressed not just a thousand but over eleven hundred homes, and was finally poised to pay more attention to preventing future abandonment than to dealing with the backlog.

In some ways, it was a classic example of data-driven management paying off. But the most important impact of the effort was unquantifiable. Hitting such an ambitious goal made it easier for residents to believe we could do very difficult things as a city, at a time when civic confidence had been in short supply for decades. As meaningful achievements can do, it raised the expectations our residents had for themselves and our community. I could feel it in the changing way residents talked about our neighborhoods—and in the higher expectations for city government. More challenges, of course, loomed in the future. But by that fall, there was a palpable sense that we could take control of our toughest problems.

The city was giving itself permission to believe.

10

Talent, Purpose, and the Smartest Sewers in the World

A short bike ride from my house, yet largely in a different world from anything in the city, sits the campus of Notre Dame. Its five vast and well-kept quadrangles are familiar turf, each a different geographic locus of memory in my relationships with family and friends. At the end of the South Quad is O'Shaughnessy Hall, where I used to toddle at my father's side to the English Department office and where the secretary, Connie, would offer gumdrops from a glass jar on her desk.

Farther south is the Mendoza College of Business, which felt like the most modern building in the world when my mother worked in its airy, newly constructed halls in the 1990s. I would accompany her there as a teenager to take advantage of the Internet connection—mostly for the purpose of downloading MP3 files of Dave Matthews songs, which could be loaded at a rate of one per ten minutes or so via the university's state-of-the-art network. Back a bit west from there is Alumni Hall, where I would hang out with old Saint Joe classmates whenever I was home on break from college, earning a decade-long distaste for gin after consuming too much of it, mixed with Mountain Dew, from a red solo cup one weekend during sophomore year.

By the time I became mayor, my father had migrated, across the leafy precincts known as God Quad, to a place I had almost never visited in my youthful romps around campus: the resplendent Main Building, topped by the Golden Dome itself, where the president sits in an oak-paneled office suite. The offices of the Hesburgh-Yusko Scholars Program, which my father directed, sat in a ground-floor corner with an outside window from which it is said Knute Rockne himself sold football tickets in the thirties.

Almost any week school is in session, there is an occasion to visit and speak—perhaps to a lecture hall full of a couple hundred engineering or MBA students, or maybe around a seminar table to the dozen or so seniors chosen for Father Scully's leadership class, or the twenty or so aspiring reporters in Jack Colwell's journalism course. It might be coffee with the College Democrats or pizza with a freshman dorm council or a full-on formal dinner with the naval ROTC midshipmen, but whatever the occasion, I always try to accept when invited there or to any of the other colleges in our area. I go partly because I just enjoy engaging students, who tend to ask the most urgent and penetrating questions, but also because they represent the key to a transformation now under way in what it means to be a college town.

I did not immediately recognize the meaning of this transformation. At first I thought of the town-gown dynamic in much the same terms as everyone else, a framework we might now call College Town 1.0. In this way of thinking, a college or university has significance that derives from its size, and the fact that it represents a certain community of people who are physically part of a larger community, the city or town. The student population is considered as just that—a population. Students are of interest mainly because they are a subpopulation with different attributes than the average resident. Specifically, they are younger, more transitory, and generally from wealthier backgrounds than the average city resident. They may also be whiter, more price-sensitive, and often more politically liberal. Taking this into account, a community deals with them accordingly. As an economy, the city will furnish less expensive food and alcohol (to accommodate students' budgets) and more expensive housing (to align with the spending power of their parents). As a municipality, the city will have a police force that must decide how much to concern itself with student drinking, an urban planning policy that pays extra attention to pedestrian mobility, and an electorate that differs in profile from a non-college town.

Notre Dame has some attributes that make it a little different. Its religious character is of course central; more than once, a student meaning to address me as "Mayor Pete" has absentmindedly called me "Father Pete" instead. The students and faculty, on average, are more conservative than at most colleges. And the university campus technically sits outside the city limits. Still, for as long as I could remember, these basic patterns of traditional city-university relations held up. If the city thought about students, it was mainly with regard to their spending habits and their likelihood of getting into danger or trouble. And if students engaged the community, it was likely to be as a place to occasionally eat, drink, or shop—or volunteer. At most, we might hope that a student would take a little time to serve food at the homeless shelter or tutor local students, just as I volunteered once a week to teach fifth-grade civics in Cambridge.

This was the framework I carried into office at first: the university as a large employer, students and other members of the university community as warm bodies, like any other resident except for a somewhat distinct economic and political profile. To be sure, Notre Dame was getting more engaged by the time I left for college. It supported a community organization that oversaw the transformation of neighborhoods south of the university without succumbing to fears of gentrification, working to make sure neighbors felt empowered rather than threatened by the school's territorial growth. Under Mayor Luecke, the city had partnered with Notre Dame to build a mixed-use development south of campus with restaurants, bars, shops, offices, and apartments that were a short walk from campus but technically in the city limits, creating more options for students and employees while also adding to our tax base. And students volunteered abundantly on worthy community causes, from the Center for the Homeless to neighborhood cleanups.

All of this was meaningful, but it didn't distinctively reflect the fact that Notre Dame is a university, not some other large organization. The volunteerism, the economic development, and even the neighborhood engagement could plausibly be something that any large organization, such a hospital or major corporation, might do on and around the campus of its headquarters.

But a university is not like any other large organization. Its students, faculty, and staff have characteristics different than any other community-within-a-community. However important their presence as residents, taxpayers, employees, and voters, the unique thing about them is the substance of their work. And if their intellectual endeavors are connected in the right way to the life of the community, the results are so profound that I now believe that a mayor who is granted one wish for any feature to add to her city—a stadium, a major corporate headquarters, a state capitol—should find the answer obvious: pick a world-class research university.

Our classic example of this was a collaboration that began before I took office, whose fruit today is my rightful boast that South Bend has the smartest sewers in the world. While wastewater management is not known for its power to fascinate, our city's experience with innovation in the field is among the most important local developments we've seen—and a model with implications for other cities across the country.

It happened because Gary Gilot, the public works director under my predecessor, understood that things going on at the university had yet-unimagined potential to solve some of the problems on his plate. Tall, soft-spoken, and deferential, bald with a crown of gray hair and a beard that he shaves below the lip, he resembles nothing so much as an engineering professor. He was a civil servant for as long as I had been alive, an exception to the norm in his field of spending perhaps half your career in the public sector before transitioning to the more lucrative realm of an engineering firm.

Impressed by his creativity and decency, I pleaded with him to stay on as my public works director after taking office. But he was ready to spend more time with his wife and focus on mentoring young engineers and community volunteers, so he declined—only to stay in the position for several months, unpaid at his own insistence, while we searched for a successor. Only once do I remember him being late to a meeting, explaining that he had come from taking the second in a series of rabies shots after being bitten by one of the many stray cats he feeds outside his home. It was a fitting metaphor for his career-long endurance of the various indignities of public service. Once, at a neighborhood meeting in someone's living room, I saw him absorb a sequence of dressing-downs by fussy residents who were demanding an unworkable gauntlet of speed bumps on their street. I observed him politely nodding while another neighbor launched into him, beginning: "Well, I'm not an engineer, I'm just an ordinary scholar of international law, but I can't understand why the city won't . . ." And that was when I realized that the patience of a consummate public servant can be saint-like.

Somehow, rather than being beaten down by his job, Gary seemed unfailingly energetic and optimistic, always searching for interesting new ideas and engaging with a younger generation of people that cares about civic innovation. This must be what made him eager to cooperate when some researchers at Notre Dame began to develop a technology for sensing water levels in sewers. Recognizing the potential value for a city that still had employees manually checking water levels under manholes full-time, he worked with the researchers to place Wi-Fi-enabled sensors across the city's sewer network. That would allow the system to automatically detect blockages, alert operators, and send instructions to smart valves that would redirect the flow of wastewater from overflowing pipes to empty ones. It was the Internet of Things, a few years before the term became popular.

The significance of this effort, Gary knew, was far greater than just relieving a two-man crew of manually checking our sewer overflows every day. South Bend, like many other Midwestern cities, had a "combined sewer" system, which means that wastewater and stormwater go through the same pipes. Under normal conditions, the system works well, but when high volumes hit the system, such as during a major snow melt, the combined sewage cannot fit through all the pipes, leading to backups that send untreated sewage into the river. This violates the Clean Water Act, which prompted the EPA to pursue several such "combined sewer overflow" cities beginning in the late 1990s. South Bend was one of those "CSO" cities, and Mayor Luecke signed a consent decree a few days before leaving office in 2011 committing the city to a series of upgrades to reduce the overflows, at a cost of hundreds of millions of dollars. It was a political no-win: inaction meant continuing to violate the Clean Water Act and courting federal penalties, but signing up for the deal meant promising that the city would accomplish unprecedented infrastructure upgrades and enact the rate increases to pay for them. By finalizing terms of a deal just before I took office, he had jumped on a political grenade for his successor.

Sewer management was not on the syllabus of my History and Literature program in college. But by the time I took office, it was clearly going to be a major part of my job. Just to comply with the consent decree, I would have to preside over the largest and most expensive public works project in the city's history. But the mandate came without funding: we were required to find the money locally. Forced to look for new ideas and better answers, our administration used the smart sewer network to get a better understanding of the situation. Using real-time data from the sensors and sophisticated models to simulate different scenarios, we were able to game out how the planned upgrades would work—and what it would take to fully implement them.

The early answers were dire. By using the sensor equipment to run more realistic models than what was available to my predecessor in 2011, we learned that the original plan would cost more than we had thought—nearly *a billion dollars* altogether. That meant almost ten thousand dollars for every man, woman, and child—in a city whose per capita income in 2017 stood at $19,818. The only way to pay for these improvements would be for people's rates to go up, meaning that if we carried out the plan with no changes, one in ten of our households would be paying 14 percent of their income on their sewer bill alone. Worse, the models showed that the highly expensive plan wouldn't actually achieve the level of control and environmental improvement that was intended—we could do the whole thing and still be in violation.

But the data also unlocked a better way. Because the simulations could tell them the likely level of water flow at every key node in the network, the team could develop a much more efficient and effective solution. Based on this information, engineers created an alternative plan, costing about $500 million less, and began a process of renegotiation with the EPA that continues to this day. The outcome is not certain, but the stakes are in the hundreds of millions of dollars; overall it stands to be a pretty good return on the $6 million or so that it cost to put the system in to begin with.

More than just a clever use of sensors, it proved how a city could gain by allowing itself to be a guinea pig for an interesting new technology. The researchers benefited from the chance to deploy their work in a real-world environment, while the city wound up getting key technology at a deep discount that ultimately saved us a tremendous amount. Best of all, in the case of EmNet, the intellectual property that was created became the core of a company that now has offices in South Bend, where skilled workers are developing this product and selling it to cities all over the world. Hoping for more positive experiences, we have since intentionally styled South Bend as a "Beta City," sitting at just the right scale and level of complexity for new ideas and technologies to be tested.

By the time we put our proposal together for the new round of EPA negotiations, it was clear that I had inherited not just an interesting technology, but the building blocks of a completely different architecture for university-community relations. This style of city university collaboration has become the pattern for what I would call College Town 2.0, a framework in which cities look to universities not only for the size of their endowment and the capacity of their students to spend money, but in terms of the substance of their work.

In 2015, I found myself speaking at a White House event, sponsored by the Office of Science and Technology Policy, to preach the value of this kind of collaboration for other cities across America. Together with officials from Pittsburgh, who had undertaken a comparable project with Carnegie-Mellon University that involved improving traffic congestion, we inaugurated the MetroLab Network, an association of city-university pairs across the country that committed to work together along such lines. Soon the network had over forty participants, working on issues from bus reliability in New York to air quality detection in Portland, Oregon.

This and other efforts have yielded a breakdown of the campus "bubble," in which the idyllic and tidy world of university students never touched the complex life of diverse and low-income areas just a mile or two down the road. Whenever possible, the city backs such efforts, as with an engineering-oriented collaboration called the Bowman Creek Educational Ecosystem that links students from multiple colleges with neighborhood groups, high schoolers, and an African-American church to pursue projects that will improve the area around an environmentally impaired underground tributary in a low-income neighborhood.

Other efforts have been generated entirely by students, who have begun to realize that they can respond to the economic inequality around them by working not just to serve but to empower others. In 2011, a sophomore named Peter Woo returned from a summer of service-learning in India and realized that what he'd observed with cash-lending practices there applied in South Bend, too. After estimating that predatory lending in our area costs low-income South Bend residents $3.5 million a year, he gathered some interested friends to launch a micro-lending nonprofit called JIFFI. Working to create alternatives to check-cashing lenders, the organization continues to serve residents on our West Side.

SOME UNIVERSITY DEPARTMENTS have fairly obvious inroads to collaborate with their surrounding communities, working in fields like urban planning, civil engineering, or law. But some of the most compelling partnerships grew out of departments that I had never expected would be so well equipped to engage in the life of the city— such as the neuroscience students I met one night while visiting a support group for mostly ex-offenders at a community center on the West Side.

The taco meat was mostly gone by the time I arrived, so I went to take a seat among the twenty or so chairs in a circle. It was a diverse group. One man looked about sixty-five years old, African-American, with jeans and a dark shirt and glasses; another did not look like he could be eighteen yet, a slim Latino kid in a gray sweatshirt with jeans and white shoes, with tattoos from the side of his neck to the tops of his hands. One woman stared straight ahead of her, talking to no one, while others made small talk with the people next to them. The only people who looked altogether out of place, besides me, perhaps, were four sunny Notre Dame undergraduates, huddling over laptops and trying to make a projector work. In addition to the usual support conversation, the evening would feature a presentation about their field, which turned out to be neuroscience. In particular, they explained, they wanted to talk to the group about neuroplasticity.

I'm about as generous-minded toward undergraduates as it gets, but I suspect my face revealed my inner thoughts at that moment, something like: *Please tell me you know what you're doing here.* Were these mostly white kids really going to inflict a PowerPoint about the finer points of neurological research on a room full of reintegrating ex-offenders who were just trying to get their lives back together?

The projector wasn't working, so three of them held laptops up while another took turns talking. The slideshow explained the development of neurons in adolescence, the electrical and chemical basis of neurotransmission, the relationship of the amygdala to other parts of the brain. They had made it fairly accessible, but it was hard at first to tell if the silent faces of their audience were showing any interest. The students talked about self-control, describing the famous study in which children capable of resisting eating a marshmallow in front of them would earn two later on—and those kids would, it turns out, go on to earn higher incomes and have generally more successful lives. They talked about Buddhist monks' ability through meditation to activate different parts of their existing neural networks, and the relationship between what you eat and how your brain works. Then the questions began.

"So, you're saying the neurons I have today are the same as the ones I had when I was a kid?"

"Yes, but they branch off and form new connections, too, and this can keep developing even in adulthood."

Another asked: "You said that a traumatic event changes your brain."

"Yes, it can cause connections between your neurons to develop differently."

"So, how do you change it back?"

A conversation transpired on how PTSD had been treated partly by having subjects train their minds to reframe the events that had harmed them from an outside perspective.

A man who said he was first incarcerated at the age of fifteen got interested. "I've seen people raped, stabbed, and set on fire. How am I supposed to think about that from an outside perspective?"

The student looked a little helpless, but another participant, a man in his twenties with a perfectly flat-billed baseball cap on, jumped in. "That's how it was for me. I got shot five times and lived, and was ready to tear up everything, but when I saw it happen from the outside I could start to let it go."

I tried not to look shocked when he went on to explain that he got shot on a second occasion as well, and that was the one that really prompted him to set out on a different path. Then he challenged the older participant to apply what he had just learned about mastering the neurological impact of his trauma during incarceration.

The students didn't have all the answers, but they had some very relevant things to say to a group of people trying to move past violence and addiction. In a different life, the students might have decided to help ex-offenders by helping cook dinner at a halfway house in town. That would have been a worthy project, too, but who knows if these kids had any special talent when it came to cooking. What they did have was real expertise in a field that directly impacted this audience. When one of them asked how long it would take the impact of addiction to be potentially reversed in the brain thanks to neuroplasticity, this wasn't a theoretical question—it was a personal and urgent one.

This could be the future of what it means to be a college town, as students and faculty at the top of their fields get more involved in the life of the cities around them. Those at the university can come to see community members not as the subjects of a service project but as genuine neighbors who can draw benefit from their work, while helping to educate them in the realities of the problems they are trying to solve. The residents can offer the students a far richer education than they can get on campus alone, and in the process the students form a relationship with our community not just as a place they passed through but as part of what shaped them, no less than the university itself. If talent continues to prove the coin of the realm in today's economy, then this is a style of development we have only begun to understand—one in which talent is reinforced through a community that knows how to connect talent with purpose.

11

Subconscious Operations

John Martinez has a problem. About my age, with a shaved head, a dark beard, and eyes that dart around looking for the next problem to solve, he is one of the stars of our Venues, Parks & Arts team (formerly Parks and Recreation). He oversees a parks maintenance staff that numbers about fifty in the wintertime and swells in the summer as seasonal workers join us to mow lawns at parks and vacant lots, irrigate soccer fields, repair lights on trails, clear storm damage, and fix whatever else needs fixing across a city with over sixty park properties.

John's problem is that the three supervisors who collectively oversee all of his operations have untold amounts of knowledge in their heads—and are all close to retirement. We're in my conference room going through numbers and flowcharts for the quarterly "SBStat" meeting for parks. Inspired by the "CitiStat" model that brought modern performance management to Baltimore under Mayor Martin O'Malley and became a template for data-driven local government everywhere, SBStat is a sequence of intensive meetings where we identify issues and vet new ideas, with rigorous analysis by city staff as the basis for our conversations. We explore lots of advanced and novel ideas in these meetings, but the title slide currently being presented bears a phrase I've not seen used before: "Subconscious Operations."

The question John brings up is how to get processes and procedures onto paper—outside of the supervisors' heads, mapping steps that they don't even know they're taking. Interviewing the supervisors and drawing process diagrams, the team has tried to get a better idea of what the supervisor does, some of it so automatically that he doesn't think about it. They have found, for example, that by the time the downtown grounds maintenance supervisor gives the daily list of jobs to his staff, he has gone through sixteen previous conscious and unconscious steps. Often without even thinking about it, he adjusts tasking based on equipment conditions, weather, or even just the day of the week. If it's, say, the first Thursday of the month, he just knows by instinct to route more resources toward preparing the area around Michigan Street, which gets more foot traffic for downtown's monthly "First Fridays" events.

ANALYTICAL WORK SESSIONS like this meeting aren't just the result of a mayor indulging his inner geek, though I admittedly enjoy them for this reason. More importantly, they are the backbone of our effort to make the city's management more rigorous, efficient, and fact-driven. When I took office, it was clear that too many decisions were still made based on gut feel, rather than data—and some operations never got rigorously analyzed at all. Old-fashioned local government is notoriously full of seat-of-the-pants operations, even as financial pressures and resident expectations should be forcing us to become hyper-efficient. No one could tell me, when I took office, how much it cost to fill in a pothole, or how many times we missed a trash pickup in a given neighborhood in a given week. If a problem arose, I would hear about it only when it became serious enough that someone contacted a council member to complain, wrote a letter to the newspaper, or buttonholed me at the supermarket to talk about it.

Fresh from a job in management consulting and eager to unlock whatever efficiencies could be found, I had promised during the campaign to set up a 311 system, so residents wouldn't have to figure out the relevant department and its own contact information in order to report a pothole or get a streetlight fixed. When the 311 center opened, a year after I took office, we gained something even more valuable than a new mechanism for customer service; for the first time, South Bend had a central, constantly updated data set on what people were calling about. Using the data, the city was able to make countless operational improvements, from cutting the time it took to get a large item picked up by our trash crews, to simplifying the way residents paid their water bills.

ARRIVING IN OFFICE, ESPECIALLY with my consulting background, I took it as a given that more data was a good thing—the more objective and analytically driven our work, the better. There was an emerging bipartisan consensus about this style of government, and I bought in. Just as Martin O'Malley had gained a reputation for excellent work modernizing Baltimore's government with improvements on everything from overtime costs to pothole patching, Republican Mayor Steve Goldsmith of Indianapolis racked up a number of wins from increased child support collection rates to the reduction of sixty-eight thousand pieces of unnecessary paperwork per year.

But this style of government also had its detractors, as I saw when Councilman John Voorde stopped by my office one day to discuss an upcoming budget vote. "Have you seen that documentary on Vietnam?" he began, in what I assumed was just small talk as he settled into a seat at the conference table. The office of mayor had once belonged to his father, Edward "Babe" Voorde, whose term ended tragically when he was killed in a car accident in 1960. Wearing his usual sweater vest over a shirt and tie, John smiled benignly and leaned forward a little in his chair. I liked him, though our styles were certainly different. John was mainly a creature of the old school—he had worked various city jobs, beginning on the street department, and was city clerk at the time I first got elected. He was one of many people of my parents' generation to support me when I first ran, and we got along well. But as a council member he was sometimes unpredictable, and I couldn't count on his vote without spending time with him to make sure I had made my case and asked where he stood.

To answer his question: I had not seen Ken Burns's new PBS documentary series on Vietnam, but it was getting a lot of attention. It seemed to be especially resonant for the generation that had experienced it as the dominant issue of their coming-of-age. As John reminisced about various people in his St. Joseph High School Class of 1962 affected by the draft, I worried that it might be a while before we came to the topic of my budget proposal. Then he said something that made clear he had been thinking of city affairs all along:

"Sometimes, Pete, when you talk about your data-driven government, I think of Robert McNamara."

I just smiled, not sure exactly where to take the conversation from here. Coming from John, or really anyone who looked back on the Vietnam War with anguish, being likened to LBJ's Secretary of Defense was not exactly a compliment. By all accounts, McNamara had been a brilliant individual, a genius even, his rimless glasses and sharp gaze embodying modern technocracy at its finest. But the outcome of the war—and David Halberstam's book *The Best and the Brightest*—made the sum total of his brilliance seem dark and ironic, as he and the other geniuses of the national security establishment led our nation into quagmire and defeat.

I could also see where the comparison was going. Before serving in public office, McNamara had been the CEO of Ford Motor Company, and the use of data and metrics on his watch escalated almost to a kind of fetish. After the Vietnam War collapsed into chaos, historians and journalists inquired into how the most brilliant minds of their generation could have led the country into such a lethal blunder, and the image emerged of McNamara as a data-obsessed manager who missed the forest for the trees. "Statistics and force ratios came pouring out of him like a great uncapped faucet," Halberstam wrote. Yet, for all the statistical brilliance of McNamara and the rest of President Johnson's inner circle, all of them were tragically late to the obvious fact that the war was a losing one, keeping America entangled there at a cost of thousands more American lives.

This must have been on Voorde's mind when he had turned the subject of our conversation to the road surface app that he had heard about. My administration was in the process of creating the first objective asset map of the city, cataloging the quantity and quality of streets, fire hydrants, signs, and anything else in a public right-of-way. This work even included an app, which could be run on an iPhone mounted on the dashboard of a supervisor's vehicle, to scan the conditions of the road and report cracks, potholes, and other deterioration.

Thinking back to his youth on the street department, John was skeptical. "You have this technology to tell you which streets need repair," he said. "But if your foreman's any good, he ought to already know that off the top of his head!"

The technology had other capabilities, and I'm glad we use it—but, admittedly, the councilman had a point. One of the reasons we have qualified, experienced individuals in organizations is to use their intuition and expertise to solve problems. If the foreman of a street crew knows every crack on Lincoln Way West and every pothole on North Shore Drive like the back of his hand, why do I need to spend money on an app to tell us where the problems are?

For all the power that data analysis represents—and I've worked to build a reputation for running one of the country's most data-oriented city administrations—it also has its limitations, and the potential for mischief. You might spend lots of time and resources gathering data that will never be used, or accumulate data that winds up telling you things you already know.

SO HOW DOES A TECH-ORIENTED MAYOR make sure that the data is serving the administration, rather than becoming an end in itself? Put another way, how does a government official interested in data come to be viewed more like Goldsmith or O'Malley, and less like McNamara? Over time, I've learned a number of rules that have helped us to make sure the use of data makes sense, and does good.

First, know the difference between reporting an issue and resolving it. In some cases, the two go so closely together that you can lose track of the distinction. For example, when we installed ShotSpotter technology using microphones to acoustically pinpoint gunshots, we were enhancing our ability to deal with gun violence. An officer could be immediately dispatched to the scene of a shooting, be it an outdoor fight or a domestic violence case, whether someone called it in or not. And this, in turn, would help in the long run to deter gun violence. But in other cases, knowing more doesn't help. At a tech conference, I once saw a pitch from a start-up that would automatically detect patterns of opioid use by scanning for trace amounts in sewage. The technology is brilliant, and may do a great deal of good in some places. But in South Bend, our problem wasn't knowing how much opioid use was prevalent in this neighborhood compared to that one; it was a lack of mental health and addiction resources to deal with the issue wherever we found it. Financing a project to tell us more about the problem could even come at the expense of treatment options, which are grossly underfunded in our county and state health systems. In cases where we have ample means to fix a problem, then we need only to find it. The rest of the time, reporting an issue is necessary, but not sufficient, for resolving it.

A second rule we learned quickly was to recognize that responsiveness and efficiency are not the same thing; in fact, they can sometimes pull against each other. Consider the example of snowplowing. The most responsive thing to do would be to ensure that anytime someone called about an impassable street, a plow crew was immediately dispatched to take care of that block. It would be an attractive thing to be able to do (think of the political credit)—but it's also clearly not the most efficient; far better to use a zone system, covering the city as quickly as possible, starting with main roads and then moving to residential streets, with added input from a parametric model that takes temperature and precipitation rates into account. Any other approach would take longer, and ultimately mean less quality of service and/or more cost. Local officials often feel pressure to deal with a squeaky wheel right away, when stepping back and considering a big-picture solution would serve people better.

Under the wrong balance of responsiveness and efficiency, data can actually make us worse at our job. This is one reason I eventually backed off from my enthusiasm for the idea of publicizing a twenty-four-hour pothole guarantee. It seemed at first like a great way to show how responsive the city was to road concerns—and doable, because in peak patching season we already get to most potholes within a day or two of them being called in. But after reviewing the concept with engineers, it became clear to me that if I instructed the staff to make sure every hole got taken care of as soon as we knew about it, I could actually reduce the efficiency of the operation. Crews on the West Side might have to drop what they were doing to go deal with a pothole on the North Side, then go chase another work order downtown, all coming to them in order of appearance. An expensive vehicle and work crew would zigzag through the city according to real-time data on which residents were first to call and complain, with little regard for whether it made more sense to have Harter Heights wait a couple days while we systematically took care of the Keller Park area for the season.

At other times, the reverse is true and responsiveness really is more important than efficiency, as in the case of graffiti. It might seem that the most efficient thing would be to treat graffiti like snow—take whatever resources we have for repainting, and have them work the city, street by street, systematically. But if a stop sign gets tagged with graffiti, leaving it there even for a couple days might motivate someone to tag something else nearby. Whether it's a gang sign or a cartoon bunny, what shows up on Falcon Street may soon be copied on Walnut, and the longer it's there, the more likely someone will seek to imitate or outdo it. So clearing it right away is the most important thing, and the team works to fix any reported graffiti almost immediately (except on a dedicated graffiti wall opposite the Emporium Restaurant, where artists are welcome to do whatever they like). The result is that people who might be motivated to deface public property find it's not worth the effort, and now it is less likely to happen in the first place.

A third lesson on data and efficiency is to be honest at the beginning about whether you are willing to follow the data where it leads. When I asked Eric Horvath, our public works director, to get creative on ways to keep solid waste billing rates under control, his team came back with options from selling ad space on city trash bins to charging customers differently by how much they throw away. The most usable idea involved a technology for partly automated trash trucks that can pick up a bin with a robotic arm, eliminating the need for a human "picker" on solid waste crews. This meant a savings for the city, keeping rates lower—and, we learned, led to lower injury rates as well. But buying the technology was only worth it if we were prepared to eliminate the jobs. It wasn't an easy thing to do, because our solid waste workers were likable and hardworking. In the end I decided to go ahead, because the city could offer the workers other jobs, provided they earned a commercial driver's license. Half the affected workers did so, and half left city employment altogether.

But in other cases, we are not prepared to capture an efficiency when we find it. For example, we continue to operate a walk-in center for paying your water bill, even though this can be done online, over the phone, and by mail. Part of me (the consultant part of me, naturally) finds this maddeningly inefficient: Why pay for a brick-and-mortar structure, and staff, at a facility whose work can be done more quickly, efficiently, and easily by other means? But the more I looked into the issue, the clearer it became that low-income residents who did not have bank accounts relied on the facility so they could pay in cash. The long-term solution would be to help them to get banked, but the reality is that this will not happen for some of our residents. The right thing to do here, it seems, is to tolerate an inefficiency for now, even though the data tells us how it could be eliminated.

A fourth data lesson came from the ShotSpotter experience: follow the data where it leads, and recognize that it could show you the answers to questions you never even asked. When we adopted the technology, the obvious appeal was that police could be dispatched immediately to the site of a shooting, without having to rely on someone quickly calling it in to 911. We knew there would be a tactical advantage, but only slowly did we realize this would also be a powerful tool for both measuring and changing the relationship between community members and the police department.

As our police chief at the time, Ron Teachman, explained, "Law enforcement projects an air of omniscience. If residents hear a gunshot and don't see an officer coming to the scene, they don't think it's because we don't know about it. They assume we know about it, and that we're not there because we don't care." With the new technology, officers appeared on the scene of shootings we simply didn't know about before. And gains in police legitimacy could be achieved by using the community policing method of "knock and talk" in concert with the technology. When the system detected gunshots in a residential area, officers would work that block the next day, letting residents know they were concerned and leaving door hangers for those who were not there, explaining why they had visited and how to follow up.

Soon the ShotSpotter data became a measure for tracking something completely different from gunshot rates: perceived police legitimacy. Since we knew from the sensors how many gunshots were fired in the coverage area, and we also knew how many times someone in the same area called 911 for shots fired, we could now tell what proportion of the time people heard gunshots but didn't bother letting us know. For the first time, we had an index of how many people thought it was worthwhile to call the police about gunfire near them, a hard number to help us measure something very difficult to quantify: trust in the police department.

Initially, we had assumed that a small fraction of gunshots went unreported, perhaps 20 percent. Instead, we learned that, shockingly, the reverse was the case. Now, we watch the ratio closely; I can log on to a law enforcement dashboard that will tell me, on a monthly basis, what proportion of shots are being called in. It's only one measure, and an imperfect one, but I use it to help get a sense of how much residents think it's worthwhile to call the police.

This leads to another concern when it comes to data-driven government, or government in general: the confusion of technical problems with moral ones. In many ways, it is psychologically easier to deal with technical problems, ones with right and wrong answers. In these cases—how to make pothole patching more efficient, or get more children tested for lead exposure—it is clear that if we find a more efficient way to proceed, by definition it should be done. But in many ways, political leadership isn't required for these technical gains, other than to give a green light to staff who identify ways to make them. Elected officials earn our keep by settling moral questions, ones where there is no way to make someone better off without making someone else worse off.

Even the most ground-level decisions can have this character, as when we switched the trucks for trash pickup. Not only did it mean some city workers losing a job, it also meant that we had to get residents to haul their trash bins to the front curb once a week, since the newer trucks couldn't operate well in narrow alleys. Moving the bins is a pain, and there's no getting around this when interacting with a resident who would rather it all stayed in the alleys. We were presented with a trade-off: keep it in the alleys and let trash pickup be more expensive for everyone, or move it to the front and make it more inconvenient for some. No math could solve this problem or present an obvious right answer; we just had to make a call, and then be willing to explain it to those affected.

A more serious version of this trade-off came up when an ethanol plant went out of business, and houses nearby found their basements full of water. It turned out the plant was such a big water user that it artificially depressed the water table—something the home builders did not take into account when deciding how deep to dig the basements. Now both the ethanol plant and the home builders were gone, and a bunch of homeowners were flooding the council chamber demanding to know what I would do to fix their problem. The city was not technically involved, but these homeowners had done nothing wrong, and it seemed we needed to do something to help.

Ultimately, we decided to re-create the effect of the depressed water table by pumping water into a ditch, to get the homeowners some relief. In the end I got lucky: a new operator took on the ethanol plant and began pumping again. But in the meantime, it seemed that we were faced with a problem that no amount of data could solve: Do we undertake a deliberate waste of water and energy costing every city resident a few cents, or let a handful of homeowners lose thousands of dollars of value on their homes through no fault of their own? Again, there was no technical answer to this problem; it was a question of who would suffer and how much.

The question of suffering brings me to one last concern around the use of data-driven techniques to bring about better government: the importance of exceptions, otherwise known as mercy. Efficiency, almost by definition, has to do with following rules and patterns; if there is an inefficiency within a rule, it can be ironed out by making a sub-rule. But sometimes our moral intuition just tells us that making an exception is the right thing to do, even if we can't explain or defend the precedent.

I knew of a council member once who got a call from an elderly constituent asking him to help deal with a dead raccoon. But the animal was in the person's yard, not quite in the street, where the city would be obligated to take care of it. The rule here was clear: too bad for the homeowner. But that didn't seem like the right answer for someone who couldn't handle it on her own. So the council member went to the home, discreetly dragged the carcass into the street, and then called it in so it would be taken care of.

Obviously this can't be endorsed as a way of dealing with these problems. But without exceptions to rules, the world would be a colder and probably worse place to live.

ULTIMATELY, THE RISE OF MORE DATA and technology presents tremendous opportunity for cities to be smarter and more efficient in their operations—and therefore become healthier, safer, better places to live. But after taking office, just as quickly as I learned the power of data, I also learned to be mindful of its limitations, and aware of the problems it will not solve. And I learned to maintain some level of respect for the role of intuition.

Good intuition, backed by years of experience, can make it possible to sense things—like whether a trash customer is telling the truth when he calls to say you missed a pickup at his house or whether he just forgot to take the trash out—often with remarkable accuracy and sometimes without even being able to explain how it is sensed. There is great power in human pattern recognition, which actually resembles big data analytics in its most important characteristic: the ability to know things without knowing exactly how we know them.

Often, discussions of performance management gloss over this crucial difference between data analysis in general, and "big data" used with artificial intelligence. Using data in general is nothing new; it is simply the application of factual knowledge to make decisions. As an approach to government, it came as naturally to Alexander of Macedonia as it did to Robert McNamara. For the purposes of using data, the only thing to change with the introduction of computers is that we can gather and apply it more quickly and precisely.

"Big data" is different. It has the potential to change government, along with the rest of our society and economy, in categorically different ways than the use of data in general. Not everyone may share my definition, but to me the difference is this: Using data means gathering information, understanding it, and applying it. Using big data means analyzing information to find and apply patterns so complex that we may never grasp them.[4]

COMPUTERS CAN NOW CRUNCH sets of numbers so vast that the patterns that emerge from them are beyond the reach of the human mind—and yet the patterns can be used. Utilities like our waterworks are beginning to tap into computing capabilities that can accurately predict points of failure in water systems without our truly understanding how the prediction was made—only that it works.

Ironically, what makes this kind of predictive technology most interesting is that it so closely resembles human intuition. More often

---

4 I am aware of taking a liberty with the term "big data," which is usually defined simply to mean data that cannot be processed without the aid of powerful computers. Here, I am talking about something more distinctive—the subset of big data analytics that involves the discovery and use of patterns beyond our comprehension.

than we realize, humans rely heavily on knowing things that we can sense, but not explain. One of the reasons it was impossible, till recently, to program a car to drive itself is that many of the mental processes we use to drive a vehicle cannot easily be defined or described (and therefore cannot be programmed). Like the parks maintenance supervisor or road foreman going through countless decisions in the back of his head, anyone driving a vehicle relies constantly on subconscious pattern recognition. I can't explain to you how I know the moment when a snowy road has become too slick for normal braking, or whether I am a safe distance from the centerline, or whether I can beat that yellow light. I just know. If I wanted a machine to gain this capacity, I would have to do one of two things: master the precise basis of this knowledge so it could be programmed, or construct a machine capable of learning it the same way I did.

The latter is becoming possible, and this is the true fascination of artificial intelligence. For government, there are extraordinary implications to a program that could anticipate road failures five years in advance, or predict asthma attacks using linked data sets on hospitalizations, weather, and car emissions to sense patterns so exquisitely complex that we will never understand them.

Now even explicitly social functions, like gauging how much anger a certain policy proposal will cause, can increasingly be achieved through social media analysis that might eventually outmatch even the finest-tuned human political antennae. The ultimate lie detector won't be designed, like current ones, by programming known patterns in heart rate and perspiration. It will be designed by machine learning, scanning millions of recordings of people saying true or false things, and using this to make predictions based on combinations of indicators beyond our comprehension.

The algorithms advance every year. This is why Netflix has a good sense of what films you would like, perhaps even doing a better job of predicting your preferences than you do, if all you have to go by is a trailer and a description. But these capabilities are also still in their infancy. My Internet TV device still sometimes shows me commercials clearly intended for a middle-aged homemaker or a teenage video-game enthusiast.

And no matter how sophisticated the programs, they will never fully learn our sense of mercy—the rule not to be applied, the efficiency not to be captured. Capable of something resembling intuition but nothing quite like morality, the computers and their programs can only imperfectly replicate the human function we call judgment. Knowing when one valid claim must give way to another, or when a rule must be relaxed in order to do the right thing, is not programmable, if only because it is not completely rational. That's why, even as reason has partly replaced divine intervention for explaining our world, it will not replace human leadership when it comes to managing it. A person aided by data can make smarter and fairer decisions, but only a person can sense when an unexplainable factor ought to come into play—when, for lack of a better expression, "something is up." And that, as John Voorde might remind me, has been the job of elected officials all along.

V

MEETING

In great contests each party claims to act in accordance with the will of God. Both may be, and one must be, wrong.

ABRAHAM LINCOLN

12

Brushfire on the Silicon Prairie

Neither mayors nor governors were in fashion when I was an under-graduate hanging around the Institute of Politics at Harvard. Discussions of nonfederal government were comparatively rare. Among the politically attuned, most eyes were on Washington, keeping tabs on national policy, or on the still-more-alluring arena of foreign affairs. When you did hear about the state or local level, it was usually in a program or study group that fused the two together in the compound phrase "state and local," pronounced almost as if it were one word, stateandlocal. These dynamics were set in opposition to national politics, and states usually got attention for the tension between them and the federal government, as if state-federal power struggles were all that mattered in federalism. Yet some of the most important policy dynamics of our time have to do with the relationships, and the tension, *between* state and local government.

I knew as soon as I took office that it would be important to form a positive relationship with our Republican governor, Mitch Daniels.

Daniels was first elected in 2004, when he defeated South Bend's own Joe Kernan, making him a villain to Democratic partisans around here. A compact man known for a powerful intellect and a temper that could flare up on occasion, he had been a protégé of Senator Dick Lugar and served alternately as a top pharmaceutical executive in Indiana and a Republican White House official.

By the end of his tenure, Daniels was popular across the state and often mentioned as a presidential prospect for the technocratic center-right. But his first term was marked by intense political battles, in which his greatest nemesis and foil was a Democrat from South Bend, Indiana House Speaker Pat Bauer. Daniels's first major and controversial policy was to lease the Indiana Toll Road, which ran through our northern part of the state, to a private entity and use the money to finance road projects across Indiana. The privatization was unpopular here, and fiercely opposed by the Democrats, led by the old-school Speaker Bauer. When the seventy-five-year lease to a private operator went through, the flow of funds to other parts of the state felt to many here like a poke in the eye. Viewing Daniels about the same way most people in the area did, I had briefly worked for his 2008 opponent, taking a few weeks off from McKinsey to help with policy research, press, and debate preparation—a fact that I hoped would not come to light while I was in the process of reaching out to him.

But in working on his opponent's campaign, I also began to realize what had made Daniels a formidable opponent—and such a highly effective governor that some national conservatives saw him as their best hope of challenging President Obama. He was a business-minded technocrat, with very little interest in the social issues that were used to rile up electoral bases in campaign years but left communities divided long after their political usefulness expired. Instead, he was extremely focused on economic issues and interested in making government work well, even achieving the improbable feat of reforming the Bureau of Motor Vehicles into an efficient and user-friendly customer service organization. (Since the BMV is the one state office that virtually every citizen uses, it was also a politically clever thing to do.)

When I had been campaigning for mayor, a frequent gripe was that the state's economic development agency had done virtually no deals in the South Bend area since Daniels had become governor. Blame went in all directions. Many believed that we were being punished, that because our northern region was far from Indianapolis and generally voted Democratic, the state government ignored us or even went out of its way to withhold opportunities from us. Others insisted that our woes were of our own making—that South Bend was so unfriendly to business and beholden to labor groups that it was impossible for even the best-intentioned Republican administration in Indianapolis to work with us.

I didn't care whose fault it was; I just wanted it to change. And I sensed that the governor might feel the same way. I had no use for the Bush administration of which he had been a part, and he would probably never agree with my full-throated support for public education and organized labor rights. But despite our differences in ideology, it seemed that he and I shared a desire to use data and good management practices to drive better government. And politically, it made sense for him to score economic wins anywhere in the state he could, including our area.

Eager to work across party lines, I gathered some community and business leaders and invited him to lunch in South Bend. The meeting was genial, and afterward he made some flattering comments to the *Tribune* for a story that ran with the headline "Governor Likes South Bend's New Attitude." We agreed that he and I should be working together to find opportunities, and sure enough, a few weeks later Daniels was back in South Bend, celebrating the expansion of a local steel-box manufacturer with help from state incentives—and an end to the dry spell of state economic development wins in our region.

It was my first major experience in this kind of bipartisan coop- eration. The most important thing I learned was that it has little to do with stretching or changing your beliefs. The governor and I did not persuade one another to become more centrist on any particular issue; rather, we found the areas where we had common goals and stuck to them. Plus, by collaborating on a specific, measured effort, we gained ground in trust and familiarity that would be helpful in the future. But Governor Daniels was in his final year, and I would have to start over again when the 2012 election yielded his successor.

I had known of Congressman Mike Pence for years, since he was a highly visible figure among the conservative warriors in Republican leadership on Capitol Hill. So when I actually first met him at the India- napolis Motor Speedway in 2011, I was surprised by how affable, even gentle, he seemed. I was with a group of candidates and elected officials attending the Indy 500, and it was a warm day at the speedway. (Then- reality-television-personality Donald Trump had been set to drive the pace car that day, but had backed out for some unexplained reason.) As we milled around near our seats, someone spotted Pence walking along the concourse to his box and introduced us. Dressed in the politician's off-duty uniform of a blue oxford shirt and khakis, he very much looked the part: a congressman going to a sporting event. We exchanged some pleasantries, and I didn't think much of it or expect to see him anytime soon. But a year and a half later, I was sitting in a folding chair in the January sun facing the west front of the Indiana capitol at his invitation, looking through a cloud of my own breath as he took the oath of office and became Indiana's governor. Afterwards, at a reception for attend- ees, I caught up to him and mentioned my eagerness to work together to benefit the city. He gave a sincere nod and heartily agreed, and a long and complicated relationship began.

There is a photo from that spring of 2013 showing me with Mike and Karen Pence in the M.R. Falcons club on the West Side of South Bend. The M.R.'s (not to be confused with the Z.B. Falcons on the

Far West Side), is one of those old-fashioned social halls and civic associations that long revolved around working-class civic commitment, neighborhood ties, and Polish identity—hence a major stop for the Dyngus Day experience. Though Dyngus Day, as I described earlier, has traditionally been a Democratic-focused affair, more Republicans have realized its value for mixing it up with regular voters. Responding to my invitation to come to town anytime, the new governor and first lady had decided to experience the sausage, cabbage, and camaraderie firsthand.

Unfortunately, his office was less responsive to my advice on exactly *when* to come during the day's festivities. Local politicians know from experience that it is best to conduct their Dyngus Day activities as early as possible, since the beer, music, and sausage are already going strong at daybreak, and things only get more, well, festive over the course of the day. The Pences turned up in midafternoon, pretty much the peak of the day's eating—and drinking.

In the photo, I have my arm around the governor as if he were an old friend. I certainly sought to be a friendly host, but the main reason my hand was at his back was that I was trying urgently to get him out of that room. Not only were the revelers into their revelry, but worse, his detail had dropped him off at the entrance that led to the bar full of some of our younger citizens taking advantage of beer specials, as opposed to the larger room containing the more elderly and sedate visitors enjoying their kielbasa and noodles.

Retail politics is never fun among the intoxicated. If a voter who doesn't like you has had a lot to drink, you get an earful. It's even worse if a voter who *does* like you has been drinking. The handshakes last way too long, they begin repeating themselves, and it takes a well-practiced art to get away from them and move on to talk to someone else—which is futile anyway, since the same person will find you later and try to have the same conversation. So my immediate concern was to get the governor and first lady out of the bar and into the dining room before they regretted coming altogether; my arm was around him in order to push him, as quickly as a mayor politely could, into the other room.

I don't know if it was because of that visit or in spite of it, but the governor seemed to remain determined to be a friend to South Bend. His office was always open to me, and he often appeared in our area for factory tours, ribbon cuttings, and other events, always with something good to say about our city. He even appointed Jim Schellinger, a well-known Democrat and architect originally from South Bend, to chair the Indiana Economic Development Corporation. Most helpfully, Pence championed a visionary economic development effort called the Regional Cities Initiative, which helped change how we position our cities for growth.

The basic idea behind Regional Cities was that economic development is no longer just a game of luring factories—what some call "smokestack chasing"—from other locations, using tax incentives essentially to buy jobs. Instead, at a time when many people first choose where they want to live and then start looking for a job, it makes sense to recruit people, not just employers. The best way to do that is to enhance the appeal of the community, often called "quality of place," and the initiative's focus was on supporting projects that would do just that.

The other main idea of the Regional Cities program was that communities in the same area should work together. For years, cities and towns would view their immediate neighbors as economic rivals, trying to lure jobs across a city limit or county line. But since many workers commute across these boundaries anyway, it does no good to add jobs at the expense of the next town over. If South Bend focused on picking off employers from nearby Elkhart, it wouldn't matter much to the regional economy. Using tax incentives to achieve this would simply give away revenue while rearranging economic value within the same area.

Sensibly, some metro areas have entered into economic nonaggression pacts, in which each city promises not to use incentives to lure employers away from its neighbors. But true regional collaboration—

proactively working with other cities by sharing resources to grow the economy—was still rare in Indiana. To incentivize better behavior, the state offered a major grant for local economic development work, not to a city but to a region. In order to compete with the funding, all the counties and cities in an area would have to band together, show they could collaborate, and submit a joint application showing how they would share the funds.

We competed for the grant, and won a $42 million package of state matching funds to help with projects in our area that ranged from accelerating the electric train to Chicago, to enhancing parks and trails along the river. I viewed it as a great policy by the state—not just because we were happy to have the funding, but because the focus on regionalism and "quality of place" helped improve the habits of local leaders and economic development players.

One spring day in 2016, I attended a press event in a former Studebaker factory being renovated into a technology center, with help from the state program. Inside a vast, empty space with high brick walls and broken windows, civic and business leaders gathered around the dream of a different economy, perhaps even a "Silicon Prairie" of data centers in our part of the Midwest. I described the governor's signature program as "visionary" and thanked him for the work he had done to make it happen. After I returned to my seat, Pence rose and spoke generously about me and our city: "South Bend, Indiana, is so blessed to have an energetic, innovative, forward-looking, creative mayor in Pete Buttigieg."

There was plenty to disagree on, as with Mitch Daniels, but once again I hoped that we could stick to common ground. While I objected to Pence's handling of early childhood education funding, labor policy, refugee resettlement, and several other issues, I saw other opportunities to work together on promoting growth. If Mike Pence had kept his primary focus on economic development, our mutual desire to work across the aisle could have anchored a bipartisan friendship that might continue to this day. Then again, if he had stuck with economics, he would probably still be governor—and would never have become vice president.

BY THE TIME PENCE CAME to our area to celebrate the Regional Cities funding, working with him had become, for me, a demanding exercise in compartmentalization. I knew that he held the keys to economic policies that would advance our city's interests and our region's growth. But he had also revealed himself to be gripped by hard-right social ideology in ways that would make even my old rival, Richard Mourdock, look moderate. It was part of my job to work well with anyone who could help the city. But Pence's fanaticism was hard to overlook, knowing how it had impacted me as a mayor—and as a person.

There was a basic fact about Mike Pence that made him deeply different from his predecessor, Daniels—and for that matter his successor, Eric Holcomb—even if all three were committed Republicans: Pence was fixated on social issues. However they felt about these matters, Daniels and Holcomb were generally strategic enough to keep them in the background while focusing on more tangible gains that could make the state better off. Whatever partisan gain they might have secured by playing to their base with red meat on issues like abortion and LGBT equality, they mostly concentrated on the kind of consensus policies that mayors and cities appreciate most, like economic development or road funding.

Pence, by contrast, could not limit himself to these issues. Maybe it had to do with the years he had spent in Congress, where the Washington environment rewards and punishes various behaviors very differently than for executive branch leaders. He had made his name in the House as a partisan warrior specializing in anti-abortion and anti-LGBT legislation, and even challenged John Boehner from the right for the position of minority leader in 2006. Perhaps this instinct was hard to shake off as he transitioned to becoming a governor. Or maybe it's just who he is, a deeply conservative politician who had shifted from Catholicism to evangelical Christianity as a young man and has described himself as "Christian, conservative, and Republican, in that order." Business leaders and mayors in Indiana had hoped that after leaving Congress, as a governor now and a rumored presidential aspirant, he might ease up on divisive social issues and focus on concrete results for the state. But, given his makeup, perhaps a divisive cultural clash was just a matter of time.

When Mike Pence told me and a few other Democratic and Republican mayors that he was planning to sign the proposed "Religious Freedom Restoration Act" because it was "in my heart that it's the right thing to do," I believed him. (Not that it was the right thing to do, of course, but that this was in his heart.) We weren't there to talk about religious freedom, gay rights, or any other social issue. As president of the Indiana Urban Mayors Caucus, I had come with a small delegation of mayors from around the state, mainly to try to get movement on road funding and make sure the legislature wouldn't interfere with our ability to use tax increment financing for economic development. In the large, wood-paneled room that is the Indiana governor's office, he hosted us graciously, warmly greeting each mayor as we stepped onto the blue carpet and saying something nice to each of us as we took a seat at his long conference table. We reviewed local priorities like tax issues and progress on the Regional Cities effort, and then, as the meeting ended, he changed the subject to the proposed bill.

I wish I could say I made a good effort to talk him out of it, but it was clear from the look in his eyes that he had made up his mind. It was also clear that he had no idea what a backlash the bill could provoke, not just from progressives but also from business-oriented Republicans. The language of the bill seemed innocent enough: "a governmental entity may not substantially burden a person's exercise of religion," unless there is a compelling governmental interest at stake. But "person" was defined to include companies, building on the legal theory of the 2014 Supreme Court *Hobby Lobby* case, which interpreted federal law as giving corporations the same religious rights as people.

Effectively, this meant that any place of business, from a restaurant to an auto mechanic shop, could refuse to serve an LGBT individual or couple, provided its owner cited religion as the motivation for discriminating. It could even be interpreted to protect an EMT or physician denying care to a gay patient. And it would wipe out South Bend's own local ordinance, passed in 2012, which prohibited workplace and housing discrimination against LGBT residents. Despite the name, its purpose was not to "restore" religious freedom—after all, religious freedom is already guaranteed in the Constitution. The bill's actual purpose, its sponsors would later reveal, was to legalize discrimination.

ON MARCH 25, 2015, a photograph appeared showing Governor Pence, seated at his desk in that same office where he had met with our little group of mayors, signing the "Religious Freedom Restoration Act" into law. Surrounding him was an anachronistic-looking group of nuns in habits, monks in cloaks, and other figures in religious garb, as well as a few men in suits whom reporters quickly recognized as the best-known anti-LGBT political activists in Indiana. The bill he signed amid that assemblage would remain intact for all of one week before Pence was forced to change course. And the national controversy he detonated from that stately desk would simultaneously destroy his credibility with many American moderates, and set him on an improbable path to the vice presidency.

The effect on our economic image was immediate and destructive: Pence had set the Silicon Prairie on fire. Until then, Indiana had managed to create a reputation as a somewhat forward-looking place to do business, thanks to a fiscally disciplined state government, low taxes, and livable communities. A nascent tech sector in South Bend was reanimating the once-moribund Studebaker corridor with data centers and start-ups. In Indianapolis, recruiting educated talent was paramount as its life sciences sector grew and was joined by a number of Internet companies drawn to the favorable business environment.

Our state was known to be a little old-fashioned—until 2018 it remained unlawful here to buy alcohol from a store on Sundays—but the growth in Indiana cities had started to make our state look like an appealingly modern place for people to build jobs, lives, and families. If anything, we had created a sense that Indiana was a place where homespun tradition and cultural modernity might coexist, like the hipster selling small-batch chocolate in a stall next to the old farmer with his eggs and pickles at the Farmer's Market in South Bend. Part of the appeal of our state was that you could work up an appetite visiting covered bridges or attending a truck pull in Owen County, then fill up on farm-to-table pub food at Upland Brewery half an hour away in Bloomington. Add in the lower taxes and cost of living, and we could even set our sights on luring young professionals from Chicago and elsewhere who were looking for a vibrant but more livable place to put down roots.

Nothing could be more fatal to this image than for our state to become known as a place that sanctioned discrimination. To many, it called to mind the ugliest demons of our state's past, hearkening back to the days a century earlier when the Indiana branch of the Ku Klux Klan became the most powerful political force in our state, with half the members of the Indiana state legislature on its rolls, largely based on a message that emphasized social issues like gambling, adultery, and prohibition.

Horrified mayors from both parties swiftly joined business leaders to denounce the bill. Greg Ballard, the Republican mayor of Indianapolis, joined four predecessors going back all the way to Dick Lugar in a statement that they were "distressed and very concerned" about the law. The CEOs of our most significant companies, from the engine maker Cummins to the tech firm Angie's List, put out similar messages. The story quickly went national. On *Saturday Night Live's* "Weekend Update," RFRA was the top story, with Colin Jost joking that any company taking advantage of the right to discriminate would be easily recognized by a GOING OUT OF BUSINESS sign.

The fallout accelerated through the week. The NCAA signaled it might drop Indiana as a venue for major events, and even NASCAR put out a statement that it was "disappointed." One of the newest major employers for the Indianapolis region, Salesforce.com, said it would cancel a major planned expansion into Indiana. And, denouncing "outright bigotry in Indiana," the governor of Connecticut went as far as to ban his employees from traveling to our state on taxpayer funds.

The next Sunday morning, I was barefoot in sweatpants at home, watching TV before getting dressed for the day's events. A beleaguered-looking Pence appeared on *This Week* with George Stephanopoulos, trying to reassure a national audience that the bill was not about discrimination. The interview was a disaster. When Stephanopoulos asked, "Do you think it should be legal in the state of Indiana to discriminate against gays or lesbians?" Pence paused, and winced. "George . . ." he began, then sighed.

"It's a yes or no question!" Stephanopoulos pressed.

"Look . . . Hoosiers . . . Come on . . ." the governor stammered, in an almost pleading tone. "Hoosiers don't believe in discrimination."

Still trying to get a yes-or-no answer, Stephanopoulos asked the question again—and then again. No matter how many times he was asked, Pence would not simply say that the answer was no. (Which means he probably believed the answer was yes, but at least knew not to admit it.) One national columnist later described it as "very possibly one of the worst appearances by a governor in television history."

The rest of the day, I tried in the back of my mind to reconcile what I had just seen on-screen with the Mike Pence I knew, a man who had always been gracious and decent to me in person, and eager to cooperate on economic matters. Most of my interactions with Republican politicians were exercises in coming to view someone more charitably, building understanding, goodwill, and appreciation as we acknowledged our differences and sought common ground. This time, the reverse was true, as I watched someone I felt I knew well go on to embarrass himself and our whole state. We all knew that the governor was very conservative, and his policy positions on any social issue were rarely a surprise. But was he really incapable of saying—even pretending—that he believed discrimination should not be legal?

My own moral outrage compounded the fact that he had just made my job, as a mayor intent on growing our community as an inclusive and welcoming place, more difficult. We suddenly appeared backward by association, along with every other community in the state. The bill would preempt local laws like our local nondiscrimination ordinance, and send a message that people living in our city could not expect to be treated equally. Notre Dame, which competes in recruiting not just with other colleges but with other college towns, would have a harder time selling South Bend. If Memorial Hospital needed to attract a specialist in pediatric cancer, or I needed to get a brilliant policy specialist to come work for the city, the state's reputation would be a new hurdle. And it wasn't just about high-flying educated experts who might turn their nose up at our state's license to discriminate. It was also a blow to some of our most vulnerable residents—like a teenager at one of our high schools, already in the incredibly difficult process of facing her sexuality or gender identity, now being told that the state would not protect her rights.

Jay Leno threatened to cancel an upcoming show here. Our Convention and Visitors Bureau director, Rob DeCleene, fought back tears at a community meeting a few days after the bill passed, insisting that he would continue to try to show that our city was a welcoming place. The alarmed director of our Studebaker National Museum forwarded me an email from one of her top donors, indicating he would likely remove the museum from his will. "I don't, for a minute, suggest that

Museum [*sic*] is complicitous," he wrote. "But I do feel it is up to every individual and institution in the state to make a stand against this kind of bigotry. . . ."

The only way to avoid South Bend getting lumped in with the rest of the state was to be vocal. Soon I was standing in a downtown diner for a quickly assembled news conference with a number of civic voices. The diversity of the group spoke for itself; an activist with dyed-orange hair, a Navy veteran, the president of our baseball team, a Jewish grandmother, and the CEO of a locally based insurance company, all stood at my side as I sought to reassure members of the LGBT community that they were safe in South Bend, and called on the state to reverse course.

My office distributed stickers reading COME ON IN: SOUTH BEND IS AN OPEN CITY and they quickly began appearing in restaurant and shop windows across town. Businesses from the South Bend Brew Werks to the Blackthorn Golf Club signed up on a list of companies reaffirming their commitment to serve all. And I found myself on national TV and radio discussing just the kind of national social issue that had rarely been on my plate as a mayor.

Like all furors, this one, too, had its comic dimensions. In Walkerton, about half an hour from South Bend, the owner of a place called Memories Pizza answered a question from a local TV reporter and unexpectedly became the first Indiana businessperson to suggest publicly that he'd use the law to avoid catering a gay wedding. The Internet erupted with angry responses, largely in the form of zero-star Yelp reviews. The content of the posts ranged from simple outrage, to obscene images composed of pizza toppings, to expressions of puzzlement over what circumstances would lead a gay couple to ask a rural pizza place to cater their wedding in the first place. Late-night TV had a field day, with Michael Keaton playing the pizza owner on *Saturday Night Live*, turning away customers with a wagged finger in a goofy spoof of CNN's reporting style.

The reaction quickly went over the top, with threats to burn the place down prompting them to close for a few days—not something likely to inspire the owners toward a more forward-looking attitude on tolerance and equality. As things grew more fierce, I began to feel a kind of regret for the owner and his adult daughter, who probably had no idea that their unguarded words to a local camera crew would make them a national lightning rod. But I needn't have worried about them. They set up a CoFundMc.com page to cover the costs of their closure and promptly raised $800,000. (The entire property of Memories Pizza, including the land and the building, had been assessed at around $40,000 in value.) Only in America in 2015 could a small-town pizza provider profess prejudice in the name of Christianity before a local TV crew, be mocked around the country on late-night television, and then be made rich beyond belief, all in a matter of days. "Indiana pizza better be good f°°°°°° pizza, that's all I can say," Jon Stewart opined in disbelief.

As I watched all this unfold, my mind turned to the people I knew—older conservatives, mostly—who were on the road to acceptance of LGBT equality but had sincere difficulty in getting there. What would my next-door neighbors think of all this? If my grandmother, who had voted for Reagan but been turned off by Gingrich, were living, would the contours of this debate make her more or less likely to embrace equality? How could we make it clear that there was no going back on equality, without seeming so ferocious to these citizens that we pushed them straight back into the arms of the religious right? The swift social change was exhilarating, but its suddenness would disorient many Americans, which increased the risk of backlash. As *New York Times* columnist Frank Bruni noted, "A 64-year-old Southern woman not onboard with marriage equality finds herself characterized as a hateful boob. Never mind that Barack Obama and Hillary Clinton weren't themselves onboard just five short years ago."

But, amid the divisiveness, the RFRA debate actually helped to bring people together across traditional party lines. Because the law's endorsement of discrimination was so naked and harmful, it aroused opposition from conservatives who may have struggled with something like marriage equality but at least recognized that it's wrong to mistreat someone because of who they are or whom they love. The activism of longtime progressives and LGBT advocates was crucial, but I believe it was ultimately the revolt of the business Republicans that changed the course of this debate.

On March 31, five days after the bill passed, the often conservative *Indianapolis Star* carried a rare front-page editorial, headlined in letters so big they almost took up the entire page:

FIX
THIS
NOW

By the time the video of Pence's disastrous *This Week* appearance was ricocheting across the Internet, it was clear that the bill was untenable in its current form. Desperate to stanch the reputational bleeding, the Republican state assembly hastily composed a clarification to the law, specifying that it could not be used to justify discrimination. The bill's original backers complained loudly that this "clarification" defeated the whole purpose of the bill, which was true—and revealing. Their objection exposed the deep truth that, contrary to Pence's protestations, discrimination had been at the heart of their project all along.

The "fix" was not exactly a leap forward in LGBT inclusion. An effort failed the next year to actually establish a civil rights policy, which meant, going forward, that in many parts of Indiana people could still be fired for being gay. Embarrassingly, we also remained one of just five American states with no ban on hate crimes. But the whole episode showed that trying to appeal to radical social conservatives no longer worked in Indiana, because it would run afoul of what most people believed, including typically conservative groups like the business community. The controversy crippled Pence's reputation as governor, and created an opening for his Democratic challenger, John Gregg, to mount a credible campaign against him for the governor's office in 2016.

What no one could have known then was the future benefit to Pence of establishing himself as a hero to the religious far right, a political martyr almost. It made him into a brilliant, if cynical, choice of running mate for Donald Trump. Nominating an evangelical heartland governor was the best way for a thrice-married, formerly pro-choice, philandering ex-Democrat like Trump to reach out to religious conservatives and begin unifying the fractured right around his candidacy. And while Trump's life story was anathema to everything Mike Pence believed in, this was the right move for Pence, too, if viewed in the cynical light of raw politics. The governor had lost respect on both sides of the aisle in his home state, and was now widely expected to lose his reelection. Strange bedfellows though they were, Mike Pence and Donald Trump needed each other. Win or lose, teaming up with Trump could give Pence a second political life.

13

Hitting Home

It was mild and hazy on the morning of June 1, 2016, as I stood on the tarmac waiting for Air Force One. I had shown up for what I thought would be a perfunctory handshake and photo opportunity. President Obama was to speak in Elkhart, about forty minutes east of South Bend's airport, which was the nearest place where you could land a 747. As mayor, I would have the honor of welcoming him as he stepped off the plane and walked over to the limousine. Standing alongside Senator Donnelly and the president of the county commissioners as the jumbo jet descended for its final approach, it was easy to be awed by the spectacle of America's presidential security apparatus. As soon as the big aircraft landed, chase vehicles appeared on the runway seemingly from nowhere, SUVs racing along its sides for some reason as it slowed to a taxi. Innumerable Secret Service and military personnel crowded the apron as the mighty white-and-blue aircraft swung around. Off to the side was a C-17; it had probably delivered the limo earlier along with who-knows-what military equipment and personnel to be at the president's side, just in case.

I thought of the day in 1988 when my father took me to peer through the chain-link fence at Ronald Reagan's plane and reflected on the nature of American strength as symbolized by the big jet, the vehicles, the personnel. The arrival of a presidential aircraft is somewhat light on ceremony, but heavy on equipment and personnel—less a show of elegance than one of power. In a sense, it was also proof of the great faith and optimism shown by our cautious Founders in placing this much authority in the hands of one democratically elected human being. Imagine the implications, I thought as I eyed the SUVs, the security men, the big graytail military jet in the distance, if all this were to fall into the hands of someone unfit to wield it.

The president descended the familiar staircase, did his requisite handshaking with the three of us smiling officials, and walked past us to greet a small gaggle of locals who had been invited for one reason or another to view the landing from the tarmac. Then an aide tapped me on the shoulder and asked me to step toward the limo nearby. Moments later, I was sitting inside, facing backward, and looking eye-to-eye at a smiling Barack Obama. I glanced down to make sure my feet did not accidentally tap the president's shoes.

President Obama was in a buoyant mood. "How are the Irish looking for this fall?" he asked me and Senator Donnelly, seated next to him. The conversation hovered on football for a while, and then ranged through what was happening in South Bend, how the auto industry had come back, how our city was positioning itself relative to the economy of Chicago. It was not a business session, though at one point Obama turned to Donnelly and pointedly mentioned that he needed the Senate to come through with funding for his opioid package.

We compared stories on throwing out the first pitch—admittedly a little different at a South Bend Cubs game than opening day at Nationals Park, but it was nice to be able to have something in common, sort of, with a president. He volunteered that one of the moments when he truly admired his predecessor was when Bush, not long after the 9/11 attacks, nailed a perfect strike in his first pitch at game three of the World Series at Yankee Stadium.

Wishing for the first time in my life that the commute to Elkhart along the U.S. 20 Bypass could somehow grow longer, I alternated between enjoying the conversation and disbelieving that it was happening in the first place. I felt I was comporting myself reasonably well, taking the opportunity to explain what was happening in our city and what our greatest needs were for support. Then, after the conversation had turned to something about my time in Afghanistan, the president interrupted me to ask, "Wait a minute—how old are you, anyway?"

And for what felt like a minute, I had no idea.

A FEW WEEKS EARLIER, I had met for the first time the person most of us assumed would be the next president. Chasten and I were at my parents' place for Sunday night dinner, as usual, when a phone call came from a friend involved with the Clinton campaign. "Hillary wants to do a campaign event in northern Indiana." Could we find a good place for her to speak? She would be here on Tuesday.

I knew right away where to send her. AM General, one of the largest employers in our community, had a great story to tell. Best known for producing Humvees for the military, it had also manufactured a number of commercial vehicles, including the well-known Hummer line and the MV-1, a new kind of vehicle for people with disabilities. Moreover, the company demonstrated how to keep with the times in ways that had escaped Studebaker. The company was in the midst of a three-year contract to manufacture Mercedes R-class vehicles, a luxury SUV sold exclusively in the Chinese market. Here was a brilliant example of how American workers could play a role, other than victim, in the globalized economy: right in our part of the industrial Midwest, we had American union auto workers building a German-branded vehicle shipped to customers in Asia. I made, as they say, a few phone calls.

Two days later I was in a folding chair on the factory floor, watching Secretary Clinton give her stump speech to the assembled auto workers and various chosen community members in attendance after a tour on the shop floor. It all went as it was supposed to, except for one oddity at the end, which amounts, in retrospect, to a major warning sign: polite applause. After Clinton spoke, everyone clapped in their seats. Then she shook hands along a rope line, and was off to the next event. This might sound normal, but I had been at enough campaign events over the years to know that a presidential campaign appearance this late in the game should never end with anything but people on their feet. At the time it just struck me as a little peculiar that a union-heavy and typically Democratic crowd was not standing to cheer; now, with the benefit of hindsight, it looks like a sign of her campaign's fatal lack of enthusiasm among workers in the industrial Midwest.

Other candidates had plenty of energy and motivation that spring, and they brought it with them to South Bend. On consecutive days in May, our Century Center downtown saw visits from Bernie Sanders and Donald Trump. The venue was the same, but atmospheres around these two visits could not have been more different. Mingling with the folks in line around the Century Center parking lot to see Bernie, I felt like I was at a party, or maybe a rock concert. Attendees were clearly serious about their values, but had also come with a cheerful, even playful spirit. Walking up and down alongside the line to get in, hangers-on hawked FEEL THE BERN T-shirts and buttons picturing the hair and glasses, Bernie with the finch, Bernie riding a unicorn.

The next day's Trump rally felt like a party, too, but one of those edgy parties where you're not totally sure if a fight will break out. Bernie had drawn about forty-two hundred spectators to his event; the Trump crowd was over ten thousand. As the rallygoers waited all afternoon to get in, protesters lined up to face them across Saint Joseph Street (soon to be renamed for Dr. King). There had been enough cases of violence around other recent Trump rallies that I was worried. Our safety strategy was twofold. Publicly, I focused on calling the community to its highest values, telling a TV crew from WNDU: "We welcome anybody who's here to express their free speech rights, even if we have vigorous disagreements. I expect the community to demonstrate our values of welcome and inclusion when it comes to responding to this campaign's arrival." Behind the scenes, I wanted to leave nothing to chance, and asked the police department to be as vigilant as possible without under-cutting the freedom of attendees and protesters.

Police set up a temporary command post in a nearby building over-looking the area, tracking online threats of violence and eyeing the parking lot for trouble. Visiting both to thank the officers and gauge the temperature of our first responders, I passed a huddle of fully-geared-up SWAT officers, there just in case, and reflected on how suddenly times had changed. This was not what it had been like when Harry Truman's whistle-stop tour came through, or Reagan or Obama, for that matter. For the first time in the modern life of South Bend, a mayor had to approach the arrival of a major presidential campaign in his city primarily through a sobering lens: not that of civic pride, or even parti-san politics, but rather the possibility of political violence. Accustomed to sizing up presidential rallies for their political impact, I now had to approach this one mainly from the perspective of safety.

The rally itself was in keeping with most of the others; nothing hap-pened that was particularly unusual by the standards of that spring. Trump was close to clinching the nomination, and his speech contained all of the greatest hits that he would repeat throughout the summer and fall. He promised to build a wall, and that Mexico would pay for it. He took jabs at his rivals, from Hillary Clinton to Ted Cruz. He attacked free trade and globalization, and vowed to deliver the most successful presidency ever: "We're going to win so much you're going to beg me, Mr. President, please, please, it's too much winning."

As a mayor, my idea of winning that day simply consisted of getting through the afternoon without incident. Checking in periodically for signs of trouble, I was reassured by our police department that the rallygoers and protesters were keeping it peaceful, if passionate. The day's last situation report from the police chief let me finally breathe a sigh of relief: "No injuries, no arrests."

THE CLINTON AND TRUMP CAMPAIGNS swapped fortunes repeatedly, up and down, through the summer. The last few days were marked by uptight but sincere confidence on the part of the Hillary campaign, mixed with a widespread sense that she was nowhere near as strong as she should be. The County-City Building is an early vote site, and as I crossed the lobby on my way to the office each morning in those last few days before the election, I wondered if this would be a close one even in our county. With its strong blue-collar tradition, St. Joseph County is normally one of the most Democratic in a mostly Republican state. But when Election Day came, she won our county only by a hair—a sign of major underperformance overall.

In the elevator the next day, I greeted my colleague Christina Brooks, and saw her face wet with tears. When we got to my floor, the staff looked bewildered. I called a staff meeting, telling everyone around the table that the most important element of our job had just become more difficult and more pressing: to hold the community together. Christina then described the experience of trying to reassure her daughter that it would be safe to go to school that morning. When her daughter showed her KKK-themed social media memes that her classmates were sending her that night while joking about Trump's victory, she thought of her own upbringing as an African-American woman and realized it wasn't just her daughter she was trying to reassure—it was herself. Another colleague, Cherri Peate, said she feared for her brother, simply because he was a tall young black man. Was he in more danger now? And also, exactly what was it this new president was promising our country? "Make America Great Again"? she asked, looking around the room as if any of us could make it less threatening for her. "When was America ever great for *us*?"

Later that day, I went to meet with the College Democrats chapter at Notre Dame. Some of them were also tearful, and for many of them, this was personal. Grace, the student co-president who was a survivor and an outspoken advocate on campus sexual assault, described the effect this was having on students in a similar situation. She had gone, concerned, to check on one student she knew who was struggling with the ways the election had compounded the trauma of her own assault—and found her suicidal.

LIFE WENT ON, BUT IT BEGAN to be punctuated by interventions from national politics of a kind I had not seen before. One day, my phone started to blow up with texts asking if there was any truth to rumors of an ICE raid on the West Side. I asked around to see if there was something going on. There wasn't, but by the time I knew that for sure, several of the small businesses in the Latino-heavy West Side of our city had shut down for the day, and families were taking refuge in St. Adalbert's Church.

Stepping into St. Adalbert's, you are immediately struck by its magnificent proportions for a church in the middle of a neighborhood. It was built in 1926 with the original intent of becoming a cathedral, only for the diocese to decide to seat the bishop elsewhere in what many considered to be a snub of the Polish immigrant community. On one interior wall, a mural depicts Christ with a background of immigrants beating swords into plowshares; an inscription above his figure reads, in Polish, "By the sweat of your brow you have earned the bread of life."

Nearly a century later, it's still the spiritual home to large, Catholic, immigrant working families—only now they mostly speak Spanish, not Polish. Father Ybarra has succeeded predecessors with names like Gapczynski and Kazmierczak. And in this first scare of the Trump era, it now became a haven for families unsure if they were safe in their own workplaces or homes. Parents had grabbed their kids from Harrison Primary Center and small shops closed for the day. After that day working the phones to verify this was all a false alarm, my staff and I added to our mayor's office to-do list the creation of a phone tree in the event of immigration raids.

One evening soon after, I walked through the doors of the Harrison school, a place I sometimes visited in order to read to second-graders. This time I wasn't there to introduce them to "Pete the Cat," but to address a "Know Your Rights" event for neighborhood residents. Hushed voices of hundreds of parents echoed off the lacquered basketball floor of the gym where they gathered. A legal nonprofit had set up a projector with a slide show. I rose to reassure the parents, in my rusty high school Spanish, that we were a welcoming community. "Our police are here to keep you safe, not to practice federal immigration enforcement," I insisted. *And not to tear your family apart,* I thought. The last thing our law enforcement needed was for Latino families to be afraid even to speak to our officers, especially if they had information needed to solve or prevent crime in their neighborhoods, all because they conflate local police with federal immigration authorities.

As I got ready to leave, a volunteer came up to me in the hall of the school and said there were some high school kids who wanted to meet me. I wasn't sure why high school kids would be around, since Harrison is an elementary school, but I said I'd be happy to and followed her into the glass-walled school library. There, I saw a group of mostly white students from Adams High School, which is over on the East Side. One was helping a group of small kids figure out a puzzle; another was distributing pepperoni pizza from boxes lined up on the side. A student explained that they were volunteering as part of their National Honor Society commitment, entertaining children while their parents were in the gym.

I choked up with a mix of emotions: appreciation on one hand for the work of these civically spirited students, and on the other hand, alarm at the world we were living in. When I was in high school NHS, our volunteer projects had to do with things like litter cleanup. Now, in post-2016 America, there were whole new categories of things you can volunteer to do—such as consoling and entertaining six-year-olds while their terrified immigrant parents gather in a school gym to get legal advice on how to keep their families from being torn apart by federal agents. It was another reminder that the reality of politics is personal, not theoretical. Tip O'Neill's dictum was right: all politics is local. Especially national politics.

For me, the politics of immigration came even more up-close and personal when I visited Eddie's Steak Shed to meet the family and friends of its owner, Roberto Beristain. Roberto had been a fixture in nearby Granger, and so was Eddie's, employing about twenty people. He had come to the U.S. twenty years earlier, without a visa, and fallen in love with an American citizen named Helen, whom he would marry. He got a job as a cook at Helen's family's restaurant, and eventually saved up enough to buy out his retiring brother-in-law. He and Helen were raising three kids, all citizens. He had been trying himself to become a citizen for years, but his path was complicated by a years-old paperwork problem from being detained at the Canadian border during a vacation to Niagara Falls. Still, he had a work permit and a driver's license, he paid taxes, and for years had been visiting an ICE office annually to check in. Other than immigrating without permission, he was more law-abiding than most of us, with not so much as a traffic ticket against his name.

Every year, Roberto would go check in with Immigration and Customs Enforcement. But when he went to an ICE office to renew his work permit in February 2017, things did not go as usual. At this gathering of alarmed friends and family members who had asked me to come meet them at the restaurant a couple hours before it opened, Helen teared up as she described waiting for him in the car outside, growing more and more concerned until someone came out to tell her that Roberto was being detained.

By the time I came to meet Helen and their friends, Roberto was being held for deportation in Racine, Wisconsin. Procedurally, things were not looking good for him. His lawyers had few options; still, the friends and family at the restaurant took turns making his case and sharing stories about him. A server spoke of how hard he worked alongside his staff, in the kitchen when necessary. His stepson explained how Roberto held up his family. One by one, they described what he meant to them and asked me what could be done.

Demographically, the crowd was typical of Granger: overwhelmingly white and Republican. Yet they were all outraged that their hardworking and honest friend was being taken away. I recognized one man, with a small white mustache and a light-colored blazer, from a Kiwanis Club appearance I had made nearby. He was a certain kind of old-school, dignified small-town gentleman for whom being Republican was synonymous with being respectable, someone who likely voted for Trump without enthusiasm but out of reflex, reinforced by a decades-long antipathy to all things Clinton. He grew indignant as he described how he and his conservative friends expected the new president to go after criminals, not members of the community in good standing. It emerged that even Helen had voted for Trump, never expecting this.

I had little role other than to listen; a mayor can't do much when it comes to immigration policy. I ached for some way to reassure the family, especially the two bright teenage daughters who were now dealing with a new dimension of bullying in middle school ("Your father is illegal!"), and their eight-year-old brother, Dimitri, who simply didn't understand why his dad wasn't there to put him to bed anymore.

The more I spoke with the people there, the more I realized it was not necessarily a contradiction for conservatives to be upset about the detention and looming deportation of their friendly restaurant-owning neighbor. As I wrote later in a reflection for the *Huffington Post*, "Think

of the favorite themes of conservatism: hard work, small business own-
ership, suspicion of overbearing government, and support for family.
Each one of those themes is at stake here, and each is insulted by the
prospect of a person like Roberto being ripped away from his business,
friends, wife and children, by a federal agency." It was because, not in
spite, of their conservatism that this room full of people felt the need to
stand up for this undocumented immigrant they knew.

They also viewed his case differently because they actually knew
him as a person, not as a stock character. Over time I've observed that
we are more generous, supportive, and pleasant toward people we actually know than toward those we understand only as categories or groups.
Humans can of course be cruel in person, too, but as a general rule we
seem less likely to hate from up close. This explains the many people I
have encountered who are noticeably racist in general but deeply supportive and protective of minority individuals they actually know personally. And it explains the sudden expansion of LGBT freedom in this
country, as people began to realize that the vilified category in question
applied to specific people they already knew and loved. This kind of
empathy was on display at Eddie's Steak Shed, as I looked at the dozens
of signatures on a petition started by employees at the restaurant, titled
"Bring Our Boss Home." And I saw it in letters from people like the
one who wrote, "I voted for President Trump because I believed he was
promising to develop a process to remove the illegal immigrants that
have done acts against the United States. I also believed that he was
going to correct the red tape that blocks the immigrants from becoming
a citizen that have been a positive contributor to the way of life here,"
meaning immigrants like Roberto.

As the story gained increasing attention, including a feature on
60 Minutes, many responded judgmentally toward anyone, especially
Helen, who could vote for Trump and then be surprised by this sort
of outcome. But to do so is to assume that voting is about ideology and
policy analysis, rather than identity and environment. For a hardwork-

ing and devoted woman like Helen with a small family business in a conservative Indiana community, most of the people she dealt with—neighbors, customers, and acquaintances—were people for whom voting Republican was simply a matter of course. If she was also a consumer of conservative news on television and social media, more liberal messages might never have reached her in the first place. We should not be so surprised that she was so surprised.

The outcome was as feared: Roberto was deported to Juárez and the family lost the restaurant. The news cycle moved on. But it's hard for me to move beyond that singular moment at the restaurant as I prepared to leave, looking into Dimitri's eyes and trying to think of something to tell him besides "You'll get your father back" or "Everything will be okay," which I could not say because I doubted it was true. Here was a kid—a very American kid—who wanted the most natural thing in the world: the company of his own father. And because of politics, he couldn't have it. A law said that he and his father were not of the same country, and a series of decisions meant that they could not live together. This—not some trading of rhetorical points on CNN or electoral up-and-down—is where political choices hit home. Not at the polling place itself, or a campaign rally, or in the halls of Congress, but in the eyes of a bewildered and utterly innocent eight-year-old boy.

VI

Becoming

Think you're escaping and run into yourself. Longest way round is the shortest way home.

JAMES JOYCE

14

Dirt Sailor

"Sir," I asked, "could you help me figure out how to answer this one on the form?"

Lieutenant Murray looked annoyed. He often looked annoyed, though over time I would learn that his deadpan style concealed a kind of gruff affection for rather clueless junior officers like myself, along with the enlisted people he oversaw, and the Navy overall.

It was time to fill in the annual "Reserve Screening Questionnaire," or RSQ, not to be confused with the "Officer Qualification Questionnaire" (OQQ) or "Navy Reserve Qualification Questionnaire" (the NRQQ, of course). Service in the Reserve will always be one of the highlights of my life, but the price of admission was an ongoing flow of administrativia. A reservist needs to be as bureaucratically healthy as an active duty service member, but has only two days a month to take care of the various requirements. The result is that during the monthly drills that make up much of your service, half of your time on base consists of filling out forms, undergoing medical checkups, running physical fitness tests, and clicking through computer-based training on everything from sexual harassment to cybersecurity. Whatever time is left over goes to "production," doing a job resembling what you would theoretically do if you were called up, which in my case meant analyzing intelligence for the European Command.

The sooner I could update this form, along with all the other ensigns and junior lieutenants seated in the carpeted and windowless room at Fort Sheridan, the sooner I could get in "the back," that is, the area full of classified computers, to do some actual work. The hang-up was that there was a question on this particular form pertaining to whether I could readily be deployed—which, of course, is the whole point of having a Reserve. The question was short, but not simple: "Are you considered a 'key' employee" in your civilian workplace? I wasn't sure what to say.

"This is mainly for firefighters and other first responders," Lieu-tenant Murray said, eyeing me through his glasses. "Why? Where do you work?"

I said what I usually said around the base when conversation went to our civilian day jobs: "I work for the city."

"All right. Can anyone else do your job?"

"Not exactly."

"Are you the mayor?" he asked sarcastically.

"Um . . ."

IT TURNS OUT THAT THE ANSWER to the question of being a key employee, in my case, was no. The reason is that under Indiana law for a city our size, a deputy mayor can be assigned to perform a mayor's duties if he (or she) gets called into active duty. There's even a spe-cific part of Indiana statute contemplating this situation, dating back to 1865, when perhaps lawmakers envisioned a mayor raising a volunteer regiment to go fight at the tail end of the Civil War. So, as far as the

Navy was concerned, I was not indispensable back home and thus fair game for deployment orders.

This seemed reasonable to me. Every reservist leaves something important behind when called to active duty—not only a job, as I had, but often a spouse and children, which I did not. Checking the box "no" was a humbling reminder that national defense has little regard for peacetime civilian hierarchy, which in a way was refreshing as well.

ALL THROUGH MY CAMPAIGNS and my first year as mayor, I continued my regular Reserve duties, usually driving two hours for a drill weekend in Illinois. Working eight-hour days, a relaxing contrast from my day job, and spending time with sailors from all walks of civilian life, was a healthy antidote to the all-absorbing work I had in South Bend. By law, I could not engage in politics or perform civil duties during the forty-eight hours a month plus two weeks a year that I was active. It was a forced, but welcome, change of pace from the constant activity of being mayor. And there was even something welcome about being a more junior employee for a while, rather than the boss. Back home, I was responsible for the conduct of a thousand employees and the well-being of a hundred thousand residents. On drill weekends, I was responsible for my own paperwork, and that of a handful of sailors and soldiers assigned to my branch.

Deployments are part of the bargain for reservists, but so is "dwell time"—the idea that the military will try to give you plenty of time in between mobilizations, so that ordinarily you only have to deploy once every five years, unless you go out of your way to spend more time on active duty. The urgency of the Iraq and Afghanistan wars put some strain on this model, with exhausted service members being called up more and more frequently, but by the time I joined in 2009, the pace was again fairly steady. I had little concern about being abruptly called up in those first few years. Besides, it was extremely rare for an ensign to be deployed, because your early years are mostly spent figuring out the basics of management and military bearing—knowledge normally not attributed to officers until they have at least made it to the rank of lieutenant, junior grade.

But as time went by, I advanced in rank and skills, and grew more likely to be mobilized. By 2013, rumor had it that the intelligence community would see an increase in deployment orders, including involuntary call-ups. One drill weekend, I encountered an unusually grumpy Lieutenant Murray, who explained that he had been abruptly and involuntarily called up for duty in East Africa. In his case, that meant suspending a successful law practice, leaving a spouse and kids, and packing his bags for Djibouti; he was very much a key employee at his solo office, but that, too, did not rate a "yes" answer on the screening questionnaire. The "Needs of the Navy" came first.

Before even taking office as mayor, I had made sure our team had a clear plan on what to do if I got mobilized. Some decisions would have to depend on the circumstances, of course, but we gathered all the information needed on legal and regulatory procedures and made several contingency plans. Now, with deployment orders coming in more and more frequently—especially for officers holding the rank of lieutenant, which was what I would become in late 2013—I told the team at home to be ready, and made sure my chain of command knew that I would rather go sooner than later, and would rather go to Afghanistan than anywhere else. Because I was a specialist in counterterrorism, Afghanistan represented the best place in the world to practice my craft. It was also a country, troubled but also hauntingly beautiful, that I had gotten to know while a civilian adviser at McKinsey. If my turn was coming up to get mobilized, I wanted it to be there.

"AN ADVENTURE IS ONLY an inconvenience rightly considered," said my friend and colleague Scott Ford, quoting G. K. Chesterton as he raised a glass of scotch. A few of us friends had gathered for one last dinner and round of drinks before I headed to Chicago with my parents, orders in hand, and then off to the sequence of bases and waypoints that would lead me eventually to Kabul. We got into the good whiskey, and shared jokes until late at night.

It was a good way to think of the coming deployment: an adventure, among many other things. But I also noted, with guilt, that this would be more than an inconvenience for my administration. We were full-steam-ahead on a number of ambitious initiatives, as I've described: addressing a thousand vacant houses, staging for the 150th anniversary celebration of the city, and redesigning the two major arteries in our downtown streetscape, to name a few. My office staff and department heads would now have to continue making progress on all of these efforts without me there to supply political cover, day-to-day guidance, or media engagement.

But by the time I got my official orders in the fall of 2013, calling me up to report the next February for duty with the Afghanistan Threat Finance Cell, we were prepared. Kathryn Roos, my hyper-competent chief of staff, had worked so closely with me that she could intuitively gauge how I would answer most questions before they even came to me. And Mark Neal, the city controller whom I had asked to assume the role of deputy mayor in my absence, would be an excellent community voice in my stead. Mark was an accomplished business leader, a former CFO of a major health company in town whose work for the city was uncomplicated by political aspirations: our original arrangement had called for him to serve the city for two years as controller before going back to private life. But right about the time he was getting ready to leave the administration, I had to approach him with an almost comically disruptive request: to temporarily take over and lead the city during my deployment. He declined—which I took as further proof that he was the right person for the job. There was no personal ambition here, no political agenda; he just wanted what was best for the city. I persisted, and eventually he agreed.

Over breakfast at my house shortly before leaving, I went over final plans with Mark. Here's what to do if there's a weather emergency. Here's the best way to get ahold of me abroad. Here are the main priorities to stick with, and the ones we can sacrifice if we have to. Then, gently smiling as he did whenever we were about to tackle a delicate issue, Mark raised the one question no one else had wanted to ask: "What if you don't come back, Pete?"

I glanced down at the table, trying to field the question the same as if I had been asked what to do if the council denied a mid-year budget appropriation. "There's a letter in the desk drawer upstairs." That was for the personal stuff. As for the city, "It would be a vacancy. They'll have to find someone new, and it will get political. I guess if it gets to that point, I won't be any help."

SOON I WAS AT NAVAL STATION GREAT LAKES, completing the first stages of mobilization and commencing the strange shift in identity and status that awaited me. The base commanding officer was away, so the command master chief did the honors of signing off on my deployment packet after I had completed the scavenger hunt of requisite medical, fitness, training, and administrative checks. He looked over the paperwork one last time in his office and asked if I felt I had everything in order on the personal side.

"Got any kids?"

"No."

"Wife?"

"Nope."

"Girlfriend?"

"No, I'm single."

"Well, that'll make it easier."

"Is your employer supportive?"

"Very," I answered, thinking of Kathryn, Mark, and the rest of my staff. "Everyone has been great."

"That's good. If you still feel that way when you get back, you can put them in for an ESGR [Employer Support of the Guard and Reserve] Award."

"I'll remember that," I muttered. But that would be like giving myself an award, I thought, so it probably wouldn't work in this case.

"You said you work for the city, right?"

"That's right."

"Well, you should definitely put them in for the award, then, especially if you need to brown-nose a little. When they do those award presentations the elected officials always come. They love standing next to military and they just eat that shit up."

A FEW WEEKS LATER, I sat poker-faced in a training room as a furious commander berated the troops at Camp McCrady, outside Fort Jackson, South Carolina. We had been there for a few days, all Navy personnel assigned to Army-style jobs in combat zones, being trained to serve as the land-based "dirt sailors" we were about to become. It came after Great Lakes, after Norfolk, the last stage before going overseas. We learned Army lingo, convoy operations, and, of course, shooting. But some officers had been underperforming, and the executive officer was not pleased.

One by one, he called up officers who had done something that displeased him, had them turn and face the others, and yelled out each of their deficiencies. One had been observed getting food ahead of the enlisted sailors in line, and disparaging the drill instructors behind their backs. He was dismissed on the spot. A lieutenant was called up for filling her CamelBak liquid dispenser with soda, also forbidden. He took it off her back and flung it across the room.

It felt like I was back in middle school, and like any bystander to the disciplining of one's peers, I kept my eyes down and waited for it all to end—not realizing my turn was next.

After dispatching his last victim, the commander glanced down at a crumpled piece of paper in his hand, then looked back up at the group: "Now. Who in the *hell* is Lieutenant. . . . Buttinger."

No one budged. Slowly and with dread, it dawned on me. I was Lieutenant Buttinger. As soon as I came to terms with this inevitable reality, I was on my feet. I stood front and center, staring dead ahead of me, getting yelled at, confused.

"You want to argue with a drill sergeant, Lieutenant?"

"No, sir!"

"You realize what these guys have been through and what they do to make sure you're ready for a combat zone?"

I sure did. I admired the drill instructors from the South Carolina Army National Guard who spent their days showing us sailors how to function as soldiers. I also had no idea what he was mad about. But I knew enough not to reveal any perplexity, let alone try to plead my case. "Yes, sir. No excuse, sir."

"Get back to your seat," he said, seeming to have unwound just a little.

"Yes, sir."

A few days later, I was back under the gaze of Commander Clark, whose countenance and demeanor gave him more than a passing resemblance to Steve Carell from *The Office*. "Well, Lieutenant Butterig, it looks like I owe you an apology." It turned out I had been confused with another trainee, and he had called me into his office to clear it up. I appreciated that gesture, though it would have been nice if he had done this in front of the others. (Our class division officer later took care of that at morning formation.)

The mistaken-identity case was the final seal on the status shift I had experienced, going from a mayor in charge of a small bureaucracy to a minor figure in the biggest bureaucracy in the world. At home, I was accustomed to people being angry at me, perhaps over a policy decision, police controversy, or pothole problem. But at least that was for things that actually happened, based on who I actually was. The one indignity I never experienced at home as mayor was someone mistaking me for someone else. But here, even as an officer, I was no one in particular. At the mayor's office, my name is printed on the door. But here at Camp McCrady, my surname wasn't even spelled right on my camouflage uniform when it was first issued to me. The rank was all that mattered; the name was a minor detail. Indeed, the most vital piece of information on me was neither name nor rank, but the letters "O POS," punched into the metal, below my Social Security number and above the abbreviation EPISC on my dog tag.

"Do not guess your blood type, shipmates!" the NCO had joked as we filled in the forms to go to the dog tag maker. We all chuckled, but when they came to pass them out, it felt like we held in our hands an emblem of our mortality as well as our military identity. I was told to separate the two tags I'd been issued. "Do your family a favor," someone had said, showing me how to lace one tag into one of my combat boots, while the other stayed around my neck. That way they could figure out who you had been even if your leg wound up in a different place than the rest of you.

"WHO HERE THINKS YOU WON'T BE going on a convoy?" asked the admiral introducing the final round of training. He was a cheerful two-star, tall and lean, seeming to enjoy having an occasion to wear the camouflage uniform instead of the dress blues of the Pentagon. His talk had been engaging, and now he let the dramatic pause linger after his question. Like all admirals, generals, mayors, and bishops, he was a politician.

Most of us figured out that the question was rhetorical, though it was also puzzling. Our group consisted of personnel specialists, medics, intelligence analysts. In theory, very few of us would wind up in a convoy. Still, it seemed like "yes" was not the correct answer here. Only half a dozen naïve hands went up.

"Guess what: all of you are probably going on a convoy."

We all understood that our deployments were not traditional naval assignments; we would be nowhere near a ship, and should be prepared for unconventional duties. We were the "individual augmentees," mobilizing one at a time to join other units, rather than with a company or a ship's crew. Still, the idea that we needed to learn convoy security seemed peculiar; we had joined the Navy, not the Army. But by now it was clear to us that we needed to be ready for anything. Months later, as I counted my hundredth time outside the wire behind the wheel, I thought of that moment. We may have started our Navy Reserve careers learning about ships and cruise missiles, but right now we needed to learn about Humvees, medevacs, and IEDs.

The culminating event of the three-week combat training sequence was an all-day convoy simulation, where we proceeded through a threat-filled third world village, a slice of Afghanistan (or Somalia or Iraq, if you preferred) in the South Carolina woods. Advice was dispensed along the way, with occasional reminders that we were not supposed to be in combat roles, but would have to learn these things, just in case. We learned the procedure for what to do when your vehicle is stopped, scanning the immediate area and outer radius for signs of an IED. But there was only time to learn the basics. None of us would be defusing bombs, but we needed to know how to act if we encountered one.

"DRILL SERGEANT, is there a standard procedure for what to do if you actually see one during the walk-around?"

"Yes: get your ass back in the vehicle."

The response was typical of the drill instructors, brusque enough to make sure we understood the stakes, but also marked by the camaraderie and gruff humor of frontline soldiers. Some of them had been through five or more deployments, even though many were younger than I was. They wanted us to be prepared for all of the things they had seen downrange. Our magazines were full of blanks, but the rifles we carried were the ones we would take to war.

There was downtime in between stages of the simulation, but every minute was supposed to be for some purpose, if only double-checking your weapon and your battle buddy to make sure they were in good shape. *"If-you-are standinaroundnotdoinnothing . . . You. Are. WRONG!"*

Halfway through the scenario, some sailors forgot their guidance, got ambitious, and decided to clear a building. Wrong move: the correct course of action here was to retreat to the armored vehicle and assess the threat. Unimpressed, a drill instructor pointed to the tallest, heaviest sailor in the group: "You're dead now."

The rest of us, left to drag him back to the vehicle as shots rang out from all around us, remembered the lesson.

After it all ended, we gathered for an after-action review. Sweating under our body armor, we shifted our weight from foot to foot, taking the occasional pull of water from our CamelBaks and holding on to our rifles as the instructors reviewed what we'd done right and wrong, blow-by-blow. Good job spotting the first IED. Don't forget to talk to your gunner. You should have had all the lines of the medevac report ready before getting on the radio to call it in.

It was clinical at first, but this last day, the tone of some of the instructors began to change from the deadpan style they had projected since our arrival. A drill sergeant got quiet and stared into the distance for a moment before naming a friend who was killed in Iraq, leaving a wife and five kids. "They have to live with that every day now." He went on, brotherly, reminding us that we were being trained to know what to do if action finds us, but were not supposed to look for combat if we didn't have to.

"Remember, if you get killed, the war's over for you. But the people you leave behind, they'll be fighting it for the rest of their lives. So before any of you decide to go off and be a hero, think about that shit for a minute." And we all did, uncharacteristically quiet, until the bus came to take us back to the barracks to pack.

15

"The War's Over"

A s soon as my war began, I wondered when and how it would end.
Hopefully in September, when my orders were supposed to con-
clude. And hopefully by then there would be further signs of success in
the American mission. But I had only been on the ground for a few days
when someone told me to leave the idea of winning and losing behind.

Smoking Gurkha cigars around the firepit with my new colleagues,
I was still finding my social bearings as we swapped stories in the light
of a Weber grill filled with scrap wood. This being an intel unit, they
had of course looked up the new guy before I arrived, but by now most
of the interest and amusement over my own backstory had already run
its course. We were back to talking, as usual, about the war and where
it was headed. I had volunteered some ideas about what it would take to
win in the border regions when Rob, an analyst, leaned back in his chair
and laconically interrupted me: "The war's over, Pete."

For a quiet moment the words hung in the air with the cigar smoke
and the dust of Bagram Air Field. My blood pressure rose as responses

flowed through my mind. What do you mean, the war is over? If the war's over, why are you here? Why am I here? If the war's over, what the hell was that rocket attack last night? If the war's over, then somebody should tell whoever keeps shooting rockets at us, they might like to know.

But I held my peace, trying to mimic the affect of the others, that tired ease and casually annoyed humor of resting soldiers, as we sat and smoked and glared at the fire. I got up to fetch more firewood from our pile of chopped-up old pallets. I wasn't prepared to argue with the most respected analyst in our unit, bearded and world-weary so that it was easy to forget he was my age, possibly even younger, and who had been working on terrorism analysis for years. Besides, he wasn't wrong. His point was that America wouldn't confront Pakistan over support to fighters wreaking havoc on the Afghan side of the Durand Line. The U.S. wasn't going to endanger its strategic, sixty-year relationship with Pakistan over some little thing like the Afghanistan War. It was 2014, and we might still be getting rockets shot at us from time to time, but there was only so much America could or would do about it. If winning the war meant sinking our relationship with Pakistan, then yes, the war might as well be over. And yet, here we were on a cold night in dusty Parwan Province, because wars like this one don't just end. I would spend the rest of my deployment wondering exactly what it means for one of today's wars to be truly over, and how anyone would be able to tell.

BY APRIL, AS THE SNOW was melting on the mountains over Bagram, I had been moved to Kabul and was starting to feel like I had my feet on the ground as an officer. As the admiral had foreshadowed, I got out more than you would expect for an intelligence analyst. I might have planned to spend my time behind a sophisticated computer terminal in a secure area somewhere, and sometimes that's just what I did. But it turned out my services were more often needed as a driver or vehicle commander on convoys moving people or gear in and around Kabul for my unit. In a ritual to be repeated dozens of times, I would heave my armored torso into the driver's seat of a Land Cruiser, chamber a round in my M4, lock the doors, and wave a gloved goodbye to the Macedonian gate guard. My vehicle would cross outside the wire and into the boisterous Afghan city, entering a world infinitely more interesting and ordinary and dangerous than our zone behind the blast walls at ISAF headquarters.

On the streets that spring and summer, I obtained the strange mental balance required of anyone operating outside the wire in a conflict zone. In order to figure out how to conduct yourself, you must hold two contradictory truths in your mind. Truth number one: The vast majority of people you see through the windshield are just regular people, just like at home, trying to get through their day, out to shop and work and study and do all the things people do. You have a moral as well as a strategic obligation to respect them, to drive carefully so you don't hit a kid on his way to school or a widow begging in the street or someone's uncle carrying home a watermelon, to act in such a way as to help or at least not harm them in their daily routines. Truth number two: With your rifle, your gear, your vehicle, and your passengers, you are quite obviously an American soldier (or sailor, in my case), and accordingly you must recognize that a small but nontrivial number of the people you see around you are spending their every waking minute figuring out how to kill you and your passengers, and will do so if given the slightest opportunity unless you avoid them or kill them first.

My first couple times out, I had prepared by practically memorizing the regular driver's briefings, page after page of information on the latest threat streams, the suspicious vehicles, the rumors and reporting. But soon I gave up on trying to understand the details of the threats. The warnings on known VBIEDs (vehicle-borne improvised explosive devices) usually boiled down to this useless advice: watch out for the white Corolla. In Kabul, pretty much everyone drives a white Corolla.

So I fell back on my training from Camp McCrady, eyes out for the known signs that we were about to get blown up. A suddenly empty neighborhood. A nervous-looking lone driver of a vehicle with a heavy trunk load. An obviously male hand coming out from underneath a woman's blue burqa.

Quickly, I learned how to drive at war. But what I saw through the windshield didn't look like a war. It looked like a city. A lively, energetic, smelly city full of children and merchants hawking things and students and businessmen with papers under their arms hustling to wherever it was they were going. Children were everywhere, and I wondered how it came to be that this boy was herding a flock of sheep grazing on piled garbage near a busy intersection, while that one was in a crisp blue oxford shirt in his own flock of identical blue-shirted classmates, charging across a four-lane road toward school. I wondered what was on the minds of the girls in black dresses and white headscarves, holding their notebooks to their chests like so many twelve-year-old girls do, never seen on the streets except in these little groups in their school uniforms.

Inevitably, I also thought of municipal services and scanned Kabul with a mayor's-eye view. I gauged what seemed to be done well (curb painting and lighting), poorly (trash pickup), and not at all (animal control). I thought of home, where people would be crisscrossing South Bend with no thought at all given to how they might obtain clean water, whether trash would ever get picked up off the side of the road, whether there were any bombs nearby.

Contrary to what I'd been told, the traffic had its rhythm, a sort of order dressed in chaos, as in Italy. Roundabouts had their flow and sometimes a counterflow, donkeys competed with tanker trucks, everyone beeped, and if you paid attention it all followed a certain logic. In the middle of it all, always there were street sweepers, anachronistic in neon-orange safety jackets with straw brooms, clearing the ubiquitous dust off the road between Massoud Circle and the airport, sweeping it nowhere in particular, never looking up at me or anyone else swerving to avoid them, heads down, fearless or oblivious. Did they think the war was over?

Of course, there were checkpoints, sandbags, soldiers, a bomb site where broken glass dangled in storefronts for weeks. And the war was busy claiming lives. One day an American duty driver got caught up at a checkpoint on the airport road (as I sometimes did) and got out to argue with the Afghan soldiers (as I occasionally would), and a Talib passing by on a motorcycle or bicycle noticed him, stopped and got off his bike, cut his throat, got back on his bike, and left while the American soldier bled out. That night, the local TV news reported the killing, showing the street sweepers with their heads down as always, sweeping bloody sand out of the roadway toward the median.

The longer I was there, unable to answer the question of how you can tell when a war is over, the more a second question rose in my mind alongside it. If you manage to get killed in a war that's "over," what does that make you?

THAT MAY, PRESIDENT OBAMA finally made his drawdown announcement after weeks of rumors. The American troop strength would fall to ninety-eight hundred by the end of the 2014, to be cut in half the year after that, and then out. The gunny sergeant walked into the office, a modified shipping container he called our tuna can. He took a seat and put his feet up, inspecting his pistol while I glanced at emails and fiddled absentmindedly with my knife. "I feel sorry for the people coming in 2015," he said. "If you're here now and something happens to you, then fine, we're late in the game but everyone understands we're here for a reason. But being here after we've said we're leaving? Getting shot at when everyone at home doesn't even think the war's going on still? Then why the fuck are you even out here, dog?"

I tried to figure out if the president's announcement meant that the "real" war was to end in 2014 when "Operation Enduring Freedom" turned into "Resolute Support" (just as "Iraqi Freedom" turned into "New Dawn" in 2010) or in 2016 when the troops would (we thought) all be gone, or some other date. Most Americans get our first understanding of wars from history books, starting with the dates each war began and ended. As with a human life, the span of a war is there in parentheses right after its name. The implication is that wars, like people, go from nonexistence to being and then back to nonexistence, all at a precise time and date. We grow up assuming wars have beginnings and endings. But that date is only the object of consensus after the fact, if at all. In the days after I had announced my deployment orders publicly, I occasionally got a puzzled response from people who seemed confused or even irritated by the idea that I would be going over. "I thought we were getting out of there," they'd say, as if I should be calling the Navy back to check if it was some kind of mistake.

At the outset of the mobilization, I had felt a sense of purpose, maybe even idealism, that can only be compared to the feeling of starting on a political campaign. I thought back to 2004 and John Kerry's presidential run, and then remembered that it was during that campaign that I saw the iconic footage of his testimony as the spokesman for Vietnam Veterans Against the War, long-haired and still in his twenties. "How do you ask a man," he had asked the senators then, "to be the last man to die for a mistake?" I did not believe the Afghanistan War was a mistake. But as I weighed my place in a war most people at home seemed to think was already ending, I couldn't stop wondering, how do you ask a person to be the last to die for anything?

THE RHYTHM OF DEPLOYED LIFE brought busy days and slow ones. Even with the extra time I spent keeping up with the home front, carrying a laptop and a cigar up to the roof at midnight to pick up a Wi-Fi signal and patch via Skype into a staff meeting at home, there was more time for reflection and reading than I was used to back home.

For every day punctuated by a rocket attack or explosion, there were five dominated by meetings, emails, and workouts. Between calls home, convoys, and meals, I sat at the computer in my tuna can and looked up the history of wars beginning and ending.

I read about how World War I ended at eleven in the morning on November 11, 1918. The armistice was signed at five in the morning, but set to take effect at eleven. In those six hours, there were thousands of casualties. An American soldier was killed at 10:59 after he decided to use the last sixty seconds of the war to charge a German position. If the armistice had been agreed on the tenth of November, or the twelfth, would anyone have bothered to set a time instead of letting it take immediate effect? Did the negotiators place any weight on the loss of life required for their tidy numerology?

By August, as my unit's only remaining officer at the thinning ISAF headquarters in Kabul, I was told in no uncertain terms that my mission now had less to do with running our little station there than with shutting it down. The gunny sergeant, my right-hand man, went home to rejoin his wife and four boys in South Carolina, leaving me with one analyst. In the fluorescent-lit chow hall with officers from another unit, I would end meals by rising from the table with mock self-importance, saying: "Well, time to go check on my troops."

This was the cue for one of the others to ritually supply the punch line to that joke: "You mean, your troop."

But the mission, which had to do with blocking the flow of narcotics funding to the insurgency, still mattered. So even as I worked to dismantle our shop, I got busy looking for people to take up pieces of ongoing work that we could hand off—a British law enforcement partner who might still be there in a year working out of the UK Embassy, a State Department civilian whose head didn't count against the ninety-eight hundred, some special units with a mission to stay throughout the retrograde, or one of the Afghan officials I had met who were going to wind up owning these problems anyway.

Letting go of the mission did not come easily, but clinging to it raised other concerns. What if I was doing something wrong by pushing too hard, risking my life and others' to keep going outside the confines of the base in order to see the mission through, while being told from on high to wrap it up? I owed it to anyone who got into a vehicle with me, and their spouses, to make sure we weren't taking any unjustified risks. In my eagerness to finish strong, how could I be sure I wasn't entering the grim tradition of officers—like the ones who had ordered those deadly advances that November morning in 1918 in order to get a few more inches of turf by eleven—who didn't recognize when their job was done, their war over?

ONE SLOW DAY AFTER CHOW, I googled "Japanese WWII hold-outs." On a Philippine island in 1945, as the war became desperate for the Japanese, Second Lieutenant Hiroo Onoda was ordered to take his three men into the jungle and come out for no one but his command-ing officer. He and his men carried out raids and lived in the jungle for decades, all but Onoda eventually dying. He continued doing this for almost thirty years. Then, in 1974, as the Vietnam War was near-ing its end eight hundred miles due west across the South China Sea, a Japanese backpacker found him, out there fighting World War II alone. True to his orders, Onoda refused to stand down unless relieved by the officer who had ordered him into the jungle. So the Japanese govern-ment actually tracked down the commander, Major Yoshimi Taniguchi, who was now an aging bookseller in Kyushu, and flew him to Lubang Island with an official set of orders relieving Onoda. Though he had effectively murdered a number of Filipinos living on the island, he was pardoned under the reasoning that he thought he was at war. He went home, quickly despaired at the sight of modern Japan, moved to Brazil, and became a cattle farmer. He died in January 2014, as I was packing my bags for Afghanistan.

Onoda's war had lasted thirty-four years. Mine was less than seven months, but it was long enough to encompass the excitement and uncertainty of two rounds of Afghan elections, and a much-anticipated change of command at ISAF. I was also there during the second un-ending of the Second Iraq War. Sitting in the offices of another unit that mine worked with closely, I watched on the big screen tuned to cable news as the Iraq War went through its third beginning, and thought of the night in college in 2003 when I witnessed its first false ending, with President Bush on the deck of the USS *Abraham Lincoln* with a MISSION ACCOM-PLISHED sign in the background. A decade later, I sat unsure what to say as the soldiers next to me, most of whom had served in Iraq, too, bitterly realized that their efforts had come to this, the emergence of ISIS. It was as though, in a war without two simple sides, war itself was going to win in the end. "The whole CENTCOM AOR[5] is a dumpster fire," one sighed.

My mind kept rotating around the question of whether there was any way at all to see the end of a war while it was being fought, or if you could only decide long afterward what had actually happened and when.

Accompanying my commander on a visit to Camp Leatherneck, structured like a giant checkerboard in Helmand Province, I saw plot after big square plot of land emptied. Just a few areas were still up and running, the rest taken back down to gravel, like abandoned industrial sites in South Bend, only much tidier because they had been removed with the characteristic thoroughness of the Marines. There, Afghans in the on-base "haji shops," who had been selling carpets and scarves and pirated DVDs to coalition forces for a decade, were bracing for the disappearance of their livelihoods. In the south, Kandahar had even more shops, arranged on a square boardwalk designed to make you briefly forget that you were on an airbase in a war, noshing in your downtime

---

5   That is, the Central Command's area of responsibility, which included the Middle East and Afghanistan.

on pizza or ice cream. But now the boardwalk storefronts were two-thirds empty, like at a dying mall back home.

One instinct would tell you to feel a little wistful, as you would naturally feel when seeing anything built with great effort come to a slow end. Then another instinct would smack you awake, as you sensed the wrongness of feeling sentimental about the end of a war. But this guilt would recede as you noticed that the war, itself, was not the thing that was ending. I'd sit in a meeting about how to posture our unit for the coming retrograde of troops, thinking the war was indeed pretty much over. Then I'd hear a briefing about the escalating count of Afghan National Security Forces killed that week, and wonder if our entire presence wasn't just a phase in a continuum of warfare that, to Afghans, did not begin when we invaded and would not end when we left.

AND THEN, ONE DAY IN SEPTEMBER, the dust, noise, beauty, and danger of Afghanistan were all in my past. A C-17 lifted me and about a hundred other Americans off Afghan soil for the last time. As our graytail eased up from the Kandahar tarmac, there was no applause, no jubilation from the tired men and women aboard. I tried to work myself into some emotion about it, to savor the moment or something, but it was just a flight.

The next day I sat with Lieutenant Jason McRae, my friend and battle buddy from training, in a surprisingly nice air-conditioned trailer made out to be a coffee shop amid the bleached bonescape that is Al Udeid Air Base in Qatar. Some six months earlier, I had walked at his side toward our barracks after the last hugs of the friends-and-family send-off at Camp McCrady. We both kept our eyes forward, but I could feel the restraint on Jason's part as he avoided looking back at his bewildered two-year-old toddling after us, not comprehending why his father was walking away, crying and confused as his mother scooped him up to carry him in the opposite direction.

Now our war was over; it was time to go home. But time had no real meaning at this stopover base, washed in sunlight and jet lag. We all carried our personal time zone around us. You might be on your way to breakfast at the twenty-four-hour chow hall and pass by a couple airmen on crew rest drinking beer in the morning sun before they go to bed. You might wake up uncontrollably at three in the morning and go to the running track to blow off energy—and find a dozen others working out there. Everyone on our side of the base had some combination of Germany or Iraq or Bagram or America standing twenty-four to forty-eight hours in their past and future. But the Navy had its way of signaling that time still existed, and that our war really was now finished: starting today, Jason reminded me, we no longer drew imminent danger pay.

Thumbing through his iPhone, Jason read a headline aloud: suicide attack in Kabul. Over there, when I heard an explosion, the quickest way to learn what was going on was usually to search #kabul on Twitter or "Kabul attack" on Google, so I did the same now. I learned that it was near the ISAF compound where I'd lived and worked, possibly on the road to the airport. Two Americans dead, no names yet. I quickly emailed the people I considered most likely to have been driving there at that time, and they promptly wrote back to confirm they were alive, and bored. It wasn't until the next day that they released the identities of the casualties—and their pictures.

Major Donahue had been with me on a trip to deliver clothing and school supplies to an orphanage. It was a volunteer mission, and everyone involved was motivated by a desire to do good but also, at least in my case, aching for more real encounters with regular Afghans even if it meant extra trips outside the wire. When we arrived a contingent of Afghan Boy Scouts came to unload the supplies, and we spent the morning with them, a group of orphans, and the NGO workers at the site. The orphans were like any schoolkids, playful and lively and noisy. I gave them my camera to play with and by the time I had it back it was full of photos. The Afghan Scouts, who were older, polite, and a little reticent, showed us the facility and explained their scouting program. Old enough to observe Ramadan, they quietly refused the candy we had brought before agreeing to pass it out to the little kids. Not having actually spoken to anyone under the age of eighteen in months, for me it was a rare taste of normalcy, the best day of the deployment.

Someone took a photo of me and Donahue standing in a classroom with a group of the kids, relaxed and smiling as one of the scouts uses the wrist of another to show us how to tie some elaborate knot they had learned. Nothing about the photo (other than our uniforms, of course) suggests that it was taken in the context of a war. Now I looked at that same face, squared toward the camera in the serious and dignified look of a standard service portrait, alongside the text of a news story announcing his death. His war and mine had both ended, very differently, just one day apart.

According to the customary recipe for a war story—baked with facts but leavened with bullshit—I ought to say that he and I were close, that he was the finest soldier I knew, a friend whose loss drew all of us who knew him closer together. In truth I neither liked nor disliked Mike Donahue. He was a coworker, a good soldier as far as I could tell. He spoke of being a father and I believe he was good at that, too. I knew him well enough to be confident volunteering to ride in his vehicle, not well enough to confide in him or ask much about his life back home.

So why was his death the casualty that affected me the most? I saw General Greene more often, admired him for his down-to-earth style, and was as shocked as anyone when he was shot and killed during a graduation of Afghan troops at a training academy. I knew Senior Chief Hockenberry much better than either of them, and, having talked with her earlier about things ranging from Navy life to her teenage son, I could vividly picture the lifelong impact of the serious gunshot injuries she sustained in that same incident. So why was the loss of this almost casual acquaintance the one my mind couldn't stop turning toward?

Perhaps it was the timing, the knowledge that the war took him just as I left it behind. Amid the drawdown, I left a few days earlier than originally planned. Otherwise I would have heard the explosion, so close to our quarters—assuming I was not out on a convoy myself. That must have been it: as different as he and I seemed, and as little as I really knew him, I could very much picture myself in his place. He drove vehicles around Kabul, just as I did. That day, he would have put on the same kind of body armor, waved goodbye to the same gate guard, signaled a turn onto the same road. So he died the way I probably would have, if I hadn't made it: the brutal luck of being chosen by an IED, never knowing who or what hit you.

Visiting the forest of white markers in the Afghanistan section at Arlington is not just for honoring the individuals lost there; it is a place to seek some reason why they should be under the headstones while the rest of us walk around on the grass. I was sorry about his loss. But my real purpose visiting his grave site and the others at Arlington is to confront the dictatorship of chance, which compounds the cruelty of loss by allocating it for no clear reason at all. To die taking a hill is one thing, but a soldier hit by an IED is basically the victim of an assassination. Like an assassin, the bomber is out to destroy a symbol, who happens to be a human being, without really knowing or caring about the most important qualities of his victim.

Looking back, I see no good reason that can be confected for why one person and not another should die at random on a routine mission. For a mind that can't come to rest around that question, the only way out is to construct a reason going forward. You resolve to build a life that is somehow worthy of emerging on the better side of luck's absurd equations, because you know that by definition your luck is something you don't deserve. Nothing that had happened during the deployment would justify the pattern by which I returned safely and some of the others did not, but I had the rest of my life to try to repay whatever debt I had incurred by coming back in one piece. It all might sound superstitious, but the search for justification was an inescapable imperative for me, and another element of propulsion for my work at home. Not that it would really be possible to ever feel like I had settled this account. But it was clear that I would have to work harder than ever to make myself useful, after these reminders of the precariousness of existence not just in war zones but in general. If this loss had happened while I was still deployed, it might have propelled me to try even harder, perhaps dangerously so, to make gains for my vanishing unit. But my war was over. If I wanted somehow to earn the luck that had brought me home safe from Afghanistan, I would have to do it from home, in South Bend.

I MAY GO MONTHS WITHOUT THINKING about the day I came home, then some event will bring it all back, like the Vietnam Welcome Home event at a smoky dive bar called Catch 22. Nestled between houses on a residential block on Fourth Street in Mishawaka, Catch 22 is a true neighborhood bar of the old school. Even though it's lunchtime, today I find it full to capacity, which means about thirty guests, taking every seat at the bar, the handful of high tops, and even the pool table, which has been covered for the occasion. Other than Mishawaka's mayor Dave Wood, and a couple staff members, a reporter, and me, just about everyone is between sixty and eighty years old, wearing a ball cap or some other clothing identifying him as a Vietnam veteran.

After Mayor Wood says a few words of appreciation, I give my little speech, something like this: "Four years ago today I landed in Afghanistan. And at the end of my tour, the reception couldn't have been better. At Baltimore Washington Airport, people lined up to shake our hands, waving flags. When I got home to South Bend, people were waiting with balloons and gave me hugs."

A little choked up, I continue to the point. "Many of you did not get that welcome home. And it's a shame. These days, as a society, we have learned how to separate how we feel about a policy from how we treat the men and women sent overseas to serve. That wasn't true for Vietnam veterans. . . . I'm sorry that not everyone got thanked properly. I'm sorry that this is coming late. But on behalf of the city of South Bend, I hope you'll forgive . . . that this message is coming late but maybe not too late: thank you. And welcome home."

Recognizing Vietnam Veterans Day has only begun in the last few years, but it quickly became another occasion for me to see how important a symbolic act can be. Some of the vets' eyes water. It's clear that to them the honor, however late in their lives, is meaningful. One of them tells me he was eighteen when he went, says he'll never forget the things he saw, but dwells on the ways in which he feels luckier than others who came back unable to move on. "They called me a baby-killer when I got back," he says, staring into the distance.

I try to picture what coming back from war was like in the 1960s and 1970s, without the benefit of email or Facebook or cell phones, your family perhaps not sure even what day to expect you until you could reach them from a pay phone on your way back. One vet describes a friend whose reunion with family happened at this very bar; he returned one afternoon, found his family's home empty, and knew that they must be at this tavern across the street.

BY THE TIME I WAS on my way home forty years later, Big Navy had learned some things about the art of preparing a service member to return. Somewhere in between Vietnam and now, the Pentagon had realized that the day after you leave a war zone is not the best time to reunite with your family. So we were given three days' interlude at a little base in rural Germany that amounted to a kind of no-frills resort. There was ample time for working out and sleep, and they even organized little trips into town. It almost felt like tourism, but the intent was to watch and help you respond as elements of normal life were gradually restored around you. As we wandered in small groups around the market square of a small city nearby, someone from the command was always on hand, to keep an eye on each little "first" of reintegration. They were normal things from home that we hadn't experienced in a while, things we might not be able to handle as easily as we expected. First walk through a crowd. First time in the presence of children. First drink.

The rest of the hours were for sessions on things like dealing with stress. As a mild-mannered captain led a session on psychological triggers, I sank into my seat at the mention of one I hadn't thought of: politics and politicians. "Remember as you go home that this is an election year. There's a lot of political advertising about war and military issues that we've found is a stressor, so you may want to steer clear of that."

Gradually, we dismantled our active-duty mind-sets and selves, and prepared mentally to return. At a folding table, I sat giving my disassembled M4 and M9 one last, exhaustive cleaning before yielding them immaculate back to Uncle Sam, along with the other gear, from Gore-Tex parkas to a gas mask. Most of the contents of the "three seabags of huah" I'd been issued in Norfolk went into various large bins and boxes to be reissued to the next person who comes along; pants, shirts, boots, and the like were mine to keep. Then, after our three-day sojourn, I was munching on ham and cheese sandwiches lovingly packed for us by the USO at Ramstein, and boarding a 747 for Baltimore.

Back at Norfolk, the focus shifted from our personal well-being to our physical and bureaucratic health. A flurry of paperwork saw to it that we were realigned with parent commands, registered for the VA, and clear of any number of physical ailments. Someone with a clipboard asked how many weeks of leave I was going to take; you were entitled to several, and urged to use them. But I couldn't be back in South Bend and not be mayor for long. I asked for the longest I figured I could get away with: one week.

At the airport in Detroit, waiting for the connection to South Bend, I realized that being in uniform among civilians is a bit like being an elected official among residents. Heads turn, a few people come to shake your hand, and others glance at you but then look away. I looked for a seat in a quiet corner of the gate, and then got to talking with a lady sitting next to me who was on her way to visit relatives. She didn't know me from Adam, and as we sat describing her relatives and my own time in the service, I felt for a moment like this might be the last normal conversation I would have for a while. Another passenger seated across from us looked up at me with a discreet, knowing smile as my new acquaintance asked, "So is South Bend home for you?"

South Bend's airport director had kindly arranged for my parents to come through security so that I could greet them before facing the crowd and the cameras. Mom held a rose, and she and Dad looked as relieved as you would expect. After a few hugs, and a few words, it was time to go out into the main concourse and start being mayor again.

It was about nine in the evening and I'd only been able to give a few hours' notice to my team, but a sizable crowd was waiting. One City Council member, who had opposed nearly every major initiative I had put forward, barreled past everyone else to embrace me in a bear hug as if I were a long-lost brother, small American flags poking out of his suit pockets. A bit more reservedly, other colleagues, friends, and strangers greeted me one by one. Mark Neal, who had stood in for me, was there, as was Kathryn Roos, who had run the office in my absence. There was Governor Kernan, Mrs. Chismar from Saint Joe High School, Father Brian from Saint James, and some young kids I'd never seen before who had made a welcome-home poster. And there were the TV cameras, of course.

I knew it was my job to give a little speech, and I had prepared in my head what to say—a thank-you to everyone who had helped run the city, to the community that had supported me, and to everyone who came to help welcome me back. I got as far as mentioning that not everyone would get to come home like this, or at all, and began to choke up, barely getting out the rest of what I had to say. I have no memory of the rest of the evening, except that Mom and Dad saw to it that I got home, and that a burger was waiting for me on the dining room table. I ate it as gratefully as I have any meal before or since.

MY STAFF HELD BACK for a few days while I unpacked my gear and reacquainted myself with my house, friends, and family. But the following Monday, it was time to get back to work. Each department had a list of updates and pending decisions.

Resuming the routine of TV appearances, meetings, emails, and decisions wasn't that hard, but regaining a civilian mentality took longer than I expected. I found myself speaking frequently with Brian Pawlowski, my deputy chief of staff and a Marine Iraq veteran, about how to make sure I was taking the residents' concerns as seriously as they did, even when everything seemed to have less urgency than what I was used to overseas.

One day soon after I returned, Kathryn came into the office with a worried expression to let me know there had been a bomb threat at the courthouse nearby. I walked over to the window and peered down at the courthouse complex, then turned and thanked her for the heads-up. "Good to know—but unless it's a huge bomb, we're probably outside the blast radius. It would have to be a five-hundred-pounder, which doesn't seem likely, so I wouldn't worry too much."

I nodded appreciatively and went back to my desk to resume working, while she gave a sidelong glance and retreated into the hall. A few minutes later, she knocked on the door again, probably after consulting Brian, to tactfully ask if I was thinking as a *civilian* when I was reacting. She wanted to see if evacuating the building might be appropriate, and I took the point; we agreed to check with the fire chief. (The threat turned out to be a false alarm.)

Getting into a car, I would sometimes pull so hard the door would fly open and bounce on its hinge, forgetting this was not the heavy, armored Land Cruiser door I was used to. And merging onto a high-way one day with my mother in the passenger seat, I caught myself just in time before barking, "CLEAR RIGHT?" to her, as I would to the gunny sergeant, to make sure we could safely proceed.

THE COMMUNITY WAS NOT JUST accommodating but effusive, too much for my comfort. Someone organized a welcome-home event at the Century Center complete with a visit by the South Bend Cubs mas-cot. I felt uneasy, especially when Joe Kernan, an actual war hero, came onstage to thank me for my service. I was proud to have served, but I was one of hundreds of thousands, most of whom had nothing like this kind of welcome. The only way to reconcile the treatment I was getting was to tell myself, and the audience, that I accepted their well-wishes on behalf of everyone else who had served, and those still out there.

There were exceptions to the kindness. One far-right blog ran a piece titled: "South Bend Welcomes Spook Mayor Back Home: What Have You Done For Us Lately, Pete?" The article said the public of South Bend "still hasn't figured out that the man they elected as mayor has likely been working for the CIA all along." A still nuttier individual showed up at a speech I was giving and demanded to know if I was prepared to admit that the CIA had introduced heroin to Afghanistan.

But there wasn't time for battling with conspiracy theorists, any more than there was time to wallow in some kind of patriotic glow. The rhythms of South Bend waited for no one, and it was time to get back to work. The budget was due for passage in a matter of days. There was just one year to go on the "1,000 houses in 1,000 days" effort. It was almost time to announce my plan to run for reelection. And, I had real-ized, it was time to get serious about sorting out my personal life.

16

Becoming One Person

If not for the deployment, I might never have found my way to Chasten. Before going overseas, I had felt comfortable being more than one person, as we all sometimes must, according to the roles we are called to play. I knew how to toggle between mayor mode, officer mode, friend mode, and so on. But something about exposure to danger impresses upon you that a life is not only fragile but single, with one beginning and one end. It heightens the desire for your life to make sense as a whole, not just from certain angles. And with this comes renewed pressure for internal contradictions to be resolved, one way or another. For me, that meant sudden urgency around a question that had lingered unanswered for all of adulthood: how to reconcile my professional life with the fact that I am gay.

In the years after I had figured this fact out for myself, but before I was ready to be open about it, dating seemed completely off the table. Even if I had sought to have a romantic life before coming out, I'm not sure I could have figured out how to pull it off. My friends and peers were all busy dating, coupling, marrying. But sitting out never felt like a huge sacrifice to me, because keeping up with my studies and work was consuming all the energy I had, especially once I was elected; the city was a jealous bride.

But that effect started to wear off as I got older. I had always wanted to have a family, and crossing into my thirties made clear that the vague and distant future in which I expected that to happen couldn't remain vague and distant forever. If I really wanted a family, sooner or later I would need to take some actual steps in that direction. The problem was that there is no way to raise a child—or in my case, go on a date in your own city—unless you are prepared to live openly.

Steadily, with each close friend's wedding or emailed baby news, the force of this simple truth gained ground against my awareness of the professional peril holding me back. But that peril was real. My military career was theoretically safe, now that the "Don't Ask, Don't Tell" policy had been repealed. I no longer stood to lose my commission as an officer merely for living openly. But what about my civilian job? South Bend had an ordinance forbidding discrimination on the basis of sexual orientation—I myself had signed it into law in 2012 after it passed in our council—but it was not exactly applicable in my case. As an elected official, your boss is the people of the city. If the people fire you for being gay, it might be discrimination, but it's not like you can sue them. I was also not eager to become a poster child for LGBT issues; I had strongly supported these causes from the beginning, but did not want to be defined by them.

So I might have kept dragging my feet through my thirties, too, if it hadn't been for the deployment. But preparing the letter on my last day before leaving home, sealing it in an envelope marked "just in case" and setting it gently in the desk drawer, had required as much of me as the hardest day of training. It forced me to think about the cohesion, or lack thereof, in my life. I had packed my bags reflecting on the possibility that I might get killed in action, thirty-two years old, single for basically all my adult life. From then on it was obvious that if I did come home all right, I needed to come out so I could get on with some kind of personal life. After I safely returned, it was simply a matter of when.

BEFORE EXPLAINING IT TO THE WORLD, I had to explain it to some people in my life. For every important step you take, certainly in politics but in life more generally, there is a "do not surprise" list. In my case, the top of the list was Mom and Dad. I felt they would be supportive, but for some reason I had not found the courage to include them in the tiny number of friends I had told. And so, at my parents' dinner table one Sunday evening in January of 2015, I found myself, a grown man and the mayor of a sizable city, sweating through my palms and pushing remnants of ice cream around with a spoon while working up the will to change the subject of conversation from an upcoming council meeting to the fact that their son, their only child, was attracted to men.

"I wanted to tell you something," I finally managed to begin.

"Okay," Dad said, both of them subtly and quietly bracing. Announcements, of any kind, are not typical at this dinner table.

Then, after a short preamble consisting of what I'm sure were a few convoluted sentences about moving ahead in life and being transparent with those around me, I made my way to the phrase that had to be said out loud: I'm gay.

They weren't terribly surprised. I hadn't brought a girlfriend home in more than a decade, and I think they understood what to make of my not mentioning any kind of romantic life in the years since. The close friends I had told included some who were surprised, some who were not, and some who had assumed as time went by that I was more or less asexual. But simply by virtue of being my parents, they probably understood all this long before I did. Both made it clear it didn't change anything in our relationship as a family.

If any disappointment surfaced at the table that night, it came after Mom looked at me, with a little light in her eyes, and asked, "Is there someone?" Only after answering no, and seeing the light fade a little, did I realize that the tone of her question had been one of hope. As moms go, she had been pretty sparing with any pressure to produce grandchildren, but I still knew that nothing would bring more joy to her life. Her hopeful question, and my disappointing answer, made for one more reason that I had to figure out a way to go public, so I could begin adding this dimension to my life. No, there wasn't someone at the moment. But I wished there were, and if I could figure out the process of coming out publicly, then one day there would be.

SOMEDAY, POLITICIANS WON'T HAVE TO come out as gay any more than one "comes out" as straight. Someone like me would just show up at a social function with a date who was of the same sex, and everyone would figure it out and shrug. Maybe it's already getting to be like that, in some coastal cities. But not in Indiana, especially not after the "Religious Freedom" debacle exploded that same spring of 2015. The very season when I was asking friends for advice on how to approach coming out publicly was the spring in which my state became nationally infamous for one of the most visible backward lurches on LGBT equality. Coming out was supposed to be a personal hurdle for me to clear, not a political statement, but doing so now meant it would be even more freighted with the complications of being openly gay in Mike Pence's Indiana.

It became obvious that no matter how I did it, disclosing this very private aspect of my life would be viewed by strangers through a political lens. And the closer I came to feeling ready, having told most of my close friends and alerted my campaign staff, the more it became not just a political question but a practical one. How, exactly, was I supposed to do this? The whole idea of having to come out irritated me—why should it be anyone's business?—but I knew that in the current atmosphere, just casually mentioning it somewhere, or being seen out with a male date, would set off weeks or months of confusion, speculation, and clarification. What I needed to do was get this out there: simply, publicly, and clearly.

The churn of life in office doesn't lend itself to reflection and preparation for important life decisions, but here again the military played a helpful role, in the form of a forced change of scene. Still in the Reserve, I owed the Navy two weeks a year of active duty for training, and in June I was to go to the Defense Intelligence Agency Headquarters in Washington for a course on military intelligence. Strange as it sounds, this stint of military duty was almost like a vacation. I would be expected to work just forty hours a week, a positively relaxing tempo compared to my schedule as a full-time mayor running for reelection. It was a kind of political Sabbath. There was time to work out, eat properly, catch up with old friends over dinner, and get a good night's sleep. My phone would not be going off constantly in my pocket; it wasn't even allowed inside the secure area. And no one, besides the occasional acquaintance I might run into from my Afghanistan days, would recognize me as anything but the rather nondescript Lieutenant Buttigieg. For someone living the frenzied life of a visible elected official, the precincts of Joint Base Anacostia-Bolling, better known as JBAB, might as well be a Swiss resort.

I reported Monday morning to DIA headquarters at JBAB, collected an ID badge, and walked in past the Scud missile on display at the entrance and through the large, daylit atrium toward the core of the enormous building. Looking for a cup of coffee, I walked a long hall wearing my khaki uniform as hundreds of civilians and other uniformed members came and went. I glanced down at the insignia on my chest, conscious that the wartime deployment had added to my military résumé, more or less readable by scanning the color code of ribbons and insignia on an officer's breast. On my right was a wall with framed pictures of the officials comprising our chain of command—President Obama, of course, and Secretary Carter. There was the photo of the director, General Stewart (his predecessor, General Flynn, had been forced out the previous year), and a succession of other generals, colonels, and other assorted senior officers. All this was par for the course at a large military installation, but when I got to the area with the coffee shop, barber, and path to the cafeteria, I was greeted by an unexpected display. It was Pride month, and a wall had been put up with colored stickers in a rainbow configuration. People were invited to write a message about how they supported their diverse DIA coworkers and stick it to the wall. Nearby, a poster advertised a speaker series on LGBT workplace issues.

Years earlier, when I'd first come out to a close college friend, he had patted me on the shoulder and teased: "Well, you didn't make it easy on yourself." Between being an Indiana elected official and a military officer, it was hard to tell which side of my professional existence was going to be less LGBT-friendly. But just a few years later, it was clear that the world was at least starting to change. After all, a bipartisan coalition had beaten back RFRA in Indiana. And the military had gone from firing any service member who tried to come out, to actively welcoming its "out" members. There was even hope that the Supreme Court would extend marriage equality across the land later that year. Neither Indiana nor the uniformed services were going to be on the cutting edge of social change, but, as I looked at this rainbow-colored exhibit in, of all places, the halls of the DIA, it now seemed being open about my sexual orientation might not be the career death sentence it had been less than five years earlier.

I had concluded that the simplest way to disclose this to my community was in writing, so during downtime in Washington I began taking notes for a short piece for the *South Bend Tribune*. I returned home and continued rewriting it over and over again, asking some friends to look over the drafts, until I felt I had gotten down what I wanted to say most. Still believing that "coming out" should someday be a non-event,

I titled it "Why Coming Out Matters, and Why It Shouldn't Have To," but the paper's editors shortened the headline to only the first half.

I asserted that sexual orientation doesn't define someone, and should be accepted simply as part of who we are. "Being gay has had no bearing on my job performance in business, in the military, or in my current role as mayor," I wrote. "It makes me no better or worse at handling a spreadsheet, a rifle, a committee meeting, or a hiring decision. I hope that residents will continue to judge me based on my effectiveness in serving our city—things like the condition of our neighborhoods, our economy, and our city services."

The question I couldn't answer for sure was: Would they?

THE ARTICLE WAS TO GO LIVE at six in the morning on June 16, and for once, I slept poorly. At dawn I was lifting barbells at the weight rack in my basement when text messages started lighting up my phone, coming in from friends, not so much in order of how close we were, as in order of how early they got up. I headed downtown as usual, where my first public event happened to be an outdoor pancake breakfast kicking off Bike to Work Week. South Bend's full complement of TV reporters appeared, asking all kinds of questions about why I had come out when I did.

Was there someone I had met?

Was something damaging about to be revealed by political opponents?

Was I trying to make some kind of statement?

So much for the pancakes. I knew these reporters well, and the aggressive questions threw me off at first. One looked hungry for a scoop as he pressed me; another seemed half-hearted, almost embarrassed that his editors had instructed him to get this personal, while his cameraman looked at me with eyes that said, "Hey, man, just doing my job." I told them that what I had to say was in the article, and returned to the importance of biking to work.

A couple hours later I was at a grand opening for a soup kitchen. More reporters, more questions—and not about the soup kitchen. I referred them to the article and repeatedly steered back to the issues of poverty and hunger that were impacting our city. Eventually they got the idea.

Around the community, people reacted in different ways. Inevitably, some of it was ugly—local TV stations covered a press conference by a newly invented group calling itself the South Bend Leadership Coalition, led by a fringe-right-wing activist who happened to live on my block. "The mayor's announcement has created a crisis that goes to the heart of our political system," their statement said. They went on to insist that this was a matter of grave political importance:

> Is homosexuality now a consideration in hiring or in the granting of government contracts? Is support for the homosexual agenda now a requirement for employment or for the receiving of government contacts [sic]? Do homosexuals get favorable treatment when they apply for jobs or government contracts? Are other members of the Buttigieg administration homosexuals? If so, would they be willing to share this information with the public and explain whether this affects their ability to function as civil servants?

There was little point in responding; either I was good at my job as mayor, or I was not. And if someone thought I was sitting around handpicking recipients of routine government contracts at all—let alone doing so based on sexual orientation—then it was unlikely that they understood our administration enough to judge it on its merits anyway.

But things like this were the exception; the vast majority of the reaction fell into two categories: those who wanted me to know they were supportive, and those who wanted me to know they didn't care. Both sets of responses were welcome. The comments from people who were impacted were certainly touching. I had not done this out of any desire to make a statement or bring about a public result, but the hundreds, maybe thousands, of emails coming into the city inbox made clear that my coming out had made it easier for at least some others. One young man from conservative Marshall County wrote of his family, "Their Christian beliefs tell them I'm living in sin and need rescued of my 'wayward lifestyle.' But having men and women like you serving the public makes it much easier for families like mine to accept their own sons and daughters." People I had served with overseas got in touch—one who had volunteered with me on a risky convoy wrote to share that he was gay as well—many to express support, and others just to say hello, to ask how I was doing, with no mention of the article at all.

A couple weeks after coming out, I returned from a few days away for a conference and went to see my neighbor, Kathy, who had been picking up my newspapers and mail. She and Irv had retired from running a small business out of the home, and had lived next door for decades; I assumed they were politically conservative, but we usually talked about neighborhood stuff, not politics. I asked her how things were going, and saw tears welling in her eyes.

"Did your mother tell you what happened?"

No, I said, I hadn't checked in with her. What was the matter?

She noticed I hadn't been getting my paper. No irregularity in our neighborhood gets past Kathy, and by the third day she figured out that the paper carrier was skipping my house. So she confronted the delivery guy, and asked him why I wasn't getting my *Tribune*. He said something about not wanting to give a newspaper to "one of those."

Wrong answer. "Has he done anything to you?" she demanded.

"No," he admitted.

I didn't catch all the details of how she proceeded to let him have it. But by the time I had gotten home, the paper was arriving faithfully every day.

In my view, the biggest thing to turn the tide on LGBT issues wasn't theological or political evolution. It was the discovery that many people whom we already know turn out to be part of this category. The biggest obstacle wasn't religion, or hatred. It was the simple fact that so many people believed, wrongly, that they didn't even know anyone who was gay. At my high school in the late 1990s, I didn't know of a single gay student.

It is easier to be cruel, or unfair, to people in groups and in the abstract; harder to do so toward a specific person in your midst, especially if you know them already. Gays have the benefit of being a minority whose membership is not necessarily obvious when you meet one (or love one). Common decency can kick in before there is time for prejudice to intervene. Of course, humans can be cruel to people we know, too, but not as often—and we're rarely as proud of it.

In the struggle for equality, we do well to remember that all people want to be known as decent, respectful, and kind. If our first response toward anyone who struggles to get onto the right side of history is to denounce him as a bigot, we will force him into a defensive crouch—or into the arms of the extreme right. When a conservative socialite of a certain age would stop me on the street with a mischievous look, pat my arm, and say conspiratorially, "I met your *friend* the other day, and he is fabulous," it was not the time for a lecture on the distinction between a partner and a "friend." She is on her way to acceptance, and she feels good about her way of getting there; it feels better to grow on your own terms than to be painted into a corner.

STILL, WE HAD NO REAL WAY of knowing in advance how coming out would affect the reelection that year. I had handily won the primary, the city was widely viewed as being on the right track, and my Republican opponent lacked a strong organization. But it was difficult to gauge whether voters would view me any differently now, as summer gave way to fall and November approached. Nor was it clear how much my popularity had been impacted by the many tough decisions of my four years in office. I still believed, as I had commented to Mike Schmuhl on election night back in 2011, that I could never be as popular as I was that night, because every difficult decision had to cost us at least a few votes.

One source of concern was an ongoing controversy over the police department, known around South Bend as the "tapes case." It became an issue in early 2012, just a few months after I took office, when I relieved our police chief of his command in response to a federal investigation, though its roots went back to before I had even taken office.

Police issues had not been a major theme of the campaign in 2011, but it was clear by the time I first took office that the department needed attention. Rumors swirled of favoritism, opportunism, and cliquishness within the police force. There was little evidence of a real promotion system or documented officer evaluations, which meant that career advancement hadn't fully outgrown the sixties-era norm in which your standing depended on popularity and political relationships. The place would need an overhaul, sooner or later.

But reforming the police department would be a major task, requiring new leadership, sustained attention, and political capital. In addition, while there were clearly management issues at the department, the current chief was well liked in the community. As the first African-American chief in our city's history, he had been uniquely able to build confidence between communities of color and the department as a whole, and his track record of youth mentorship programs and other community work had paid dividends for the department's vital neighborhood relationships. So, after interviewing him and two competitors for the job, I decided during the transition phase that I would reappoint him, and save major police department reforms for a future year.

It turned out to be my first serious mistake as mayor.

Somewhere during that transition phase, in the months before I took office, the internal politics of the department had boiled over. The chief, believing that some other officers were gunning for his job, allegedly confronted them with tape recordings that could embarrass them if disclosed. He had access to these tapes because some phone lines in the department were connected to recording equipment used for interviews and investigations, and the officers had been recorded on that equipment without their knowledge. As court filings would later document, the chief threatened to take action against at least one officer he had come to consider disloyal. Perhaps the chief didn't realize that I was already leaning toward reappointing him; or perhaps it just seemed like an insurance policy.

Enter the Federal Wiretap Act—a set of very strict federal laws about recording other people without their knowledge. In fact, making such recordings or disclosing their content can be a felony, punishable by prison time as well as fines. There are state laws, too, against recording a conversation without the knowledge of either party, absent a warrant or other legal clearance. The recorded officers knew it, and complained to federal authorities, who took the issue seriously. So that's how it came to be that, a few weeks into the job of mayor, I learned that my newly reappointed police chief was being investigated by the FBI. Eventually a message came through, thinly veiled but quite clear, from federal prosecutors: the people responsible for the covert recordings needed to go, or charges might be filed.

Why did they send me that signal, instead of just acting on their own? Was the intent to do me a favor, giving me a shot at resolving this quietly and helping my young administration without getting bogged down in the scandal of indictments just a few weeks after we got started? Maybe. Or perhaps they just understood the politics of all this before I did. Why should a U.S. attorney shoulder the responsibility of taking down a beloved African-American police chief, if he can get the mayor to do it for him by removing him from his position? Justice would be served and compliance would be established, while charges and a messy trial could be avoided.

In any case, whatever had led to this point, the choice now lay at my feet. I sat at the end of the conference table in my office, and contemplated which scenario was more likely to tear the community apart—a well-liked African-American police chief potentially being indicted over compliance with a very technical federal law, or me removing him for allowing things to reach this point? There was no good option: the community would erupt either way.

Maybe the chief would step down on his own, I thought. I called him. (Another mistake; things like this should be done in person. Since that day, I've never removed a direct report without sitting down with him or her for a face-to-face discussion, however painful and awkward.) After I explained the situation and my view of it, he did offer his resignation, and I accepted it.

The reaction was instant and fierce. Community activists demanded to know more details about what had happened, but I was worried that going into too much detail would get us sued. (Eventually I did go into more detail publicly, and a lawsuit quickly followed, teaching me another important lesson.) By the next day, he had changed his mind and withdrew his resignation. Allies in the community, including many African-American leaders whose support and respect I had counted on before, had convinced him to change his mind—and now wanted me to change mine.

But the status quo was not an option. Even leaving aside that I believed removing him was the best way to avoid him facing potential legal action, I had lost confidence in the leadership of a chief who had not come to me the moment he realized he was the target of an FBI investigation. The hiring and firing of officers in our city is ultimately up to a civilian Board of Public Safety, but the mayor decides who ascends to senior rank. Acting on that authority, I demoted him from the position of chief to that of captain.

Then something happened that I did not see coming. Local press began reporting on rumors that the tapes contained evidence of officers using racist language to describe the former chief. (All of the five officers known to have been recorded were white.) The content of the tapes had not come up when I was talking with staff or with the chief about the issue. If true, this was explosive, and serious. The credibility and legitimacy of our police department depended heavily on the expectation that officers did their job with no racial animus. And since so many of the worst race-based abuses in modern American history happened at the hands of law enforcement, policing was the most sensitive part of the entire administration when it came to demonstrating that we acted without bias.

Infuriatingly, I had no way of finding out if this was actually true. The entire crisis was the result of the fact that the recordings were allegedly made in violation of the law. Under the Federal Wiretap Act, this meant that it could be a felony not just to make the recordings, but to reproduce and disclose them. Like everyone else in the community, I wanted to know what was on these recordings. But it was potentially illegal for me to find out, and it was not clear I could even ask, without fear of legal repercussions. As of this writing, I have not heard the recordings, and I still don't know if I, and the public, ever will.

Overwhelming pressure mounted for me to disclose the recordings, especially from the African-American community. Protesters picketed my first State of the City address. A group calling itself Citizens United for Better Government formed and appeared in public meetings with custom-made T-shirts reading RELEASE THE TAPES.

I invited a number of the most prominent community and faith leaders to meet in my living room, so that I could explain the legal constraints I was under. They viewed my protestations skeptically, as did the *Tribune*, but legally I was stuck unless a court gave me room for maneuver.

The story dominated media coverage of my administration for most of our first year, and affected my relationship with the African-American community in particular for years to come. A legal drama ensued, with the council suing the administration to release the tapes, while the officers sued the city over the fact that the tapes had been made in the first place. The technicalities became dizzying, with one branch of the city government suing another; some parts of the case are still in litigation years later as we look to the courts to answer the basic question of whether I can lawfully authorize the recordings to be released.

The most important lessons of this painful episode were not about the finer points of federal wiretapping laws, but about the deeply fraught relationship between law enforcement and communities of color. This issue, previously an abstraction for me, was now hitting home. Ferguson and everything that followed in the Black Lives Matter movement came after the tapes controversy exploded locally, but their urgency grew from the same root: the fact that many of the worst historical injustices visited upon black citizens of our country came at the hands of local law enforcement. Like an original sin, this basic fact burdens every police officer, no matter how good, and every neighborhood of color, no matter how safe, to this day. To the many people in the community who rose up to demand that the tapes be released, this wasn't a question of whether I was right or wrong in fearing that doing so would violate state and federal wiretap laws. It was about their belief that not everyone in the community could trust the men and women sworn to protect them. Like so many police officers and Americans of color dealing with the long reach of such past wrongs—and the present-day wrongs that flow from their legacy—I found myself answering not only for myself but for history.

ANOTHER CHALLENGE IN the reelection campaign would be the mixed popularity of my approach to our streets downtown. While this entailed far less moral anguish than the police tapes situation, it was in the headlines just as often, and led to even more critical letters to the editor and challenging conversations. Even many of my supporters weren't so sure of my approach, stopping me at the Farmer's Market or the sidelines of an event to say, "I love what you're doing with the city . . . except for your 'Smart Streets.'"

Unlike our famous smart sewers, the program I had decided to call "Smart Streets" had little to do with sensor technology. It was about the hope of a better downtown, and the role of street design in making it happen.

I had gotten a crash course in urban planning after becoming mayor—both literally, in the form of a seminar organized by the National Architecture Foundation and the Conference of Mayors, and figuratively, in meetings and meals with members of my administration trained in architecture and New Urbanism. All of them seemed to agree that our city's downtown was nothing less than a tragedy of misguided "urban renewal."

Old photos corroborated the memories of people like Bob Urbanski, showing people crisscrossing busy downtown streets full of shops, theaters, and hotels. But by the time I took office, downtown streets were about one thing: cars. The two main north-south roads in town had been converted, decades earlier, into a pair of four-lane, one-way streets that shunted traffic as quickly as possible through—and out of—downtown. The result was a quick commute through the heart of the city, but also a central business district that felt hostile to pedestrians. Going between my office and a restaurant a couple blocks away felt like walking alongside a highway, which is technically exactly what it was. The roads functioned to evacuate the very area I was trying to fill in.

Other cities, from West Palm Beach to Louisville, had begun reversing this sixties-style road design, restoring two-way patterns to slow traffic a little and encourage more of a pedestrian- and bike-friendly downtown. The idea seemed radical to many, since it often involved actually reducing the carrying capacity of roads. Growing up, I had only ever heard of roads being widened; now my planners were speaking of "road diets," a concept that I knew immediately would be difficult to sell.

The plan also required us to install roundabouts, in order to properly distribute traffic through the redesigned road network. These were particularly controversial among residents who refused to believe that drivers could learn to use them, or that trucks and snowplows could fit through them (even though, obviously, we had checked).

Still, to me it was clearly the right way forward. And after over a year of refinement, dozens of public meetings, and a series of council votes to approve the vision and arrange the funding, it was set to become a reality. It also quickly became a campaign issue. Kelly Jones, my Republican opponent, made opposing it a central part of her campaign. One op-ed writer in the *Tribune* predicted that it would "kill any prospect of true revitalization and future growth above the ground floor." A man-on-the-street interview for a TV station yielded this plainer assessment: "I think the roundabouts are stupid." And in a debate, Jones sarcastically invoked my policy of public downtown Wi-Fi access as she predicted such long traffic jams that people would turn to in-drive entertainment. "I'm glad we'll have Wi-Fi, so those people stuck in traffic will have something to do."

I was convinced that the community would eventually embrace the vision once they could see the results—an improved downtown and more business investment. Indeed, now that the project is complete, the result has been an estimated $90 million in new investment that has come to downtown from businesses saying the street projects were a major factor in their decision. Traffic, meanwhile, has only slowed by a minute or two in most cases. But during the 2015 reelection campaign, most of the improvements hadn't been completed, and people couldn't yet see the results. This, too, would cost some votes—but how many?

FORTUNATELY, EVEN FOR A VOTER who disagreed with my decisions in the police matter and was skeptical of the plan for roundabouts and two-way streets, there was no denying the city's accelerating transformation. Unemployment had been cut in half, and had gone from well above the national average to within one point of the U.S. rate. Meanwhile, census estimates showed population levels increasing after a decade of contraction.

Experience corroborated the numbers. The twenty-five-story Chase Tower, the tallest building in our city, had gone vacant after a bankruptcy and receivership, its condition deteriorating so quickly that I had asked staff to estimate the cost of blowing it up. Now a buyer had emerged and was investing over $30 million to restore the building and open a new hotel there. Another problem property, the eerily empty former College Football Hall of Fame, also saw a buyer emerge and build a hotel on adjacent land, mentioning that our streetscape plan had helped motivate them to invest. A new owner had acquired the South Bend Cubs and invested millions to enhance our baseball stadium. Customers were dining on sushi in what had been a vacant former chicken wing restaurant downtown, while in one of our lowest-income neighborhoods, newly built co-op housing was emerging on formerly vacant lots in the wake of our "1,000 houses in 1,000 days" effort.

No less promising was the activity around the industrial area that formerly hosted decaying Studebaker buildings, largely thanks to industries that had not existed when cars were being manufactured there. On a grassy expanse so serene that it was almost impossible to imagine the decade of work it had taken Mayor Luecke's administration just to remove the collapsing factories that once covered it, a sleek new building had now been built for a data-hosting and analytics company first incubated on the campus of Notre Dame. It would soon receive a neighbor, in the form of a high-tech laboratory for turbomachinery research, drawing top aerospace companies to the area. Meanwhile, another data-center entrepreneur had purchased the eight-hundred-thousand-square-foot main assembly building of Studebaker—a six-story brick mass extending a fifth of a mile, long quiet but almost too stout even to demolish—and was proposing to create a mixed-use technology center in what had been literally the biggest physical symbol of our city's decline.

Progress was palpable. Especially after the city's 150th anniversary celebrations that spring of 2015, I could say with a straight face that our city was experiencing not just a comeback but something akin to a miracle.

WOULD VOTERS AGREE? If applause at the debate and general sentiment among people I ran into were anything to go by, I was in good shape when the sun came up on November 3. I knew what it felt like to go into a losing battle and a winning one, and this felt like the latter. But what if I had misjudged my popularity? It seemed at least possible that voters might say one thing out loud but feel another when it came to my sexual orientation, my handling of a sensitive issue, or even my leave of absence for military duty. We would only truly know when the results came in.

Huddled with a few key staff and loved ones in a small room off to the side of my office, home to the only working television set on the top floor, I fiddled with the antenna as the signal cut in and out, watching the local news. When the numbers finally did appear, they disproved what I had said to Mike that first election night: we won with 80 percent of the vote. It didn't only vindicate the work we had done over those four years; it showed that I would be judged based on that work alone. Our socially conservative community had either moved forward in its acceptance of minority sexual orientations, or decided it didn't care. Either way, I had a mandate to continue our work, and a deep sense of acceptance in the community.

Of all the speeches I've given, the short one I offered in the West Side Democratic Club that night was perhaps the most heartfelt yet:

Four years ago, I turned up as a political unknown, a rookie proposing a fresh start. And when I showed up asking for that fresh start, you gave me an opportunity to, you endorsed me as a leader and you supported me as a friend. A year ago when it came time for me to step away from the job and the home that I love to go overseas and take up arms under the colors of our nation you supported me as a brother. Earlier this year when I was at the most vulnerable moment in my public and private life, you embraced me as a son. The City of South Bend means the world to me. I love South Bend.

Analytical by nature, I surprised even myself with the emotional tenor of my words to the crowd that night. But I was moved by the support at the polls, which felt not only like a mandate for my administration's work, but also an affirmation of my relationship with the city that had produced me, welcomed me home, and accepted my sometimes novel way of doing business. A close observer might also have detected an additional influence on my tone and words that night. Most would see only the effusiveness you'd expect in a candidate relishing an overwhelming electoral margin. But those who knew me best would recognize something new in my countenance that night—the proverbial glow of a young man in love.

17

Becoming Whole

If you saw Chasten next to me at a restaurant or a party, with his tortoiseshell round glasses and gingham shirt with rolled-up sleeves tucked into a pair of jeans, you might assume he was in politics, too, or a young lawyer, perhaps. You might guess that he and I met at Harvard, or that he was finishing up his doctorate at Notre Dame. You wouldn't realize, at first, that you were seeing an avatar of Middle America and of the challenges of millennial life. You wouldn't know that you were looking at a 4-H boy turned theater kid, a small-town product who found his way alone to Germany as an exchange student, or that he was the first in his family to complete college and move on to cannily survive alone in a big city, a graduate student with top grades whose teenage years had included a period of homelessness in Michigan. I hadn't seen any of that, either; I just saw a nice-looking guy on an app, and wanted to meet the man behind the big smile and blue eyes in the photo of him by the lakeshore. So I tapped the box on the right.

Chasten (pronounced to rhyme with "fast in") was living at the time in Chicago, pushing through coursework for a master's in education at DePaul and paying his way by working as a substitute teacher in Chicago public schools, sometimes crashing on a friend's couch while letting out his apartment on Airbnb for extra income. I was a mayor, newly out of the closet and ready, at long last, to start dating, prepared that summer of 2015 to begin to experience the thrills and setbacks that most of my friends had gone through fifteen years earlier.

I had come out of the closet in order to make it possible, at last, to create a meaningful personal life. I was already well into my thirties, and hoping, as I've described, to have a family someday. The politics were what they were. Now that I didn't have to worry about being spotted or outed, it was time to start dating. But how? How is a gay mayor—or any mayor—supposed to go about getting a date?

The closer to home I looked, the harder it seemed. It could be an ethical minefield; a mayor in his own city can certainly get his calls returned, but there's also the risk that someone will completely misunderstand why you're inviting them to meet for a coffee at Chicory Café or a pint at Fiddler's Hearth. Farther afield, friends from college were willing and eager to introduce me to people they knew. But most of the eligible guys in question lived in New York or Washington. To most of them, I was lost in the expanse of "flyover country," probably even more remote than if I were overseas. Since I wasn't moving anytime soon, I was going to have to think closer to home.

But when it came to South Bend, it wasn't even clear where to look. I thought of the countless local doctors and business leaders of my parents' generation who had seemed intent over the years on fixing me up with their bright and lovely daughters. Where were these would-be matchmakers now, and how was it that not one of them had a son or nephew that they wanted me to meet? My city had never felt so small.

In the military, sometimes they talk about "training age" to describe the difference between longevity and experience. For example, if you are a forty-year-old major trained in field artillery and then switch to intelligence, you might have the same training age as a private first-class twenty years your junior when it came to a specific skill like cryptography.

That's how I felt about dating and romance: I was in my thirties, but my training age, so to speak, was practically zero. On my thirty-third birthday, I was starting my fourth year as the mayor of a sizable city. I had served in a foreign war and dined with senators and governors. I had seen Red Square and the Great Pyramids of Giza, knew how to order a sandwich in seven languages, and was the owner of a large historic home on the St. Joseph River. But I had absolutely no idea what it was like to be in love.

I'M FAR FROM THE FIRST PERSON to find himself in that kind of strange and embarrassing position—years in the closet have done that to millions of people—but my situation was still more unusual. In fact, it was unique: the scenario of a thirty-something mayor, single, gay, interested in a long-term relationship, and looking for a date in Indiana must have been a first. Luckily, for this twenty-first-century problem, my generation had invented a ready solution: a proliferation of websites and apps promised to connect me to datable guys within any radius I chose.

I was young enough to try it, but also just old enough to consider it newfangled and a little risky. I wasn't immune to a previous generation's stigma when it comes to online dating. But I was living through the tipping point when it was becoming clear that many, perhaps most, new long-term relationships and even marriages had begun online. So I logged on. Now came another set of puzzles. What do you put down for "occupation"? What do you do if the best photos you have of yourself depict you in a suit with people standing around clapping? The pictures on my phone all looked great for politics, terrible for dating. Ribbon cuttings. Groundbreakings. Graduation speeches. Do you hide that you're a politician? Maybe, but you need to tell someone your name in order to date them. Then what? People have Google, and they're not stupid. Coming out as gay had been a hard thing to do in the political world; coming out as a politician in the online dating world was even more perplexing.

Confronted with the puzzle of how to describe my day job, I went for a middle ground—not to conceal that I was an elected official, but not to lead with it, either. Friends helped me pick out the right photos for a profile—most of them doing something social and looking casual, but one giving a speech, an obligatory one from a beach, and, of course, one in uniform. (Anyone who claims to be above using military service for dating purposes is lying.) I looked mostly for people in Chicago, near enough to drive but far enough to be outside the viewing area of our TV stations, where most people had never heard of me. After setting up accounts one by one on websites and apps like OkCupid and Match.com, I started matching with people. A few chats led nowhere, then I found some guys who actually seemed promising, and started arranging dates.

On that August weekend when some algorithm served Chasten and me up to each other, I had more time than usual to spend on my phone. I'd just been through surgery to address a hernia that had probably resulted from my deployment-inspired weight-lifting regimen. So I was spending a lot of time on the couch with an ice pack, binge-watching *Game of Thrones* and checking for updates, when Chasten and I started chatting through an app called Hinge. This app talks to your Facebook profile and is supposed to introduce you to people with mutual friends, though in our case it didn't reveal any common acquaintances but just vaguely said, "connected through your social network."

It started with the usual small talk, something about weekend plans and watching TV, but it became clear to me that he had a quicker wit than most. Our first conversation is lost to the recesses of the deep web now, impossible for either of us to retrieve, but I remember being intrigued, then wanting to meet him in person. It helped that he neither dwelt on my position nor pretended not to notice it. A FaceTime conversation followed—his idea—another nice modern convenience that previous generations might have appreciated, to get a feel for whether you were about to go out with a jerk or an ax murderer. Each of us must have passed that test: we decided to meet up.

Other than the same-sex aspect, our first date was something our parents could have recognized as typical, almost vintage. He rented a car to drive in from Chicago for what was supposed to be a coffee but, thanks to slow eastbound traffic, turned into a beer at Fiddler's Hearth, our downtown Irish pub. I talked about South Bend, he talked about his family and his experiences in the classroom. In my pocket were two tickets to that night's baseball game, in case the date was going well, which it was. After some pub food, I proposed that we walk down to the ballpark to see our own South Bend Cubs take on the Great Lakes Loons. Somewhere around the sixth inning, we ditched the game to take a long walk along the river, through downtown, and over to the churning and multicolored River Lights display that I had just inaugurated a few months earlier at the climax of the SB150 celebrations.

Crossing back toward downtown along the railing of the Colfax Avenue Bridge, I felt the slight brushing of his hand coming closer to mine, and I took hold of it. Nothing in my life, from shaking hands with a president to experiencing my first rocket attack, matched the thrill of holding Chasten's hand for the first time. I was electrified. We got back to the car just as the post-game fireworks began, and as the explosions and lit colors unfolded over us, he went in for a kiss. We began to see each other every weekend, and it only took a few weeks for me to acknowledge the obvious: I was in love.

BEING A SOCIALLY AWARE YOUNG PERSON, Chasten follows and cares about politics, but his background was not political at all. His parents, who have a mom-and-pop landscaping business in Traverse

City, have voted for candidates from both parties but rarely discuss politics at home. Unlike mine, his political awareness came not as a dinner-table inheritance but as a response to how his world was shaped by the attitudes and decisions of those in power.

As I saw in those first photos online, he has two tattoos. On the back of his right calf is a black infinity symbol, which he got to honor his mother, Sherri, after she was diagnosed with cancer. On his left tricep is a rectangular tattoo that resembles the flag of a country, red, green, and blue—it's one of the first things I noticed in that first picture of him that showed up on my phone, smiling brightly someplace overlooking Lake Michigan. Actually it is not a flag, but the logo of Jif brand peanut butter, in honor of his father, Terry, who lived out of a car for much of his younger years and went on to build a stable middle-class life, home, and business. For Terry, Jif had once been a luxury; having it on hand in the cupboard was the measure of a decent life-style. Terry would repeatedly promise to his three boys that no matter what, he would see to it that they would have Jif on the shelves. If one thing was immediately obvious about Chasten, it was his loyalty when it came to family; in addition to the tattoos he wore a ring that, he explained, was one of a set of three he had purchased, one for each of the Glezman brothers.

Sometimes supplementing his wages with food stamps, Chasten worked his way through community college in Michigan and, later, the University of Wisconsin at Eau Claire, where he earned a degree in theater education with a global studies minor. I joke with him about the number of jobs he's had; once I asked him to recite them to me so I could write them down. Not counting helping around the family landscaping business, licking envelopes, and making copies for his mom from the age of twelve or so, his first job was at a veterinary hospital, where he scrubbed kennels, cleaned surgery and exam rooms, and walked and fed the dogs. By sixteen he added a second job busing tables in the aftermath of taco and burrito dinners at La Señorita, working until eleven some nights. Then he got a job at Cherry Republic, a touristy store in downtown Traverse City offering cherry preserves, cherry cookbooks, aprons with cherries printed on them, cherry salsa, cherry horseradish . . . you get the idea. He stained wood as the shop was being built, then worked customer service there. As he contemplated a career in health, he got a job as a home health care aide, taking care of a boy with cerebral palsy, getting him off his school bus, feeding him, helping him stretch while watching *The Ellen Show*, bathing him, feeding him dinner.

At eighteen he enrolled in Northwestern Michigan College for nursing, and on top of his full-time course load he worked a complementary gig as a nursing assistant at Munson Medical Center in Traverse City. With a move to Milwaukee came another job, as a waiter at the short-lived CJ's restaurant. There was Christmas-season work as a cashier at Toys "R" Us, and during the semester a slot as a site coordinator for a tutoring service. In the summer, he taught theater classes for Upward Bound. He served drinks at a bar, worked retail at Eddie Bauer, poured coffee at Starbucks, and taught theater to children with autism at First Stage, then back in Chicago found himself tending bar at a comedy club and recruiting for a performing arts academy.

By the time I met him, he had realized that his future was in teaching, not nursing. He'd followed up his hard-earned bachelor's degree by enrolling in the Master's in Education Program at DePaul, fitting coursework in between work hours and maintaining perfect grades. In the absence of substitute work during the summertime, he made ends meet (and scratched the itch of his fondness for travel) with a job guiding exchange students through O'Hare Airport, driving a herd of German or Korean teenagers from one terminal to another, while checking the phone in his downtime for Airbnb customers and people to date.

The resourcefulness and work ethic, if not the restlessness, clearly came from his parents, Terry and Sherri. For them, income was never the guaranteed fruit of a lifelong career with one employer, but rather the yield of ingenuity, relationships, and hard work. As they raised their three boys in their one-story house just off Route 37, Terry was also constantly improving and rebuilding it with his own hands. Sherri works part-time helping other small businesses with their books, while Terry plows snow in the wintertime. Their landscaping business gets work throughout the year but specializes in Christmas decorations; in a peak year, Terry and Sherri sell over a thousand wreaths and eighty thousand feet of garland after making it in the garage at their house or in their pole barn nearby.

SPEAKING IN FRONT OF ANY-SIZED political crowd has never bothered me, but I was as nervous as a middle-schooler onstage when we pulled up in the Glezmans' driveway for the first time after a four-hour drive north to Grand Traverse County, a few days before Christmas 2015. Earlier that day, I had been in full mayor mode, cohosting an event with Governor Pence to celebrate a major economic development grant. Now, sitting in my sweater and jeans in the passenger seat of the Jeep, with a sleigh's worth of presents in the back for Chasten's uncountable slew of extended family relatives, I had become a living cliché from a holiday-season romantic comedy: the boyfriend coming home to meet the parents for the first time.

I don't know who was more anxious, him or me, but at least Chasten had the advantage of being at home. The front yard was a Christmas wonderland, complete with lights and Santa figures. (When the boys were young, Terry was known to go out while they were sleeping and use deer hooves to create "reindeer prints" in the snow on the roof.) Chasten beeped the horn as we came to a stop in the driveway, and within seconds a yellow Lab came bounding out of the garage door, followed by an equally energetic Sherri and Terry.

"Hey, Bubby!" Sherri enthused, looking younger than her pictures as she emerged from the garage to greet Chasten with a big hug. Next it was my turn, and the hug was just as big, followed by a generous handshake from Terry before he instinctively began helping carry in our things.

It quickly became obvious that I had nothing to be nervous about. Almost immediately I was on a sofa in their carpeted living room, answering questions about home and hearing about what Chasten was like as a kid. Since we hadn't been dating that long, it had been decided that I would sleep in the guest room, which had previously been Chasten's own; he, meanwhile, was relegated to the couch in the basement.

By the next day, to Chasten's chagrin, we were reviewing embarrassing home videos of his boyhood. Sitting cross-legged on the carpet in sweatpants as the smell of homemade cinnamon buns wafted out of the kitchen, watching VHS footage of my goofy boyfriend-to-be at age fourteen in a school skit, while also playing one-handed tug-of-war with the dog, I felt more at home than I would have thought possible. The walls of the cozy living room ricocheted with the sound of Sherri's high, contagious laugh as she threw back her head of long jet-black hair to relish one joke after the other. Terry was quieter, sitting in a recliner and smiling more with his eyes than his mustachioed mouth, occasionally patting beads of sweat off his shaved head with a bandanna and contributing details to the family stories being swapped.

We'd been dating only a few months, from that August night at the ballpark to this Northern Michigan holiday, but I felt immediately welcomed into the family. I got just as far as discovering the shoe box with the potty-training videos before Chasten felt compelled to intervene in my bonding with his parents, and proposed we go to the kitchen table and play cards or something. Later, when we arrived at the pole barn for the extended-family Christmas dinner, too big to fit in a house, a giant stocking with my name on it took its place on the inside of the garage door alongside those for the two dozen aunts, uncles, and cousins, filled with peanut butter cups and Slim Jims.

SO WARM IS THE BLANKET of love in that household, wrapped around Chasten and me both, that I struggle to visualize the darkness of a time in which he did not feel welcome there. Chasten, braver than I, came out at the age of seventeen. Hungering to understand the world, he had enrolled in a student exchange program against his parents' wishes and gone to Germany. In that year abroad, he gained a command of spoken German, a little weight on his scrawny teenage frame, and a deeper awareness of who he was. Incapable of self-deception, he fully understood by the time he came back that he was gay, and needed for his family to know.

They thought it was a choice. It made no sense to them, hardworking and churchgoing people who did everything they knew how to set a strong foundation in life for their three boys, that the youngest could select such a destructive and immoral path. How could he harm his family like this? Or was it somehow their own fault, something they had done wrong when he was little, or even before he had been born?

In the weeks of turmoil that followed, it became Chasten's turn to sleep in a car, as his father had. Working two jobs, enrolling at community college, and rotating between nights on friends' couches and in a discreetly parked 2004 Saturn Ion, he was too busy and disoriented to contemplate the word "homeless" or apply it to his own case. He worked, he studied, he slept, while back home some kind of battle played out between things believed, things felt, things assumed, and things discovered. That battle took place out of view, but it ended when love and acceptance asserted their victory in the form of an unexpected phone call asking him to come back home.

• • •

THOSE PAINFUL DAYS SEEMED impossibly distant by the time I met the family that warm Christmas, and only more so across the visits that followed and led naturally to a Thanksgiving morning that saw me rise before dawn at Chasten's side in the guest room, and tiptoe out to head for the deer blind with Terry. A kind of adoption was in progress, communicated that morning in a different way than Sherri's big hugs and loud laugh but just as clear, in the coffee and jerky proffered on the way out, the companionable silence as we shivered and scanned the woods for hours, and the wide-ranging chatter as we made our way back. I was made to feel the unique sense of welcome that comes from someone whose love for a son means love for whomever he loves, given on the sole condition that he be trustworthy.

After dinner, Terry and some of the boys went out for a second round of hunting, but in the traditional post-turkey drowsiness I decided to stay talking in the living room with the others, as the conversation turned to Sherri's battle with skin cancer. She described her new treatment with a topical chemotherapy that came in the form of a potent cream that she applied, wearing gloves, to burn off the cancerous areas—then she produced a package of the stuff from the bathroom so I could see how mundane this lifesaving medication looked. I blinked in disbelief as she held up what resembled a tube of toothpaste, and explained that each one cost over two thousand dollars. Or that's what it would cost, if not for the insurance she had purchased through the health insurance exchanges that had been set up as part of Obamacare. I thought—and spoke—of that moment often, later, as I talked about why health policy was not a theoretical question for our family.

And it was, each passing holiday, more and more *our* family, a different one than the one I'd grown up with, but surprisingly compatible, too. One summer weekend, my parents came up to Traverse and we went out on the Glezmans' pontoon boat together, nibbling on Terry's smoked fish and motoring among different favorite swimming and fishing spots.

If the stereotypes of our divided society in 2016 were to be believed, there would be little hope of my liberal, intellectual parents relating to Chasten's gun-collecting, working-class, small-business-owning rural Michigan mother and father. But five minutes on the boat made it clear they would get on famously. Their rapport got a boost from the universal language of fishing, both social and introspective, which is capable of uniting people of almost any style and background. But mostly it was because of the simple, transitive effect of love: my parents for me, his for him, and therefore all of theirs for each of us and for each other, all rooted in the strong desire for us to be happy.

CHASTEN'S PARENTS ARE THE KIND of people who sometimes pay for the customer behind them at the drive-thru window at McDonald's, just to put a little good out into the world, so it isn't surprising that I am showered with gifts whenever I am at their home. Anything I have admitted to enjoying will make an appearance—from Reese's peanut butter cups left under my pillow at night to offerings of dark-roast Keurig pods that Sherri will save in between my visits, knowing I'll enjoy them more than anyone else in the household.

But I really knew I was a member of the family when I became the object of their truest expression of fondness: teasing. As we filled up at a Shell station one Labor Day weekend amid an extended family camping trip in Michigan's Upper Peninsula, I volunteered to run inside and fetch breakfast supplies for the next morning at the campsite.

"Could you pick up some blinker fluid while you're in there?"

"Sure," I agreed, not processing the question too actively and somehow not detecting the conspiratorial telepathy among Chasten, Terry, and Sherri.

"For this car you gotta make sure it's the E-50," Terry added. "The purple kind." Chasten nodded in solemn agreement.

I committed the specs to memory. "Uh-huh. E-50, purple." Got it.

Inside, I found bacon and eggs in the refrigerated section, then made my way to the car supplies. Not finding anything purple or marked "E-50," I worked back along the aisle a second time, without success, and then started to look for the clerk. Just as I began asking for help, I heard the chime at the door as Sherri came inside. As the other two chuckled in the car, she couldn't resist making sure she was on hand to witness the interaction. That way, later, around the campfire, she could describe the look on my face at precisely the moment it dawned on me, while repeating myself to a quizzical store clerk, that there is no such thing as blinker fluid.

BACK HOME, AS CHASTEN AND I had become a couple, it was not readily clear to either of us how we were supposed to act in public. But we quickly formed the habit of conducting ourselves like any other couple, and found that we were generally treated that way. The harder part for him was the challenge that awaits any political plus-one: dealing with the volume of positive and negative attention coming to you and to someone you love, as a consequence of a life that he, not you, has chosen.

One day, not long after we had begun to live together, Chasten was making an evening grocery run to Martin's. In the refrigerated section, he pulled open a glass door to select a carton of yogurt. Eyeing his choices, he suddenly heard a tapping sound next to his ear. Startled, he turned to the right and found someone knocking on the glass.

Abandoning his yogurt selection for a moment, Chasten closed the door between them and asked how he could be helpful.

The constituent's request was simple enough: "You tell your *husband* to stop fucking up the streets downtown!"

Evidently the gentleman was not a fan of our Smart Streets initiative. It was beside the point that he may not have fully appreciated the economic benefits of a complete-streets policy, or that he was unaware Chasten and I were not yet married. In that moment, Chasten realized that he, too, had become a public figure, and would have to answer for me as well as himself.

Even as he lives his own demanding professional life as a classroom teacher and head of junior high at the same Montessori school I attended as a child, Chasten has found that he constantly has to represent not just me but also a city administration in which he has no formal role. As we flop down in the living room after a long day of work, most of his stories are about the school day, but some are inevitably about how my work has invaded his. A day won't go by without some kind of intrusion. It can occasionally be endearing, but just as often it will be frustrating, such as the staff meeting where an idea he mentioned was met with the response, "Is that your idea, or the mayor's?" Or it's just peculiar, as when a stranger lobbies him to get the city to stop putting fluoride in our drinking water.

PERHAPS IT IS THE FEAR of any queer person preparing to come out that he or she will be marked as a kind of other, isolated from the straight world by virtue of being different. No doubt many have that kind of experience—indeed all do, at least a little bit. But the main consequence for me of coming out, and especially of finding Chasten, is that I have felt more common ground than ever before with the personal lives of other, mostly straight, people.

Before, I could rarely relate to the stories I heard from others when it came to adult domestic life or romance. Today, being in a committed relationship with Chasten just might be the most normal thing about my life. I no longer have to extrapolate or use imagination to understand what colleagues are describing when it comes to their wives or husbands. Our world at home is full of the blessings of domestic life—and the frustrations, too, from my irritation that it's hard to get him to fold the laundry as I do, to his bemusement at my stubborn indifference to expiration dates on items in the cupboard.

For this reason most of all, it is mystifying that some persist in describing sexual orientation as a "lifestyle." In those fragments of our days that aren't dominated by work, our lifestyle revolves around meals, friends, exercise, housekeeping, sleep, extended family, and the care and feeding of our dog. Trying to visualize it from the outside, it strikes me that my partnered, gay "lifestyle" is a lot more normal, sustainable, and fulfilling than my prior lifestyle consisting almost entirely of work and travel. In that context, something as simple as taking care of a dog would have been inconceivable.

TRUMAN, OUR RESCUE MUTT, was named Lamar when we went to visit him at the foster family that had been keeping him for weeks after a couple failed adoption attempts. A hound and beagle mix said to be about four years old, he had come from Kentucky by way of an animal rescue that specializes in getting dogs out of shelters in high-kill states. He had clearly been badly mistreated, and was at first extremely skittish. As his foster owner in Granger led him out on a leash to meet us in her yard, he avoided eye contact with either of us. As soon as Chasten went to pet him, he pancaked onto the ground in a passive slouch. Maybe the earlier adoptions hadn't worked out because he just didn't act very dog-like. But Chasten was convinced there wasn't anything wrong with him that a few months of love couldn't fix.

Trying to think ahead, I was more reluctant. Once, weeks earlier, he had wondered aloud about whether we were in a position to responsibly take care of a dog, and I had pointed out that we didn't even seem to be in a position to responsibly take care of cheese. After all, things constantly went bad in our fridge as we went days at a time without a meal at home. Taking good care of a pet would mean a change in, well, lifestyle.

But the dog was irresistible, and Chasten reminded me that we had a good support network despite our work and travel schedules, especially since my parents lived around the corner. The next thing I knew, we were the loving owners of a four-ish-year-old hound whom we rechristened Truman, after the president who had quipped, "If you want a friend in Washington, get a dog."

Early in my relationship with our new family member, I often thought of this saying with irony. For the first few weeks, he would get up and go to a different room if I so much as made eye contact. After that habit subsided, he still tended to run away and hide under a table anytime I tried to leash him. He wasn't exactly man's best friend. But over the months he bonded with Chasten and eventually with me, becoming the class pet in Chasten's schoolroom and curling up in our bed with us at home. Now I return home to a serenade of barks and howls, a wagging tail, and all of the goofy excitement that you'd expect from a four-legged canine companion.

CHASTEN'S LIFE AND MINE had become so fully intertwined that I was completely unprepared for the jolt of a winter afternoon text, which led to seven minutes in which I doubted I'd see him again. He was abroad, getting an early start on a winter vacation in which I was to catch up to him a couple days later. I was working when the unreal-seeming text message lit up my phone: "Problem on plane—lots of commotion—don't know what's going on. Captain said making landing for 'secret reason'—love you love you love you."

I texted, paced, and waited, for seven inordinately long minutes, until another text came. He had landed, he wasn't sure where. (It turned out to be Bucharest.) There had been a bomb scare on board. He was fine, but shaken; passengers had been crying, shouting, and a few were running in the aisles even as it landed.

When I finally caught up to him in Berlin, he asked me to walk with him to the Brandenburg Gate. Lit splendidly in the cold night, it was one of those landmarks that looks exactly the way it is supposed to. It was also, Chasten explained, a place he came to while he was figuring himself out as a teenage exchange student, watching the people come and go and fitting himself into a bigger world.

He described the terror as the plane made its steep and sudden descent. "All I could think about was how unfair it was that I would lose the chance to have a life with you," he told me, and reached into his bag. "I'm not going to get on one knee, but . . ."

Now I was afraid again, for a different reason. I really did love him, and no other attraction or relationship had compared to the feeling of wholeness I had with Chasten. But it had been less than two years, and I still felt new at this. Our first date wasn't just our first date; it came at the beginning of my dating life altogether. Now, it seemed, my boy-friend was proposing—and I wasn't sure what to say.

What he said next made it clear he knew me better than anyone. He opened the box. "I know you're not ready for marriage, but I want you to know how I feel. So instead of giving you a ring, I'm giving you . . . time."

In the box was a watch.

A YEAR LATER, it was my turn to fumble for a box, and now it was definitely a ring. We were on another New Year vacation (the days between Christmas and New Year's are the nearest it gets to a quiet time in the mayor's office), and I had lured him to Gate B5 at Chicago's O'Hare Airport, the spot where he said he was killing time between herds of exchange students when he first noticed my profile on his phone and began chatting with me. I had worked out what kind of ring he wanted—a platinum band with a little square diamond in the middle—and made sure his parents and mine knew about my plans. All that remained was to ask him.

This won't sound romantic to those who don't know us, but I had selected the space behind the gate agent's desk, a three-foot-wide zone against the window where you have something resembling privacy while looking out on the tarmac. In a way, O'Hare had brought us together. Plus, the halfway-secluded space in the midst of the busy concourse was symbolic for how our life together would be. "I can't promise you an easy life or a simple one. And sometimes privacy for us will be like this, stealing away a quiet moment even with people all around us. It won't always be elegant. But I promise it will always be an adventure, and I promise to love you forever." I went ahead and got on one knee.

Through the tears, he said yes.

THE DAY BEFORE THE WEDDING, Terry Glezman sized up the parking lot outside the enormous building known as LangLab. This was not exactly your traditional wedding reception venue—a disused former furniture factory slowly being turned into a mixed-use arts and entrepreneurial space, complete with a chocolate maker at one end, a print shop in the basement, and on the far side, a makeshift office for student interns working on soil samples for water quality projects.

It was quirky, but LangLab had ample space, a stage, and a bar. The price was right, and it perfectly captured the things we love most about South Bend: creativity, art, and transformation. We arranged for local art to be displayed in one room inside while a band and, later, DJ played in another. Dinner would be served outside, where guests could eat it in a tent or bring their tacos and sliders into the building.

Sweating in the morning heat, as he assessed the scene, Terry scanned the ground and concluded that the parking lot was not sufficiently level. So, of course, he decided to fix it. He somehow procured a wheelbarrow and a load of gravel, press-ganged a couple relatives into helping, and spent that Friday personally leveling it so it would be ready by the time of our reception, while Sherri hauled in boxes of wine from Traverse City and wrapped gifts for members of the wedding party.

Saturday afternoon, it was even hotter outside, but cool inside the Cathedral of Saint James. Chasten and I sat holding hands as friends gave readings, from poetry selections to the ending of the *Obergefell v. Hodges* decision that, just three years earlier, had made this wedding legally possible to begin with. Father Brian Grantz, my pastor since I had moved home a decade ago, gave a moving sermon, assuring us that we were made for one another by God and reminding us to look for love in the spaces "between the divine and the mundane."

At the altar, my voice dropped by an octave as I fought to get the words of the vow out before my emotions could stop me. Then came the customary yet unreal sequence: the rings, the kiss, the applause and cheer of our friends and family, the bishop's blessing, and the summing-up by the deacon as the service came to a close: "Life is short, and we do not have much time to gladden the hearts of those who travel with us; so be quick to love, make haste to be kind, and go in peace to follow the good road of blessing."

Like most newlyweds, I remember the reception itself mostly as a blur. There is the face of my mother, the happiest I have ever seen her, dancing with me to the Beatles' version of "Till There Was You." There is Chasten savoring a victory after besting me in a lopsided contest of Skee-Ball, on a pair of machines we had rented for the occasion. There are our friends singing in unison on the dance floor, seamlessly picking up for Bon Jovi as "Livin' on a Prayer" is interrupted by a short power outage triggered by the taco truck outside. And there is the note from Sherri that I had found in my room while getting ready, rolled up in a BEST SON-IN-LAW EVER coffee mug, welcoming me to the family and ending, "Take care of my baby, he may be on a permanent loan to you but he will always be mine."

VII

BUILDING

Hold to the now, the here, through which all future plunges to the past.

JAMES JOYCE

18

Slow-Motion Chase

I wish it had not required a victory by Donald Trump for the political class to renew its interest in the industrial Midwest. Still, better late than never. For all the reasons I've described, the challenges and the promise of communities like ours belong nearer to the heart of our national discourse. When swing states like Wisconsin and Michigan punished the Democratic Party for its inattention by voting for Trump, for better and for worse our part of the country forced itself back onto the country's political center stage.

To some, the 2016 election was a kind of revenge by "flyover country," long ignored and misunderstood by the coastal elite in general and by the Democratic Party in particular. I certainly felt that our region had been ignored and misunderstood, but to me that did not have to lead to this kind of electoral outcome; our own story in South Bend showed that an honest and optimistic politics could resonate just as well in economically challenged communities. The 2016 election, it seemed to me, only made it more important for the national Democratic Party to take stories like ours on board, while better communicating shared values in terms that would make sense to people who live around here.

I wasn't the only one who thought this way, and said so, after the 2016 election astonished and traumatized my party. So perhaps I shouldn't have been so surprised when more than one acquaintance in politics called after that election to ask if it had crossed my mind to run for chair of the Democratic National Committee.

It had not. From the moment I had become mayor, and then even in the toughest weeks, it was easy to see why Governor Kernan had told me it was the best job he ever had. Every day was different, and everything mattered. Among elected roles the job is uniquely stimulating, compelling you not just to form opinions about issues but actually to craft—and implement—solutions. You are held accountable for results, and rarely have to deal with "alternative facts" because the good, the bad, and the ugly are plainly visible to everyone who lives in the city.

I was in no hurry to be anything but mayor of my hometown—and even in moments of reflection about what might come next when my time as mayor inevitably ends, being a political party chair had never been on the list. It's a thankless job in the best of times, balancing tough customers, big egos, political jostling, and constant fundraising in order to hold the party together and meet its mission of supporting candidates. By definition, the chairmanship also represents an extremely partisan existence—the opposite of a mayor's typical experience, in which working across the aisle is a critical and often gratifying means of delivering results for residents.

But, looking at the landscape of the party as it now stood, I also recognized a moment in which I could make myself useful. Like South Bend in 2011, the Democratic Party in 2016 was in need of a fresh start. And many of the party's greatest weaknesses were in areas where it seemed I was uniquely able to help. The party was struggling to engage young people, it was out of step with areas like the industrial Midwest, and it was failing to prioritize the hard work of government and party-building at the state and local levels. Who better than a millennial, Midwestern mayor to try to guide the party in a better direction?

RUNNING FOR CHAIR MADE SENSE from a generational, regional, and structural perspective. And because I belonged to no faction, it seemed that I could help the party transcend an emerging internal struggle between its establishment wing and its new left. As I contemplated entering the race, the main candidates were increasingly coming to be seen as representing the two sides of the party. On one side was Keith Ellison, a Minnesota congressman who had the support of Bernie Sanders and some labor groups, cheered by many progressives but viewed skeptically by those who saw our party's coalition resonating only in coastal states and big cities, our base shrinking at the moment when it most needed to grow. The other major contender was Secretary of Labor Tom Perez, who entered the race in December. Rumor had it that President Obama himself had persuaded him to seek the post, and as NBC News put it, once he got into the race he immediately became "the de facto candidate of the party's establishment."

Though each of them entered the race with heavy-duty backing from major figures in the party, neither candidate managed to quickly assemble a commanding majority. Perez was weighed down by the fact that many Democrats who revered Obama as a president were nevertheless resistant to him as a party leader, perhaps because he had shown less interest in traditional party-building and fundraising than other Democratic presidents. Ellison, meanwhile, struggled to gain supporters beyond the most progressive precincts of the party's leadership. And by refusing to defer to the forces in the party most aligned with Obama (and, for that matter, Hillary Clinton) he contributed to the sense that the race for chair would turn into a proxy fight.

In my view, reliving the 2016 presidential primary was the last thing our party needed to do. Yes, we needed to debate some of the questions at stake in that race, like how to cement our core progressive values and still connect with independent voters. But a factional fight in which the party focused on its own inside baseball would be missing the point. From developing better infrastructure to navigating the toughest issues around race and policing, experience at home had taught me that the best policy and political solutions were emerging far from presidential politics, and far from Washington in general. Both leading contenders were impressive figures, but if the race were left to a member of Congress and a Cabinet Secretary, no one would be seen as speaking for the dynamic, hopeful communities whose stories could be distilled into an antidote to the prevailing cynicism about Washington-driven politics.

To gather my thoughts, I wrote an essay on the future of the party, called "A Letter from Flyover Country," and published it online. Seeking to offer a Midwestern, millennial mayor's perspective on where our party had gone wrong and how we could do better, the essay suggested a values-oriented approach and a much greater concentration on the stories and lived experience of Americans getting through life in our hometowns. I also believed that this kind of approach could move us beyond a superficial political strategy based on capturing constituency groups individually, with no unifying theme. I wrote:

> The various identity groups who have been part of our coalition should be there because we have spoken to their values and their everyday lives—not because we contacted them, one group at a time and just in time for the next election, to remind them of some pet issue that illustrates why we expect them to support us.

The article circulated quickly, and the response was tremendously encouraging, enough that I felt it was time to look at a run. But the vote was just weeks away, and I would have to decide quickly.

To gauge if the idea was crazy or not, I needed to talk to someone who had actually done the job. Howard Dean was among the most effective and well-regarded former DNC chairs, and someone passed me his number so that I could reach out to him. Dean had briefly gotten into the race for chair himself, but then made clear he was mostly just interested in making sure of a break in the business-as-usual pattern of the party, preferably in favor of a newer generation of leadership. (An established elder who nonetheless craved change, he made me think of some of my earliest supporters for mayor of South Bend.)

"It's a long shot," Dean told me. "But it's not a ridiculous long shot."

A CONTESTED RACE FOR NATIONAL party chair is unique in American politics. Highly personal and idiosyncratic, it in some ways has less in common with other contemporary elections than with the bygone era of brokered political conventions we read about in histories of the 1960s—or 1860s. In a sense, vying for the votes of committee members is a consummate insider's game that calls to mind the proverbial smoke-filled rooms of old-school politics. But in 2017, this setup collided with the transparency created by social media and Internet organizing, giving party activists across the country an unprecedented level of visibility in a race that would come down to the votes of just a few hundred people.

The race was nationwide in scope, with appearances on national television and in person from coast to coast. It would require heavy-duty fundraising, at a pace at least on par with a congressional race. But the whole process would play out in a matter of weeks, and the vote itself was completely in the hands of the 447 members of the committee, an electorate not that much bigger than when I had run for class president at Saint Joe High.

I got a list and started calling the members one by one, pacing in my South Bend dining room as I asked for their views on the race. Most were encouraging, or at least not discouraging. Surprisingly few said they had committed to any candidate just yet, and many said they believed the race remained "wide open." The more people I called—

from freshly-voted-in Bernie delegates in California to dyed-in-the-wool Washington operatives who had been in the party for decades—the more I sensed that people were looking for something different. And as I made the case for more attention to the struggles and successes of communities like mine, I found that even coastal members were coming to understand why this was an important perspective for the party to better take on board.

In the course of the conversations, as I tried to engage national party officials on the perspective of my hometown, I also found that my own viewpoint widened into a broader account of where our national party needed to go, and several changes that would need to happen.

First, it had become clear, we needed to stop treating the White House like it was the only office that mattered. By the end of 2016, Democrats were shockingly at the lowest level of congressional and state capitol influence in nearly a hundred years, having lost over a thousand state and federal seats in less than a decade. As the Obama White House learned to its great frustration—and as I was experiencing firsthand as a mayor in a state with a Republican legislative supermajority—even when you are in power you can only get so much done without control of legislative seats and governorships. Much of the anguish in Democratic circles at that time understandably focused on the disaster of losing the presidency, but for these reasons it seemed clear to me that the party would have been in serious trouble *even if we had won* the White House in 2016.

Conservatives, by contrast, had patiently and cleverly built majorities around the country from the bottom up, fortifying their state and local power bases over the decades while presidencies from either party came and went. Partisan gerrymandering made these legislative majorities self-reinforcing, all but locking them in, a decade at a time. Meanwhile, in parallel to their campaign work, the right's think-tank apparatus also paid careful attention to the power concentrated in offices from school board to state senate.

I pointed to the example of ALEC, the American Legislative Exchange Council. Funded by the Koch brothers and other conservative and corporate interests, it has grown to become one of the most influential think tanks in America—yet it doesn't engage on federal policy at all. Instead, it generates model legislation for adoption in state legislatures and finds sympathetic state house and senate members to carry the bills. Legislation is often nearly identical from state to state— so much so that journalists sometimes find copy-paste errors where the wrong state is mentioned in the text of a bill. Tellingly, by 2014, ALEC had decided to expand its model beyond the state level—not by going federal, but instead targeting *local* policy through a new offshoot called the American City County Exchange. Those on the left were belatedly catching up to this kind of organizing after realizing the cost of short-changing state and local policy work over the years.

In addition to overlooking state and local government generally, it had also come to feel that the Democratic Party was neglecting the industrial Midwest in particular. Every restored house, improved street, and good job we helped deliver in South Bend had shown me that practical leadership guided by progressive values could deliver results in a part of the country that had simply been written off. In political terms, there was great opportunity to present a hopeful economic message to blue-collar workers experiencing major economic disruption, as an alternative to the litany of resentments being offered by the other side. Beyond South Bend, many of the smartest and most original politicians I had met were state and local elected officials, quietly doing impressive work in the American heartland. But as a party, we had become less likely to put forward leaders from the region, and less likely to compete at all in some parts of the country once known as bellwethers. If a place like northern Indiana was proving steadily less likely to vote Democratic, that called for more, not less, engagement by the party.

We had come to look at the politics of different American regions— the Republican "red" states and liberal "blue" states—as immutable.

But I had seen from close up how important it was that Democrats continue to compete in tougher territory. Joe Donnelly had proven this in Indiana, getting elected to the Senate in 2012 as a Democrat even as the state went decisively "red" in the presidential race that same year. Joe carried fewer than thirty of our state's ninety-two counties. But he prevailed, because he won the most populous areas and made sure not to ignore the others. He took pride in the hole that a reporter once noticed in the sole of his shoe as he worked his way through countless parades, county fairs, and dinner speeches in conservative counties. This strategy served him well, even—or especially—in those counties he couldn't actually win, because losing them 60–40 instead of 80–20 helped make it possible for the bluer counties to put him over the top.

Yet national Democrats seemed increasingly to write off red states— or red areas within blue and purple states—completely. The result was that many parts of our country had heard so little from Democrats and progressives that anyone living there who sympathized with our party might assume they were totally alone. If that loneliness prompted them to keep quiet about their values at coffee after church or on the local radio call-in shows, then the sense of a Republican monopoly on opinion in these communities would become self-fulfilling.

Yet this conservative dominance was relatively new. As late as 2005, the Democratic leader in the Senate, Tom Daschle, was from South Dakota—the same state that had produced Democratic presidential nominee George McGovern a generation earlier. Go back even further in history, and figures like Eugene Debs of Indiana and Bob La Follette of Wisconsin show that a century ago the American political left was arguably being led from the Midwest. Treating the middle of the country like unshakably Republican territory would serve us poorly in the long run.

Worse, a culture had begun to take hold in some Democratic circles that addressed our part of the country with condescension, bordering on contempt. A party once built on looking after ordinary Americans was now beginning to feel like the preserve of comfortable, educated, upper-middle-class city dwellers. Often I would hear a well-heeled fellow Democrat shake his head at how a low-income conservative voter could be so foolish as to "vote against his self-interest," oblivious to the easy retort that would be available to such a voter: "So are you!"

I knew that bedrock Democratic values around economic fairness and racial inclusion could resonate very well in the industrial Midwest, but not if they were being presented by messengers who looked down on working- and lower-middle-class Americans.

TO ME THESE IDEAS SEEMED CLEAR, almost to the point of being obvious. But few others in the national conversation seemed to be making that case. So, as a second-term urban mayor just a few days shy of my thirty-fifth birthday, I did something that would not have crossed my mind two months earlier: began organizing a national campaign.

You might think such a small number of voters is easy to approach, but in some ways it's harder, because each of them expects to hear from you personally. The election was in late February, which meant I had about two months to reach them all. Mathematically, this is certainly possible . . . if you assume half-hour calls at a rate of ten or fifteen calls a day. But that also assumes they actually pick up.

What happens, instead, is an enormous, nationwide game of phone tag. Of course, a few really do pick up, and you can have a straightforward conversation and ask for their support. But more likely you leave a message, or several. Or you try to schedule a call. Or they call you back, but you miss it because you're on another call or they're calling from Hawaii and it's three in the morning.

Late to the game and racing against the deadline, I put together a staff to help bring order to the phone-call operation—not to mention logistics, press, volunteer management, and finance. On January 5, 2017, two weeks before the inauguration of President Trump, I officially

314 / PETE BUTTIGIEG

became a candidate. Since this was a party post and not a public office, there was no big speech to give, or even a county clerk's office where I could ritually go file papers. Instead, unglamorously, I just printed out a statement of interest in running, signed it, scanned it, and emailed it to someone at the DNC.

The dining room of our house on North Shore Drive became the initial headquarters. With Chasten and a couple soon-to-be campaign staff members around the table tracking social media and filling my call schedule, I spent my first day as a candidate on the phone with reporters, party figures, and potential supporters. Looking through the window at the sidewalk in the early January gloom, I told CNN that "not being afraid to talk about our values will resonate in places where we as a party have been struggling." Pacing around the living room on rugs I'd brought back from Afghanistan, I told Tom Perez that I was getting in and why, and listened as he responded graciously and welcomed me to the race (as did each of the other candidates I would be competing with). Between bites of a Chipotle burrito, I tried to stay lucid through call after call, all the way through to a trip to the nearest satellite studio for a 10:40 p.m. appearance on MSNBC.

What followed was an eight-week sprint that took us to every corner of the country, with major candidate forums at a Phoenix hotel ballroom, a Houston college campus, a Detroit auditorium, and a Baltimore convention center. I held fundraisers in San Francisco, Los Angeles, New York, and Washington and made appearances in Miami and Chicago in the run-up to the big final DNC meeting in Atlanta where the vote would take place—all while continuing to go to my office on non-travel days to perform all the functions of mayor.

Every couple days we took on a new hire until the team grew to about a dozen. We attracted more and more attention as we went, and it became impossible to stay on top of all the incoming communication. My email in-box became impenetrable. If the phone rang and the caller ID said "Unknown," I knew it was either a telemarketer or some one very important. At one point I picked up a call from an unfamiliar Vermont number, thinking it was Howard Dean (who had been encouraging me to run), and instead heard the voice of Bernie Sanders (who was calling to suggest I drop out and make room for Ellison). National figures I had never even met took an interest, as word reached me daily of new endorsements from figures ranging from North Dakota Senator Heidi Heitkamp to Cher—neither of whom, unfortunately, turned out to be voting members of the DNC.

As I went with my fellow candidates through debate after debate, TV appearance after TV appearance, it became clear that my approach was hitting a nerve. People responded to the idea of a values-led message. They wanted us to compete in red and purple states, and to pay attention to local races. Most understood that a healthy strategy would involve emphasis both on racial justice *and* an economic message, not choosing one over the other. And to the extent that a candidacy from someone my age was itself a kind of message, the idea of mobilizing a new generation of voters and organizers, through fresh leadership and tactics, resonated strongly. As we engaged party faithful far from Washington, I could see in the faces of the audiences that a fifty-state strategy and a willingness to compete everywhere was already important to those on the ground.

IT WAS ALSO EVIDENT that the party itself was at a moment of truth, its future role unclear. In the suddenly antiquated twentieth century model, political parties had had a near-monopoly on information, access, and money. A volunteer list, a campaign finance account, or even just a way to get the word out about an event was difficult to build on your own. I thought of Butch Morgan back in South Bend, and the influence that he had once wielded from that landline phone on his desk at the party headquarters. But now online organizing and outside spending had eclipsed many of the functions of a traditional party organization—local and national alike. To be useful in the digital age, the DNC would have to figure out a new division of labor across party operations, campaigns, and causes.

An episode in Houston, during the heat of the race for chair, dramatized this humbling new reality for the party. We had come to Texas for one of four regional gatherings of DNC members, and the competitors for chair were at a reception after completing a forum (effectively a debate) before an audience of committee members and party activists. Earlier that day we had learned of President Trump's travel ban on residents of certain Muslim countries, and word had begun to spread of a grassroots movement to protest the policy at airports around the country.

As appetizers and drinks circulated among candidates and party leaders in a hotel ballroom, my campaign staff learned that Texas was not immune to the grassroots pushback: a protest was getting under way at Houston Airport. Having spent the better part of the day advocating for a party leadership that could better engage with the grassroots, it now felt like I belonged there, with activists at the airport, not here at a reception with party functionaries, donors, and hors d'oeuvres.

A few minutes later, I was in a rented minivan with Chasten and several staff, racing to George Bush Intercontinental Airport, Terminal E. We were going as fast as we could—which, owing to pre–Super Bowl traffic, was not fast at all. I kept refreshing Facebook and Twitter to see how the protest was going, while also monitoring the news as accounts spread of an ACLU effort to stay the ban in court. After twenty minutes or so, we learned that Tom Perez had had the same idea, possibly after I tweeted my whereabouts, and soon another candidate, South Carolina Democratic Party Chair Jaime Harrison, was en route as well. All of us were literally racing to join those standing up for our values. But nothing was moving quickly on these logjammed roads.

As I looked out at the bumper-to-bumper traffic on the freeway, it hit me that we were enacting a highly metaphorical version of what was going on with the party at large. Here was a young mayor, a former Cabinet secretary, and a state party chairman, with their respective campaign entourages, all in hot pursuit—rushing into a comically slow-motion car chase, trying to catch up to a group of activists and citizens organized just hours earlier by a twenty-six-year-old restaurant server using social media.

When we finally arrived, over a hundred people had gathered, chanting, cheering, and singing. Joining with them—and with my competitors—was a heartening moment after days of despondently watching news coverage of the first few days of the Trump administration, wondering with each new outrage if it would soon be accepted as normal.

But the moment also demonstrated how much had changed from a few years ago, when it would have taken weeks, not hours, to stage simultaneous demonstrations at dozens of locations in cities across America. To be relevant and useful to those who shared our values, the party would have to figure out a way to be part of a new flying formation.

THE SECOND MONTH OF THE CAMPAIGN for DNC was even more fast-paced. Routinely, Chasten and I would wake up in a hotel room and each ask the other if he could remember which state we were in. James Mueller, now my chief of staff, made sure the city team made the most of the time I could put in at the office in South Bend, while the campaign staff ensured that whatever time remained was spent as effectively as possible on the road, on TV, or on the phone. Each day brought encouraging press coverage and more followers online. But as the last days approached, the phone calls yielded little but noncommittal members, saying they liked what they heard but hadn't decided yet, or indicating they had already promised to vote otherwise but would consider me on a second ballot.

I did secure a handful of supporters among the DNC membership—along with the endorsements of Dean and four other former DNC chairs—but as we entered the last week of the campaign, I still didn't have the number of hard commitments it would take to survive a first round of voting and make it to a viable position on the second ballot. My last chance was to move large numbers of members in the final seventy-two hours of the race, as all of the voting members converged for the run-up to the vote at a meeting in Atlanta.

We arrived in Georgia with tremendous energy. About a hundred volunteers in blue PETE FOR DNC shirts crisscrossed the halls of the big Westin Hotel, affixing campaign placards and putting stickers on people. But the front-runners had their supporters out in force as well, and Perez was getting extremely close to the magic number needed to win. I had expected that becoming more viable in the wake of the endorsements would help me add to my vote count, but in fact the opposite was true. Wavering members who were expected by their friends or employers to vote for Perez or Ellison reported increased pressure to commit, and rumors spread that President Obama himself was making phone calls on behalf of Perez.

We kept working to gather support until the morning of the vote itself, but by the time I huddled with the team after a predawn *Today Show* appearance from a plaza across the street from the hotel, it had become clear that I couldn't win. While many DNC members signaled agreement with my platform and appreciation for South Bend's story with its broader implications for our party, it wasn't enough to override years-long friendships, institutional commitments, favors called in, and countless other reasons to support one of the more recognizable and established candidates. It just wasn't going to happen.

EVERY CANDIDATE HAD A FEW MINUTES to address the full voting body, gathered for the vote in a big room at the convention center downtown. Standing at the podium, I looked out at the faces of the Democratic National Committee, from famous elected officials to obscure party activists, cleared my throat, and explained that I was standing down. But before leaving the stage, there was one last chance to press for the ideas that had motivated me to run in the first place. I urged the next chair to lead a party that would look beyond Washington, engage a newer generation, and compete in regions like my Indiana home. I asserted one more time that politics was ultimately about impact on everyday life. Invoking my military reserve status, I sought, even in this process-heavy and insider-oriented environment, to call for renewed focus on the concrete impacts of political decisions rather than on horse races and palace intrigue. "My life depends on the decisions that are made by elected officials," I reminded the hushed committee members. "So does yours."

Reflecting on the experience of running, I also had something to say about the moral basis for leadership. It had been on my mind ever since allowing myself to call President Trump a "draft-dodging chickenhawk" during one of the DNC forums. While true, that statement was not in keeping with how I publicly speak about political figures, or anyone else, and afterward I reflected that this president was inspiring a loss of decency not just in his supporters, but also in those of us who opposed him. It was another way of looking at the moral stakes of politics as it filters through to millions of lives: that we might all be growing into harder and perhaps worse people, as a consequence of political leadership that failed to call us to our highest values.

After the speeches came the voting, the counting, and then the revoting. Tom Perez won on the second ballot, and I lingered backstage long enough to congratulate him on his victory. Then Chasten and I found our way to a room where my staff and volunteers had gathered—over a hundred people in blue T-shirts whom I had taken to calling the "Happy Warriors" of our campaign. Emotionally drained but also gratified that we had made an impact on the debate over our party's future, I slept well that night in Atlanta. But other than the last day of the deployment, I can't think of a time I looked forward more eagerly to going home.

I WASN'T SURE HOW PEOPLE would respond back home in South Bend, passing by in the aisle at Martin's or spotting me on Jefferson Boulevard on my way into work, after the campaign had ended. From the very outset of my first run for mayor, some had doubted my commitment to local government in South Bend, suggesting that I wouldn't even finish one term before seeking another office. At one house-party appearance after another in the 2011 campaign, I had fielded questions from residents that included, in one context or another, the word "stepping-stone."

In fact, I had always intended to serve a full term, and hopefully then earn and serve another one. Actually doing the work reinforced my belief that I belonged in the mayor's office, and over the years I had learned to quickly deflect the occasional phone call from a party recruiter in Washington or a local journalist about running for Congress. By 2016, as I came off reelection and showed little interest in the chatter about me as a potential lieutenant governor nominee, the "stepping-stone" talk had at last quieted. But now, in early 2017, at the outset of my sixth year in office, I had unexpectedly sought a new job. The whirlwind of the DNC race had only deepened my love for South Bend and for my day-to-day work guiding its recovery, but I knew that returning now, I would be the equivalent of an employee meeting his boss after applying for another job. What would people say?

I had my answer when I headed in to work at the County-City Building for the first time after coming back from Atlanta, and someone stopped me on the sidewalk: "Congratulations, Mayor!"

I was taken aback. A little confused and trying to smile, I said, "You . . . know I didn't win, right?"

"Yeah, but you got out there, you told our story, you had us on the map."

Several times, I had variations of this conversation. Another time, as I emptied my pockets at the metal detector in the lobby of our building, a resident said, "It was so great to see you on TV!" as if noting something unusual. It was an odd thing to say to a mayor who turns up on local television practically every day. But what he meant was that they had seen me—and our city—represented on *national* TV in the course of the DNC race, and he took pride in the publicity for our hometown.

In a sense, we had won by losing. I had influenced the national conversation about where our party needed to go, but also got to return home to the rewarding work of the mayor's office, where compelling second-term projects awaited, from guiding a new route for the train to Chicago, to building out affordable housing options in low-income neighborhoods, to spearheading a transformation of our most recognizable parks. Meanwhile, Americans (at least those who closely followed a process like this) saw that there was more to the emerging leadership of our party than blue-state federal officials—and more to my Indiana home than intolerance or nostalgia. In the course of arguing that the party needed to better vindicate itself in the heartland, I also found myself telling our city's story as a way to insist to the party and to the nation that the fundamental sentiment moving people in my corner of the industrial Midwest was not resentment, but hope.

19

Not "Again"

There is no going back.

South Bend cannot and should not rewind to the Studebaker heyday of the 1950s, just as America cannot restore the old order in which families obeyed a single, male head of household, each race had its so-called place, average weather was the same from one decade to the next, and a job was for life.

For those who remember if not mourn an epoch of lost greatness, it may be impossible to accept that there is no return. But for those of us who were raised only among its shards, and who grew up questioning if it was ever as great as advertised, embracing the permanence of change is the only thing that can liberate us to move forward.

I never did see those factories off Main Street and Indiana Avenue throbbing with activity, or the thousands of people who worked there pouring into Robertson's Department Store on a Thursday evening for a family night out. If I had ever witnessed the Studebaker assembly building as a hive of production instead of as that silent hulk overshadowing our baseball park, maybe I would dream of nothing but restoring it to its original use and former glory. But for a generation that knew it only in its post-1963 decay, the building's potential as a home for data centers and glass-walled tech company offices is more vivid and believable than any thought of a return to its automaking past.

True hope for our city never lay in returning to some nostalgic prior state, some literal or figurative return of Studebaker. Rather, the first vision of the resurgent South Bend in which we now live was expressed all the way back in that bleak December of 1963 when the store owner Paul Gilbert defiantly told the assembly of alarmed fellow city leaders, "This is not Studebaker, Indiana. This is South Bend, Indiana." At the time, it might have sounded like wishful thinking. No doubt many in his audience, knowing how dependent our city was on that industry, exchanged skeptical glances at one another, supposing that he was in denial.

But the real denial, and the more costly, was to persist in believing that South Bend could only thrive as an old-school, automaking company town dependent on a single, massive employer. I would encounter this thinking even a half century later in 2011 when I was running for mayor. I heard it as a refrain among those who said that what we needed was to land that one mythic giant factory, to lure "something big" here from somewhere else, and get some version of Studebaker taking root again. This was the impossible promise that held us back—and, seeing this promise go unkept, my generation grew up suspecting that our only hope was to get out.

Progress could begin only once the loss had been fully metabolized. Nothing is more human than to resist loss, which is why cynical politicians can get pretty far by offering up the fantasy that a loss can be reversed rather than overcome the hard way. This is the deepest lie of our recent national politics, the core falsehood encoded in "Make America Great Again." Beneath the impossible promises—that coal alone will fuel our future, that a big wall can be built around our status quo, that climate change isn't even real—is the deeper fantasy that time itself can be reversed, all losses restored, and thus no new ways of life required.

To defeat this temptation is to see what actually lies on the other side of acceptance: not diminished expectations, but still greater ones. For us, paradoxically, the only way to relive anything like our hometown's former greatness is to stop trying to retrieve it from our vanished past. If manufacturing is to grow around here now, its growth will not come by reverting to a world of cut-off trade routes and pre-computer production methods. It will come from those of our employers who seek to compete in new ways—and from new arrivals, like the Silicon Valley–based start-up that bought the entire facility housing the old commercial Hummer production line where I sent Hillary Clinton a few years ago. Backed by investment from China, the company is making partially automated electric vehicles, using local union labor. Enterprises like this take globalization and automation as their point of departure, and work through these forces rather than against them. The founders of car manufacturing here would scarcely recognize this industry as their own—but it echoes their originality and audacity, showing that the less we concentrate on emulating our forebears, the more we begin to resemble them at their best.

I WOULD LOVE TO BE TRANSPORTED, for an evening, back in time to the South Bend of 1960, 1940, or even 1920. I would love to stroll the pavements of the past, and see Michigan Street fronted by an uninterrupted wall of active building façades, rather than the urban missing teeth left by Nixon-era demolitions. I would see the pedestrian and vehicle bustle downtown that we have only now managed to create anew through the politically and fiscally expensive Smart Streets initiative. I could watch passengers step off an electric train from Chicago at a station that was foolishly moved out of downtown before I was born, and which we are still working to restore to the heart of the city. I would look at the most elegantly dressed gentlemen walking past and try to guess which among them was a senior executive at Bendix or South Bend Watch or one of the other towering companies of South Bend's past. Then I would jump on a streetcar, along tram lines long since torn out, and let it carry me into the West Side, to step off in a neighborhood and wander into a bakery full of East European delights or a tavern where people were swilling Drewrys beer and speaking the language of the old country.

But only for an evening. If I stayed any longer, I might become depressed. The saddest thing would not be the foreknowledge of loss, though it would be a little poignant to look on the buildings, shops, and companies that would soon be gone and envision their demise through the second half of the last century. But no, the depressing thing would be pity for the people I would see on the train platform, in Robertson's, or along Main Street, because any one of them would actually be much better off in the South Bend of today.

On those streets of the past I would see people who knew a kind of job security we might ache for. But I would also be seeing people—an African-American laborer or a female clerk—who might be consigned to the same job for life even if they had the gifts to become a great doctor or scholar (or mayor), because admission to a place like Notre Dame was still unimaginable for someone of their race or sex. I would see people living dignified and interesting lives, but know that they did so in a city that was also shortening those lives, its river water and air quality toxic by today's standards. I probably would not find any sign of gay life, but if I did, it would be nowhere near the Episcopal Cathedral of Saint James, completed in 1894, where I would one day get married to Chasten. Instead, it would be in some sketchy bar or alley where men fearful of exposure would exchange coded and furtive glances, totally unable to imagine that in a future generation they might have known the incomparable joys of authentic love and marriage.

Even the most prosperous men to cross my path would be ignorant and unhealthy compared to the average middle-class South Bend resident of, say, 2015. And while the fruits and meats at the Farmer's Market then might well have tasted better than today's, those shopping there would never know the simple pleasure of a taco de chorizo, a chicken pad thai, or a California roll—all now taking their place alongside cheeseburgers and goulash as part of South Bend's twenty-first-century menu. In short, I would see a world that was as good as it got by the standards of the day, but one in which virtually every person's everyday life was worse, in absolute terms, than his or her counterpart's today.

To reverse the thought experiment, imagine if I could fetch someone off the downtown street in one of those bygone years and bring him into the present. Never mind inviting a female or black or gay or Jewish resident to show them the transformative opportunities that might have awaited them. Just imagine one of my own counterparts, a mayor from our city's heyday. On some level, I ought to envy them. The population and economic growth that, by tremendous civic exertion, we are proudly achieving today is still slower than it would have been in their time, and for them it was comparatively effortless as modernity carried our city on its wave tops.

Certainly men like Mayor Carson (1918–1922) or Pavey (1938–1945) or Bruggner (1960–1964) would be saddened by some of the changes to the city they led. They might look at the factory remnants, or the vacant lots in our neighborhoods, and ask if South Bend had been struck by air raids in some dreadful war. And they would perhaps have little use for Thai food, same-sex marriage, or even racial integration. But as I toured them through the city, they would see what civic gifts time had brought to our hometown, despite its many unkind turns. As only mayors could, they would surely appreciate the sewer sensor system, the 311 center, and the law enforcement technology. If I explained it well, they would see what the railroads that developed here on their watch had in common with the fiber-optic connections that flash stock trades and emails around the world and enable a data-analytics industry to employ residents in whole categories of well-paying jobs that did not exist in their day.

WE DON'T ACTUALLY WANT TO GO BACK. We just think we do, sometimes, when we feel more alert to losses than to gains. A sense of loss inclines us, in vulnerable moments, to view the future with an expectation of harm. But when this happens, we miss the power of a well-envisioned future to inspire us toward greatness. Here, someone will say I should be careful, as a progressive, to go around speaking of greatness. Especially in this moment, when "make great" is the mantra of a backward populist movement, the word seems associated with the worst in our politics, its champions consumed by a kind of chest-thumping that seeks to drown out any voice that would point out the prejudice and inequality we still must overcome.

Yet South Bend, for all our struggles, has formed my faith in a great future. Any of my counterparts from decades ago would look at our city and, even after noting that it had been diminished in some ways from the one they knew, would have occasion to use the word "great" to describe what they saw.

There is nothing necessarily wrong with greatness, as an aspiration, a theme, or even as the basis of a political program. The problem, politically, is that we keep looking for greatness in all the wrong places. We think we can find it in the past, dredged up for some impossible "again," when in reality it is available only to those who fix their vision on the future. Or we think it is to be found in some grand national or international adventure, when the most meaningful expressions of American greatness are found in the richness of everyday life.

A marriage can be great. So can a meal, a recovery from illness, or a song. We are shown greatness on the news, but it is also found in everyday lives, and then in the neighborhoods and communities that take on the character of those lives added up. When the potential greatness of our country first flickered early in the last century, it was intertwined with that of our cities. When a kind of greatness in our society became a beacon for others around the world, helping us to prevail in the Cold War, it did so because of a global admiration not only for our space program and our skyscrapers but also the everyday prosperity, however imperfect and unequal, that could be observed in so many of our neighborhoods.

THE PRIMACY OF THE EVERYDAY is brought home to me every month or two on the lacquered floor of a middle school basketball court, where I set up shop for the simple democracy of an event we call Mayor's Night Out. We invite residents to meet with each other, local council members, city department heads—and me. Sleeves rolled up and taking notes, I sit with my colleague Cherri at a folding table and meet anyone who wants to talk, one-on-one, a few minutes at a time. We may see twenty people or more a night this way, back-to-back. After the first hour and a half, the department heads are welcome to go home, and the council members usually take off. But Cherri and I stay until we've seen the last resident waiting to sit down and talk. By the time we leave, it's usually down to her, me, a handful of other staff, and the school janitor carting off the last of the folded tables and chairs.

Absolutely anything can come up in these conversations, I have learned. A woman is at her wits' end because of the drug house on her block and asks what else we can do about it. A taxi driver wants to know whether I am going to allow Uber to continue growing here. A landlord says he had no idea that the vacant house with the tall grass on Fassnacht Avenue was on the demolition list when he bought it, and swears he can fix it up if we could just ease up on code enforcement for six more months. A wide-eyed fellow has miraculously invented a perpetual motion machine and just wants me to review his schematics. Another wants to know if I have personally accepted Jesus Christ as my Lord and Savior. Curbs and sidewalks. Aquaponic fish farming. Deteriorating greens on the city golf course. A Boy Scout troop, eager to earn a new badge, waits to get their picture taken.

It's like changing channels every five minutes between *The Wire*, *Parks and Recreation*, and, occasionally, *Veep*. It wears me out, and the follow-up keeps my team busy for days after. But it also renews us every time.

It's not that we handle most people's issues this way; if I've seen 500 city residents at these meetings, that leaves some 99,500 that I haven't. More people call our 311 system in a day than I can meet this way in a year. But it matters, not only as a venue for problem-solving but as a refresher on why we even have governments and politics in the first place: to support people going about their everyday lives.

Our city administration's mission is to "deliver services that empower everyone to thrive." A government process can't single-handedly decide whether people will thrive or not. But we can make it more likely that they will, sometimes by acting and sometimes by getting out of the way. I see our role reflected daily in the faces of fellow residents. A seven-year-old smiles, exuberant, as she runs through a splash pad we installed in the low-income Kennedy Park neighborhood. A mother of three from the Southeast Side weeps at an act of gun violence we failed to stop. A family's eyes reflect the red, then blue, then green glow of a light pattern painted by LEDs across the cascading whitewater behind the Century Center, a new kind of public art for our city. So many things that will happen today in any one life are possible only because of a functioning local government: mundane yet vital things like a hot shower, a drive to work, a stroll under the streetlights at dusk. The more people can thrive in daily life here in our once-rusting town along the St. Joseph River, the better our city can make a claim to greatness, and the more its example becomes useful to others.

On deployment in Kabul, I encountered the Afghan proverb that says, "A river is made drop by drop." It must have been inspired by the

Amu Darya on the Tajikistan border, but of course I pictured instead the St. Joseph, as it coursed by my house in South Bend some seven thousand miles away. It is usually invoked at the outset of a big undertaking that requires countless individual steps. But it also captures the importance of working at the local level as part of building a better nation: tearing down obstacles to a good everyday life in a single community, knowing how the small adds up to the great.

I've learned that great families, great cities, and even great nations are built through attention to the everyday. That lesson, once I began to understand it, proved to be the unexpected and consistent theme of two decades' education and work. Seeking wisdom and purpose at the age of eighteen, I rushed to escape the hometown that had shaped me. Then, slowly and imperceptibly, like one of those muted winter sunrises over South Bend, a pattern became visible across all I'd learned in philosophy and literature, business and service, politics and love. At last there is now enough light to see that the meaning I sought was to be found very close to where I had begun, on a path that proved in my case to be the shortest way home.

ACKNOWLEDGMENTS

No one invents himself, and a good South Bender is raised to know that his achievements rest largely on the support and indulgence of countless others. This is particularly true for a mayor who decides to write his first book while in office, and I am in debt to all those who made this possible.

They are, of course, too many to name, stretching back through my career and formal education all the way to the cradle, where my mother, Jennifer Anne Montgomery, and my father, Joseph Buttigieg, first gave me the gift of language as well as that of their love.

As this concept went through its first iterations, my agent, Chris Parris-Lamb, gave me the insight and guidance needed to venture into the literary world.

My publisher, Robert Weil, made an author of me, patiently reading draft after draft and forcing me to find an authentic storytelling voice on the page. His faith in this project and in me as a writer propelled me, and this book is the result of his expert, energetic management of both text and author. Bob's colleagues at Liveright and Norton, especially Marie Pantojan, provided me with vital support, and the copyediting by Dave Cole was uncannily precise and perceptive.

Jennifer Huang is a superb research assistant, catching inconsistencies and running down references to corroborate or correct my recollection at every turn. A brilliant interviewer, she also gathered many of the stories that make this book worth reading, and her insights helped throughout. Of course, any factual errors that did survive into the published edition are my sole responsibility.

From the earliest conception of this project, my friend Ganesh Sitaraman provided expert guidance, unvarnished advice, and steady encouragement. Trusted friends and colleagues read drafts, and I am thankful to Mike Schmuhl, Kathryn Roos, Nathaniel Myers, James Mueller, and Lis Smith for their time and insights.

South Bend's story is far from mine alone to tell, and I am indebted to South Bend residents and others who shared their own stories in interviews for this project, including Pete Mullen, Gladys Muhammad, Chuck Hurley, Bob Urbanski, Mayor Greg Goodnight, and Governor Joe Kernan. In a broader sense, the book belongs to the people of South Bend, since they have shaped and authored the city's story and, in so many ways, my own.

Writing a book places monstrous claims on a politician's most precious and contested resource: time. Members of my staff including Laura O'Sullivan, Yesenia Garcilazo, Andre Adeyemi, Suzanna Fritzberg, Matt Cruz, Cherri Peate, Mark Bode, and others went to great lengths to help me carve out enough time to undertake this work amid all the demands on our office. And I would not have a very good story to begin with if it weren't for the brilliance of current and former office and campaign staff members, phenomenal department heads, and more than a thousand dedicated employees doing great work for our city. Among them, Aaron Perri, Stephanie Steele, Santiago Garces, and Eric Horvath also helped me to verify factual and technical information about their excellent work.

While writing this book, I gained a new family in the Glezmans, whose love has enriched my life and buoyed me, and whose story I have been honored to share.

No one has sacrificed more for this book than Chasten, my love, who has put up with countless hours of lost time together, even as I worked to express on the page what our time together means to me. His loving scrutiny of my text and of my heart has made me a better writer, a better mayor, and a better man.

ILLUSTRATION CREDITS

INDEX

"PB" indicates Pete Buttigieg.

ABOUT THE AUTHOR

PETE BUTTIGIEG has served as mayor of the city of South Bend, Indiana, since 2012.

As mayor, Buttigieg has reduced the number of vacant and abandoned properties by over one thousand, led a major reconstruction of downtown streetscapes, and initiated the largest investment in parks and public spaces in the city's history. Elected at the age of twenty-nine, he was for a time the youngest sitting mayor of a city of over one hundred thousand residents.

Born in 1982, Buttigieg grew up in South Bend and attended Saint Joseph's High School there. He attended Harvard, earning a bachelor's degree in history and literature, and went on to study philosophy, politics, and economics at Pembroke College, Oxford, as a Rhodes Scholar.

He is the recipient of the New Frontier Award from the John F. Kennedy Library Foundation and the Harvard University Institute of Politics, and serves on the advisory board of the U.S. Conference of Mayors.

An officer in U.S. Navy Reserve from 2009 to 2017, Buttigieg took a leave of absence to serve in Afghanistan during a seven-month deployment in 2014, earning the Joint Service Commendation Medal for his counterterrorism work.

An active musician, Buttigieg plays piano and guitar, and has performed with the South Bend Symphony Orchestra. He lives in South Bend with his husband, Chasten Glezman, and their dog, Truman.

From Byron, Austen and Darwin

to some of the most acclaimed and original contemporary writing, John Murray takes pride in bringing you powerful, prizewinning, absorbing and provocative books that will entertain you today and become the classics of tomorrow.

We put a lot of time and passion into what we publish and how we publish it, and we'd like to hear what you think.

Be part of John Murray – share your views with us at:

www.johnmurray.co.uk

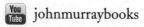 johnmurraybooks

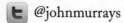 @johnmurrays

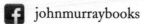 johnmurraybooks